PALM ISLAND

Aboriginal and Torres Strait Islander people are respectfully advised that this publication contains names and images of deceased persons, and culturally sensitive material. AIATSIS apologises for any distress this may cause.

Note: The Manbarra are Traditional Owners of Palm Island. The Bwgcolman (pronounced Bwook-a-mun and meaning Palm Island) are historical residents. They and their ancestors were deported to Palm Island reserve from across Queensland.

The terms Palm and Palms are also used on the island in reference to both the land and the Indigenous community, reflecting the strength of the connection between the two.

For Wagina

PALM ISLAND

THROUGH A LONG LENS

Joanne Watson

Aboriginal Studies Press

First published in 2010
by Aboriginal Studies Press

Reprinted 2010

© Joanne Watson 2010

All rights reserved. No part of this book may be reproduced or transmitted in any form or by any means, electronic or mechanical, including photocopying, recording or by any information storage and retrieval system, without prior permission in writing from the publisher. The *Australian Copyright Act 1968* (the Act) allows a maximum of one chapter or 10 per cent of this book, whichever is the greater, to be photocopied by any educational institution for its education purposes provided that the educational institution (or body that administers it) has given a remuneration notice to Copyright Agency Limited (CAL) under the Act.

Aboriginal Studies Press
is the publishing arm of the
Australian Institute of Aboriginal
and Torres Strait Islander Studies.
GPO Box 553, Canberra, ACT 2601
Phone: (61 2) 6246 1183
Fax: (61 2) 6261 4288
Email: asp@aiatsis.gov.au
Web: www.aiatsis.gov.au/asp/about.html

National Library of Australia
Cataloguing-In-Publication data:

> Author: Watson, Joanne, 1960-
> Title: Palm Island: through a long lens / Joanne Watson.
>
> ISBN: 9780855757038 (pbk.)
> ISBN: 978 0 85575 720 5 (ebook PDF)
> Notes: Includes index.
> Bibliography.
>
> Subjects: Aboriginal Australians — Queensland — Great Palm Island. Aboriginal Australians — Legal status, laws, etc. — Queensland — History. Aboriginal Australians — Government policy — Queensland — History. Aboriginal Australians — Social conditions — Queensland — History. Great Palm Island (Qld.) — History. Queensland — Race relations — History. Palm Island Aboriginal Reserve (Qld.) — History.
>
> Dewey Number: 323.11991094436

Front cover: Map of Palm and Surrounding Islands, 1937, courtesy of Queensland State Archives; view to Fantome Island, courtesy of the author; *Silhouette at sunset* by Lakeisha Ryan, courtesy of Bwgcolman Future Inc., Palm Island.

Printed in Australia by BookPOD

Palm Island: Through a Long Lens *is a masterly rendition of historical facts, situating 90 years of blighted government and erratic officials within the movement towards Indigenous rights during the twentieth century. Anchored firmly in the knowledges and experiences of Palm Islanders through the decades, this book illuminates not only their hellish existence under government controls, but their unquenchable spirit and unflinching determination to prevail.*

In this compelling living history of Palm Island and its people, Joanne Watson takes the reader from the idyllic pre-contact times of the original occupants to the ongoing trauma of the death in custody of Mulrunji Doomadgee.

This book is a vital corrective to the facile sensationalism of commentators who continue to define the people by the circumstances imposed upon them. It is an important caution to those who mistake official statements for historical truths.

Dr Rosalind Kidd

This is an outstanding contribution to Indigenous history — especially the history of Palm Island. Watson has made great use of historical records, media reports, discussions with Palm Island people alive today, and historical recollections from family members.

Stephen Hagan, University of Southern Queensland

This book is essential reading if we are to confront and understand Queensland's shameful record of Aboriginal removal and segregation, and the profound deformation of human rights it bequeathed to the Australian nation during the twentieth century. Joanne Watson, with an astute combination of exhaustive research, insight and empathy, has encapsulated here the entire tragedy of Palm Island, as well as the inspiring capacity of those caught and imprisoned within this history to confound and transcend it.

Dr Raymond Evans, Adjunct Professor with the Centre for Public Culture and Ideas, Griffith University

These stories are our children's inheritance. The stories passed on by their parents, grandparents and great-grandparents will provide the 'fire in the belly' to move forward. This book will offer sustenance, strength and solace. Like me, they will read this book and know the stories. They will be present in the period and feel the emotions that are stirred. PI. Good or bad, this is our home. They come from within and they form who we are. Bwgcolman.

Rachael Cummins, former Deputy Chair,
Palm Island Aboriginal Council

Joanne Watson captures the spirit and history of Palm Island in a way that helps make sense of the past and the present and also provides important pointers for the future. Understanding the full detail of the trauma and pain that many people have endured on the island over many decades is crucial to the process of recovery. For those of us who only hear about this remote tropical island when shocking events give it 'news value', Joanne Watson's detailed research and oral history fills many gaps. The shameful policy that created Palm Island has an enduring legacy, yet the warmth and humanity that percolates through this story is a remarkable testament to the capacity of people to survive and prevail. Understanding the past is the essential first step to making the future.

Dr Julianne Schultz AM, Editor *Griffith REVIEW*

Foreword

When Jo contacted me some years ago and said she wanted to do her PhD on Palms history, I knew that this is what Palms had wanted for a long time. Bwgcolman people needed their history documented so that their children would not forget their beginnings, their old people and their place. They needed to leave an inheritance for their children.

Of course there were pieces written about Palms throughout the years. Mostly these were written by those who had some position of authority in the administration, churches or other institutions. Bwgcolman people poked and prodded in the name of law, God and science. Then, over the last 30 years or so, the community and individuals featured predominantly in the local rag — the *Townsville Bulletin*. But what was being said — the interpretation of events, the social, cultural and political context of Palm Island — was told by others, many of them far removed from the consequences of their words.

In some of those writings, Palm would be portrayed as a God-forsaken hellhole — a penal colony where only the savage or brave live. It was certainly not a place for nice people and definitely not a place where their children should be. Other stories were of an idyllic paradise. Balmy, carefree nights, where the fishing is good and the Aborigines received silver spoon service. A certain paradise!

But Bwgcolman people have their own stories. These stories capture daily events of life on Palms — past and present. These stories tell of the individuals' and families' journeys to Palms made a long time ago. They tell too of the families and countries left behind. The kinship structure – who was related to whom — and importantly, who carried responsibility for what. These stories also carried people's happiness and pain. Their hopes and fears and for most, their dread. They told of psychological trauma, the impacts of degradation and subjugation and the dichotomy of powerlessness and resilience.

These are some of the stories that Jo was able to document in this book: oral history as told by the people. Jo's writing style, her pace and presentation have captured brilliantly the environment and manner in which these stories were told. As I read each chapter, I am transported into that time and all my senses are taken back then.

These stories are true. I knew them to be true before I read the supporting evidence. These are the stories I heard as I was growing up on Palms. I heard about Superintendent Curry from the mouths of people who were there. I head about Mr Pitt in whispered conversations. The rations — I know what was in it and how little we got — because I lined up for it and grew up on it. The violence I witnessed. Not in the homes but in the streets. For crimes of 'impertinence' or 'inciting' behaviour, aka: waving to girlfriends in the dormitory or simply being late to work. These lawbreakers were beaten with pick handles because they refused to go to jail quietly. I accompanied my parents too to Bartlam's office to ask for a travel permit to Townsville for shopping. And the account of Roy Henry Bartlam! I swear I must suffer some post-traumatic stress disorder — I'm getting chest pains as I write this. He would have to have been the most controlling Superintendent on any of the Aboriginal settlements. Settlements — now that's a play on words. Bit like the 'settlement' of Australia.

As a child I felt the authority and absolute domination of this Superintendent, and I don't think I was particularly sensitive or intuitive. Yet, this was the same man who provided the Christmas dinner rations. Believe me, it was Christmas. Tinned ham, stone fruit and tinned steamed pudding. Hallelujah. This was also the crimson-faced man mountain who donned the Santa suit and us kids lined up (yes, again!) and he gave us our Christmas presents. I can tell you I wasn't the only child who was breaking out in a sweat and prepared to forfeit Christmas. But I'm not old and I had a blessed childhood. I came from a family of hardworking, law-abiding God-fearing people. If I'm feeling this way what must others feel? My age meant my experience of Palm during that period was only brief. What of people of my grandfathers' and mother's age? What do these people feel? How do they cope?

And how do other children of my generation cope? I had dormitory kids in my grade at school — from year one to year seven. Throughout these years most of these kids did not see their parents. Many had countrymen on Palms but it was the exceptional occasion that any of the kids saw their parents. Many had no one except camp people who would take them out for the day. I didn't understand then but years later, I cried for all my mates from the dormitory. Many of them gone to an early grave. I still cry when I think of them and their stolen childhoods.

But I suppose we got our freedom of movement and in the seventies when the dormitories closed many people left to go back home. Most I know hoping to fit back in but never making it. Others never made it past Townsville. There, they met up with young men, kicked off — exiled from Palms — refusing to be tamed blacks. They slept rough, on the strand looking over the water to Palms, the only home they knew. These were the Drones. They did it hard. There were no government-funded support programs for shelter or meals. The Catholic Church provided comfort both physical and spiritual for those who came. I remember though, no matter what their circumstances, there was a real bond between the Bwgcolman Drones and a behaviour code which is lost today. I remember too, there was a special whistle and a 'hey Bwgcolman' greeting.

At this time there were also Bwgolman people living in Townsville — now exempt from 'the Act'. These ex-Palm Island families would help each other out and they kept an open door policy for any of the 'Bwgcolman mob'.

Self-determination and self-management came with both celebration and frustration. For all the blood sweat and tears that people put in over the decades fighting for our human rights, when the administration moved out, government ensured that there was no smooth transition to community governance. Despite having total support from the then Queensland Minister for Aboriginal Affairs, the churches, non-Aboriginal supporters and the 'whole world watching', control was as present and poignant on Palm Island in the 1980s as it was in the 1930s and 1950s. Meeting under cover of night was as fraught with danger in any period. Getting the message out comes with a cost.

The uprising in 2004 got the message out. No more whispered conversations. People shouted their demands for answers. The meetings were announced and open but still the threats and the exiles continued. The difference now was that the orders were not made under the 'protection' laws but under laws which are (supposed) to protect us.

These stories are our children's inheritance. The stories passed on by their parents, grandparents and great-grandparents will provide the 'fire in the belly' to move forward. This book will offer sustenance, strength and solace.

Like me, they will read this book and know the stories. They will be present in the period and feel the emotions that are stirred. P.I. Good or bad, this is our home. Oral history accounts of Palms are personal and precious. They come from within and they form who we are. Bwgcolman.

It's been an honour. Thank you Jo.

Rachael Cummins

Contents

Foreword		vii
Illustrations		xii
Abbreviations		xiii
Acknowledgments		xv
Maps		xviii
Chapter 1	Sorry Time 2004: 'A Duty to Protect Everyone on the Island'	1
Chapter 2	Out from 'the Big Swag'	17
Chapter 3	Kenny's Time: From Carpet Snake Country to Hull River Reserve	24
Chapter 4	Curry's Time: 'A State of Constant Apprehension'	36
Chapter 5	The 1930 Rampage: 'As Straight as A Gun Barrel'	55
Chapter 6	Gribble's Time: 'Fiscal Restraint'	76
Chapter 7	Fantome Island, Phantom Welfare	92
Chapter 8	Bartlam's Time: 'We Couldn't Tolerate Any More', the 1957 Strike	102
Chapter 9	Whistleblowers' Time: 'A Certain Paradise for Certain People'	121
Chapter 10	Campaign Time: 'Heady Days'	135
Chapter 11	The Inquest and its Aftermath: 'Our Day in Court'	146
Conclusion	Calling Palm Island Home	157
Notes		162
Bibliography		180
Index		197

Illustrations

(between pp. 108–109)

Palm Island jetty
Carpet snake painting
Bêche-de-mer fishermen, Challenger Bay, 1885
Butler's Guest House
Group of inmates — Hull River Settlement
Women and children — removed to Hull River settlement
Early Reserve housing, Palm Island, 1930
Henry Wilson and grand-daughters •

Mango Avenue and site of Curry residence
Administrators with Palm Island children
Robert Curry and Palm Island Brass Band
Corroborees, 1925
Palm Island, 1925
Matron Ethel Pattison and Dr Charles Pattison
Site where Robert Curry was shot, 1930
Map of removals
Tom Morgan Snr
Palm Island football team, 1941
Sister conducting laboratory medicine, Fantome Island
Construction work, Fantome Island, 1940s
All Souls' Day Mass Fantome Island, 1948
'Taking Their Daily Medicine'

Golden jubilee to strikers

Lakeisha in the car, community photography project, 2009
Silhouette at sunset, community photography project, 2009

Abbreviations

ABC	Australian Broadcasting Corporation
ACC	Aboriginal Coordinating Council
AIAS	Australian Institute of Aboriginal Studies
AIATSIS	Australian Institute of Aboriginal and Torres Strait Islander Studies
AMIEU	Australian Meatworkers' Industry Employees' Union
ANU	Australian National University
ANZ	Australian and New Zealand Book Company
A&R	Angus and Robertson
ASA	Australian Sound Archives
CJG	Criminal Justice Group
CMC	Crime and Misconduct Commission
CUP	Cambridge University Press
DAA	Department of Aboriginal Affairs
DAIA	Department of Aboriginal and Island Affairs and Department of Aboriginal and Islander Advance¬ment
DOGIT	Deeds of Grant in Trust
DNA	Department of Native Affairs
DPP	Department of Public Prosecutions
FAIRA	Foundation for Aboriginal and Islander Research and Action
FCAA	Federal Council of Aboriginal Advancement
FCAATSI	Federal Council of Aborigines and Torres Strait Islanders
HRC	Human Rights Commission
JCU	James Cook University, Townsville
MUP	Melbourne University Press
PIAC	Palm Island Aboriginal Council
PCYC	Police Citizens Youth Club
QPD	*Queensland Parliamentary Debates*
QPP	*Queensland Parliamentary Papers*

Abbreviations

QPS	Queensland Police Service
QPU	Queensland Police Union
QPUE	Queensland Police Union of Employees
QPSU	Queensland Police Service Union
QSA	Queensland State Archives
QVP	*Queensland Votes and Proceedings*
RAAF	Royal Australian Air Force
RCIADIC	Royal Commission into Aboriginal Deaths in Custody
SERT	Special Emergency Response Team
SMH	*Sydney Morning Herald*
SWAT	Special Weapons and Tactics
TB	*Townsville Bulletin*
TDB	*Townsville Daily Bulletin*
TLC	Trades and Labour Council
UQP	University of Queensland Press
UNSW	University of New South Wales
VD	venereal disease

Acknowledgments

This book could not have been written without the support of a series of Palm Island Aboriginal Councils. I thank these councils for their cooperation, with a special thanks extended to Mayor Alf Lacey, former Mayor Delena Foster for her help in 2007 and to Ricky Clay and the late Sylvia Reuben for their assistance as chairs of council when I began conducting oral history research on the island almost twenty years ago. Qwanji (the late Pastor Don Brady) and former Deputy Chair, Rachael Cummins, first alerted me to the nature of Palm Island's history in my teenage years. I am grateful to them for forging an interest which has finally led to this recording of some of the voices of the Palm Island people. To Rachael, I am especially indebted for introducing me to the community and providing solid support when my confidence waned. Staff at Aboriginal Studies Press were a pleasure to work with and the Director, Rhonda Black, offered detailed editorial advice that was invaluable.

Members of the Bwgcolman community shared their lives and perspectives with me in a spirit of enormous generosity and kindness. I will always remain immensely grateful to the following elders, now deceased: Woodja (Annie Tallis), Ivy Sam, Jack and Jean Sibley, Silas Prior, George Ryan, Johnny Jumbo, Bill Congoo, Paddy Tanner and Tom Morgan Snr. Still resident on Palm, Blokey (Henry) Wilson also shared his precious knowledge of Palm Island history. On the mainland, ex-residents of the island, now deceased: Bessie Lymburner, Cliff Wyles, Sissy Miller, Bill Seaton, Monty Prior and Arthur Burns were equally hospitable, and I will always be grateful for the time that they spent with me. Thelma McAvoy (deceased) and Virginnia Wyles also provided invaluable assistance while I was in Townsville.

Raymond Evans' groundbreaking work in teaching Australian race relations history at Queensland University was fundamental to my ability to pursue this project initially as research for a doctorate which he supervised. Sandra Phillips offered consistent support and interest and visited the island with me in the early 1990s. A special gratitude is extended to Jan Smallwood for her help in the Townsville-Ingham region and for her friendship and support. Non-Aboriginal residents of Palm Island in the 1980s, Father Mick Peters and Janelle Byrne, also provided support and interest, while David Horton of the Australian Institute of Aboriginal and Islander Studies (AIATSIS) provided valuable editorial comment on the original thesis. In the Brisbane Indigenous community, the late Maureen Watson, Lilla Watson, Mary Graham, Bob Weatherall, Jeanie Bell and Kev Carmody taught me and a great many others a good deal more, I am sure, than they will ever realise. With patience and tact and in the examples that they set, these people enlarged and enriched our understandings and our perspectives.

Richard Buckhorn of Brisbane and Paul Turnbull of James Cook University kindly shared their resources. Staff at the Oxley Memorial Library, the Queensland State Archives, Fryer Memorial Library, James Cook University Library, Mitchell Library (Sydney), the South Australian Museum (Adelaide), and in Canberra, at AIATSIS, the Australian War Memorial, the National Film Library and the Film and Sound Archives provided their expertise and guidance in the research for this project. Kay Saunders, Ann McGrath and Jackie Huggins facilitated publication of an edited version of the chapter on the Palm Island strike in the journal *Labour History* and Joanne Scott provided an opportunity to publish a brief biography of Superintendent Robert Curry in the *Australian Dictionary of Biography*.

Bruce Sims contributed his expert copy-editing skills. Thanks are also due to Rene McBride, Sheryl Cornack and Leonie Daisy for providing accommodation and support during my stays in the Townsville/Palm Island region, to Lonnie McBride for his photography, and to James McAvoy (deceased) for allowing me to reproduce his painting.

Members of my extended family and friends contributed to this work in a variety of ways and I am grateful to them all for their assistance. On the island, Leonie Daisy and Abe Johnson shared with me more than I can ever return. Memories of our fishing trips together, of Turtle Rock and North East Bay, will remain with me forever, and I thank them deeply for the privilege of participating in the Bwgcolman way of life. Finally I thank my dear friends Rachael, Sandra, Kym, Heather, Jenny, Jan and Bill, Kerry and Marg, my sister Jill and Aunty Ann O'Rourke, with special thanks to my daughter Wagina for her extensive patience, love and support.

Permissions

Thanks are extended to the following people for their permission to use illustrations contained in this book: the late artist James McAvoy, (with assistance from Joanne Bulmer, Vina Palmer and HJ Wilson) for *Carpet snake painting*; Christopher Anderson for permission to use his 'Map of Removals'; the State of Queensland through the Department of Tourism, Regional Development and Industry for photographs of the Palm Island dormitories; the Oxley Memorial Library, State Library of Queensland for photographs as noted in the list of illustrations; the Premier's Department, State of Queensland for photographs and illustrations from Queensland State Archives as noted in the list of illustrations and AIATSIS Library for photographs as noted in the list of illustrations.

Location of Queensland Government Settlements, Church Missions and Torres Strait Island Reserves. Map by Damien Demaj, demap. Map based on Queensland Parliamentary Papers, Vol. 2, 1958–59. Courtesy of Oxley Memorial Library

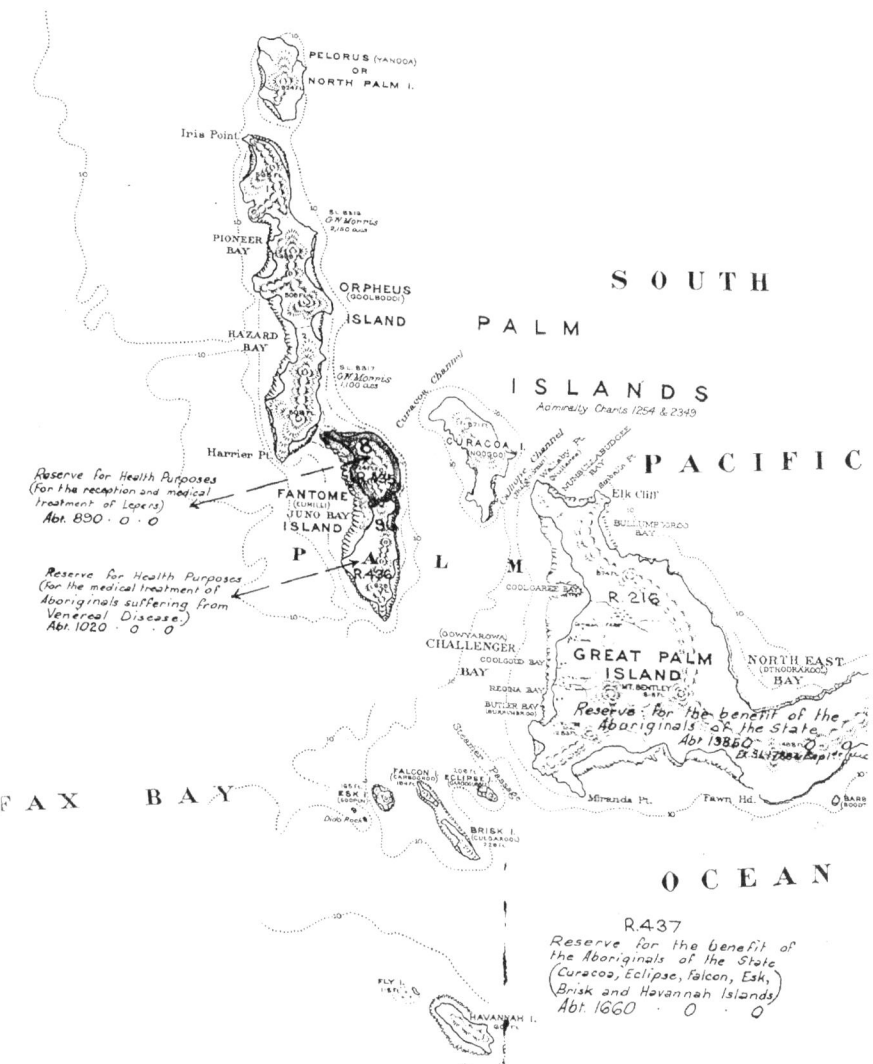

Palm and surrounding islands, 1937. Lands Office, Palm Island Bundle. Courtesy of Queensland State Archives

If we had only written records, our knowledge of the past would often be both extremely partial and extremely shallow. We can say this with certainty because of the few but significant white people's accounts of self-censorship, and we can say this with even greater certainty because of the oral histories. Once we know that people regularly conspired to conceal public knowledge of their actions, the importance of oral histories is clear.

Deborah Bird Rose, 'Oral histories and knowledge'[1]

---

1. Bain Attwood and SG Foster (eds), *Frontier Conflict: The Australian experience*, National Museum of Australia, Canberra 2003, p.127.

Chapter 1

Sorry Time 2004
'A Duty to Protect Everyone on the Island'

In the summer of 2004, planes and helicopters, loaded with journalists and camera crews, flocked to the remote settlement of Palm Island, 65 kilometres northwest of Townsville, in Halifax Bay, North Queensland. They hovered like buzzards over the island's burning courthouse and police station. The community had mobilised and in a mood of desperate anguish many engaged in dramatic acts of civil disobedience. Flames tore through buildings, glass cracked and smoke billowed in a circular signal of distress. Television viewers could not help but hear the recorded cries of human beings in pain.

Some of us felt physically sick as we watched, sensing the imminent repercussions. I remember thinking that these people were taking action because they knew that no one else would. Later I recalled the proverb that says, 'A slave is also a man who waits for someone else to come and free him.' Yet I failed to grasp the extent to which the Bwgcolman people were making history, for their actions then, and in the months that followed, would lead to the first prosecution of a Queensland police officer, in relation to a death in custody.

In the weeks before the events of that summer, Erykah Kyle, then Mayor of Palm Island, and Councillor Rosina Norman had tried to alert government representatives and the media to the perilous state of people's lives on their island home. Speaking of mass unemployment and poverty, substance abuse and violence, Rosina Norman noted that 'all these people here are walking time bombs waiting to explode.'[1] Their words were prophetic, for only a fortnight later the community did indeed explode, with the spontaneous eruption of grief and anger over the shocking death in custody of 36-year-old Mulrunji, less than one hour after his arrest for a petty misdemeanour.

Mulrunji was a popular member of the Palm community. A traditional Waanyi man, he took his son Eric and his friends fishing, to teach them his ancestral and traditional ways. He worked part-time for the Palm Island Aboriginal Council. Once each week he would go fishing, returning with turtle, crayfish and other seafood, and once a month he hunted for goat and possum to support his family. Mulrunji was a regular babysitter of his nieces and nephews and was often the carer for his mentally-impaired nephew Dwayne. He lived with his partner, Tracey Twaddle, who described him as 'a loving husband and father'. A generally fit and healthy man, he was regarded by the then Mayor, Erykah Kyle, as 'a well-known, lovely person, who went about his business and was one of the top hunters in the community'.[2]

Mulrunji had been walking along Dee Street, Palm Island on the day of his arrest. It was Friday morning, 19 November and he had never before been in trouble with the law on Palm Island. That morning he had been out crabbing with a friend and afterwards had been drinking. He was described by those who saw him as having been in 'a happy-go-lucky' mood.

At around 10am, he was ambling along the footpath and singing, when a police van, driven by Senior Sergeant Chris Hurley, accompanied by Police Liaison Officer Lloyd Bengaroo, drove into Dee Street. Gladys Nugent was also in the van and police were assisting her to obtain her medication from the Bramwell house, because of an earlier conflict with her partner, Roy Bramwell. Patrick Bramwell, 24-year-old nephew to Gladys and Roy, was outside the house and intoxicated when the van arrived. He began swearing at police and Sergeant Hurley arrested him.[3]

Mulrunji was walking past as the arrest was made and he chided Bengaroo for locking up his 'own people'. Bengaroo advised him to keep walking or he would be 'locked up too'. When both police officers were back in the van, Sergeant Hurley asked Bengaroo what Mulrunji had said, and on the strength of that exchange he decided to arrest him. The police would later claim that Mulrunji turned and swore at them. Others would recall that Mulrunji was singing, 'Who let the dogs out?' — one of his three favourite songs.

Noby Clay would later testify that Mulrunji had stopped singing when Hurley drove up to him, placed his hands on Mulrunji's arms and pushed him 'into the back door of the paddy wagon with force'. She stated that she saw Hurley 'throw him head first into the rear inside of the paddy wagon' and that as the van drove away, she could see Mulrunji's 'legs sticking up in the air'. Another witness, Edna Coolburra, wept as she told a later inquest that 'he was minding his own business' when he was arrested for 'causing a public nuisance'. Others stated that he was not obstructing the vehicle or other pedestrians and that 'he was not making a nuisance of himself' when arrested. Coolburra stated that Mulrunji tried to resist arrest but that Sergeant Hurley 'was too tall and powerful'.

Chris Hurley was 33-years-old and more than 200 centimetres (6 feet and 7 inches) tall, and weighed 115 kilograms. He had worked in several Aboriginal communities over his sixteen-year career and from 2002 was in charge of the Palm Island police station — 'the ultimate figure of power and authority on Palm Island'.[4] He had gained a reputation in Burketown for drinking, womanising and being 'good with his fists'[5]. At around 10.20am on 19 November, the van Hurley was driving pulled into the police station as Sergeant Leafe came through the back of the garage with Roy Bramwell. Hurley told Leafe to take him into the station for questioning over an earlier assault on his partner.

Mulrunji was still complaining about his arrest when Sergeant Hurley went to the back of the cage to bring Patrick Bramwell and Mulrunji inside. As he was let out of the van, Mulrunji punched Hurley in the jaw. Two witnesses later claimed that Hurley responded by punching Mulrunji in the ribs. Penny Sibley was in close proximity, having arrived to talk with Lloyd Bengaroo, and stated she saw Hurley punch Mulrunji 'in the side, or the rib'. She would never waiver from this in repeated testimonies. Alfred Bonner was walking past the rear of the station and looked into the garage area, where he claimed to see two men struggling and what appeared to be Hurley moving his arm over, in an action suggestive of striking blows. Hurley would later deny these claims.

Hurley wrestled with Mulrunji as he tried to drag him into the police station. What happened next has been hotly contested. The lack of clarity is exacerbated by the contradictory statements provided by some of those involved. Lloyd Bengaroo initially claimed to have opened the back door of the police station and stood there; on another occasion, that he went straight inside and down the hallway. His response to the initial police investigation was that he wasn't watching what happened at that point because 'if I see something I might get into trouble myself or something. The family might harass me or something' — a response left unexplored during subsequent questioning by Inspectors Weber and Williams. In the later courtroom setting, Bengaroo was 'reticent' and 'almost inarticulate', but did claim to have seen Hurley and Mulrunji fall 'side-by-side' across the doorway — that no part of either man had come into contact.

Hurley would later state that Mulrunji tripped over the 7.5cm step as they entered the doorway and the pair fell. Constable Steadman stated that from outside the station he heard Hurley yelling 'in an abusive tone' at Mulrunji.[6] Not far from where the two fell, Roy Bramwell was seated on a yellow chair in the 'dayroom' waiting to be questioned. Although his view was partially obscured by a filing cabinet, he later stated that he saw Hurley's elbow going up and down three times, as if striking Mulrunji, and that he heard Hurley saying 'Do you want more, Mr Doomadgee? (Mulrunji) Do you want more? Have you had enough?'

Hurley would later refute these claims, stating that he had tried to lift Mulrunji up by his shirt (although he did not mention this in his initial interviews with investigators) and that he and Sergeant Leafe had dragged him by the hands to the cell. He stated that he thought Mulrunji was 'foxing' when he had to be dragged in this way. In the cell, Mulrunji 'just laid there then'.[7] At 10.26am, Hurley completed the custody register, recording that Cameron Doomadgee (Mulrunji) had been charged with causing a public nuisance and was in custody.

The police station's video surveillance tape starts at 10.17am and covers only the cells. The tape had been taken by police during the initial investigation and its later analysis as being several minutes 'out of time' was attributed to a 'glitch in the power system'. No Palm Island Aboriginal residents have, to my knowledge, confirmed that they experienced any problems in the generation of power on the day in question. On 1 February 2005, journalist Jeff Waters revealed that the Crime and Misconduct Commission (CMC) had confirmed that evidence had been collected by serving police officers, seconded to the role.[8] The tape of the cells shows Patrick Bramwell and Mulrunji lying next to each other. Mulrunji has at this stage sustained massive injuries — in addition to a black eye, scalp and jaw injuries, he had four fractured ribs and a completely ruptured liver and portal vein, with the liver 'cleaved in two.'

As he lies bleeding to death internally on the concrete cell floor, he writhes, moans and calls out for help — with words that sounded, on the station's tape recorder, like 'Help me, I'm dying' — but no one comes to his aid. After fifteen minutes — at around 10.30am — he is still. Patrick Bramwell, almost comatose, pats his dying friend. It is a harrowing image that it many ways typifies the abandonment of Palm Islanders by mainstream Australia. Lawyer for the Doomadgee family, Andrew Boe, would later comment, 'Anyone wishing to assess the grief felt and held by the family and close members of the community must look at this video recording. The family have.'

At 11am, Hurley walks into the cell, looks down at Mulrunji and kicks him lightly on the right shoulder. There is no response and he kicks him again. One can only imagine the horror for the family viewing this scene. When there is no response, he bends down to check his breathing. A second seven-seconds check was conducted on both inmates. Forty-two minutes after that, Sergeant Leafe reported to Hurley that Mulrunji appeared to be cold and unresponsive. Hurley enters the cell and checks his breathing and pulse. An ambulance is called but no attempt is made by police to resuscitate, despite that at this stage there is uncertainty as to whether Mulrunji is dead. About fifteen minutes later a paramedic arrives and pronounces Mulrunji deceased. The tape shows Hurley slide down the wall with his head in his hands.[9]

Lloyd Bengaroo claimed to have considered that the family should be notified, but that Hurley told him to 'keep quiet'. A short time after this, Mulrunji's partner, Tracey Twaddle, and his eldest sister Carol, visit the station with food. They are told to go away and are not advised that metres away from the inquiry counter their loved one lies dead. Mulrunji's sister Jane also visits with another sister and a niece and sees three ambulance officers leaving. The women question police as to what had happened and if Mulrunji was all right. Hurley tells them to go away, that Mulrunji is asleep, although he knows he is dead. Hurley would initially deny these claims, but later accepted them as true.

At 3pm that afternoon, a policeman from Townsville visits to tell the family that Mulrunji has died. Later that day rumours circulate that Patrick Bramwell had been released and that he claimed to have been given $50 by police and told to 'keep quiet.'[10] The police investigation that followed was widely condemned as having shown little concern for even the appearance of impartiality and for ignoring established legal procedures.

While all deaths in custody, according to Queensland State Coroner's guidelines, are meant to be investigated by the state Homicide Investigation Group, this did not happen. Instead, in response to a phone call from Hurley, Townsville Regional Crime Coordinator, Inspector Warren Weber, sent over Detective Senior Sergeant Raymond Kitching from Townsville CIB and Detective Sergeant Darren Robinson, in charge of CIB Branch on Palm Island. Both were friends of Hurley, Robinson a close friend. Coroner Christine Clements later noted that their investigation failed to meet established standards and guidelines.[11]

Moreover, Robinson has previously investigated and dismissed two serious complaints against Hurley, both made by Palm Islanders accusing him of assault causing injuries. The appropriate form regarding Mulrunji's death was not sent to the Coroner until 22 November and it failed to include any reference to the alleged assault on Mulrunji, which Roy Bramwell had raised in an interview with Detective Kitching. This meant the first autopsy report was compiled without access to 'crucial information'.

Senior Sergeant Hurley picked up the investigators from the airport on Palm and was seen by the community to be driving them around. That night, after having interviewed Hurley, they shared a meal at his house. They failed to secure the site where Mulrunji had been fatally injured. 'Off the record' discussions were held between Hurley and other important witnesses, including Bengaroo and Leafe. Even after the Ethical Standards Command took over, Weber and Williams engaged in further 'off the record' discussions with Hurley, including an exploration of discrepancies about times. This was not documented and only came to light incidentally through Hurley's answers to the later CMC investigation.[12]

The detonation of the news of Mulrunji's death reverberated in shock waves across the community. On Monday 22 November, 200 Palm Islanders had marched to the police station demanding answers. The crowd was surprised when Hurley came out and shouted that he'd 'done nothing wrong'. Other police came out in his support. A community resolution called for his removal from the island. The crowd dispersed. Hurley and also Bengaroo did leave, erasing any chance for the community to meet with their Police Liaison Officer. When Mulrunji's family received the autopsy report, a week after his death, the state government failed to provide counselling and instead sent eighteen extra police to the island, who proceed to 'strut around the community, looking intimidating'.[13]

On the Tuesday, the council shut down alcohol supplies in response to the death and calls were made for the government to meet the community on the island to discuss their concerns. On Wednesday an autopsy was conducted by Dr Guy Lampe and the report released to the Queensland Police Service Commissioner, who requested that the CMC assume responsibility for the investigation. Police were directed to take their weapons to the barracks and to sleep with them by their sides. No direction seems to have been offered that might have established a pathway to conciliation.

Moreover, during the week various episodes of intimidation and harassment occurred, including an armed police 'raid' — ostensibly in search of contraband alcohol — on a peaceful gathering at Butler Bay and the removal by carloads of large policemen of a small child from one of the homes nearby.[14] Barrister Mark Donnelly would later have it put onto court record that he had been informed that Sergeant Robinson made a threatening phone call to Jacob Baira Jnr on Thursday evening, 25 November.[15] While some have speculated that police were being deliberately provocative — especially given their later acknowledgment that they had intelligence of a possible riot, from conversations overheard on the island — it seems more in keeping with the history recorded in the following chapters, that they simply felt themselves immune from scrutiny or repercussion in this isolated community.

On Thursday 25 November, another protest was held outside the police station, the community now inflamed as the government refused to speak with the council and the Coroner's office refused to publicly release the autopsy report. That same evening Mulrunji's family received the report and the following day, on Friday 26 November, the report was released to the media. A crowd of several hundred Palm Islanders gathered at the town square to hear the findings.

In this context and in a setting where rumours of police brutality had begun to circulate, the official report declared that Mulrunji had died from an 'intra abdominal haemorrhage caused by a ruptured liver and portal vein'. His ribs were broken and a lung had been punctured. These injuries were the result of a scuffle and an accidental fall 'onto a hard surface such as the steps outside the watch house'. There was, the report concluded, 'no evidence to suggest' the injuries had 'resulted from a direct use of force'. Emotions ran high. 'This is cold bloody murder,' one person yelled at the crowd. 'I am not going to accept it and I know a lot of you other people won't.' The crowd stormed the courthouse and in the heat of the unfolding melee stones and fire starters were hurled.

Civil unrest on Palm Island culminated in the burning down of the police station, the courthouse and police barracks, the evacuation of local police from the island and the declaration by the Queensland Premier of a state of emergency under the *Public Safety Preservation Act 1986*. At the opening of the twenty-first century, Palm Island and its people were suddenly catapulted out from under the obscurity of 'the big swag' of silence and secrecy[16] and onto the front pages of our daily newspapers.

Photographs of smoke billowing from the roof of the police station accompanied the headlines TROPIC OF DESPAIR, PARADISE LOST, QUEENSLAND HELL HOLE and ISLAND OF SORROW. In the weeks that followed, television news reports subjected viewers to thrice-daily images of one resident bearing a shovel and marching with the crowd, in a repetitive relay not seen since the Twin Towers fell. Reports were published in Europe and Canada, in England and in the United States.

Buildings targeted were those representing the legal and justice system on the island. Yet fear soon swept across the whole of the white staff, particularly those disconnected from the community. Some of the teachers made the students 'duck for cover' under the desks of the classrooms — as if entertaining visions of Palm Islanders attacking their own children. Eighteen police officers had already fled the station prior to its destruction and moved into the police barracks as the courthouse burnt. Glass at the station's day room shattered. Sergeant Robinson had removed all unlocked weapons. As police took up residence in the barracks across the road, someone yelled out that the crowd was moving towards the fenced-in quarters.

Rocks were hurled across the fence and police used wheelie bins and a pool table to deflect them. A gas bottle exploded at a nearby police residence. A member of the crowd told police they had one hour to leave the island. Sergeant Darren Murphy phoned through a Code 2 alert to the Townsville Police Communications Centre demanding back-up. At the barracks Inspector Richardson advised officers that they would 'be justified' in using their weapons after the hour elapsed. 'Do what you have to do.'[17]

Police stationed themselves in the storeroom at the back of the police barracks where ammunition was shared around and plans were made to fire 'a warning shot at the crowd'. Meanwhile white school teachers, nurses, public servants and contractors fled in frantic droves, evacuated by a passenger boat able to take a hundred and fifty people. During a lull in the disturbance, police left the barracks and headed to the hospital on Mango Avenue where a group of them formed a line across the emergency entrance at the back. One of the officers was armed with a shovel — though readers should note that this was not the shovel that was captured and replayed endlessly on television in the weeks that followed.

A crowd gathered at the ambulance entry and police sought to negotiate with Lex Wotton. Sergeant Robinson would later testify that he went to talk with Wotton with a gun in his pocket and that 'I decided that if he wasn't going to give us more time, I was going to shoot Lexie.' Police Alsatian dogs were harangued by Palm Islanders' brave little chihuahuas, who barked furiously at their much larger opponents. A resident 'dog whisperer' managed to calm one of the police Alsatians, and was later charged with assault[18] — one of the gentlest assaults in human history, incurred for patting a dog.

The only female police officer involved later stated that she was also prepared to shoot Lex Wotton, when 'a male dressed as a woman came towards me'. Senior Constable Kathleen Richardson claimed that 'She was yelling abuse in a falsetto, woman's-type voice and saying he knew about racism (sic).' Richardson claimed to know the name of 'him' through photographic identification. Barrister Mark Donnelly later questioned the validity of this, noting 'the problems Caucasians sometimes have identifying Aborigines, but you had to decide on the gender of a cross-dresser to boot. What was he wearing, a two piece ensemble, a dress or what?' It was, she replied, 'a frock'. Richardson noted she had her hand 'on her Glock' at the time and she was 'weighing up' whether to shoot one of the protestors 'if he hurt someone'.[19] Since she wore a Glock, and her castigator 'a frock', it is difficult to feel compassion for Richardson's suggestion that she was the subject of threatening aggression.

In contrast to later allegations made by police against Wotton and their pressure to have him charged with attempted murder, police at this point asked Wotton to organise a bus and accompany police to the vehicle 'to guarantee their safety'. Shortly afterwards senior officers announced that reinforcements had regained control of the island with police flown in from Townsville by Chinook helicopter and from Cairns by plane. The crowd was told to 'Piss off and go home, the police are back in charge.' Within 20 minutes the crowd had dispersed and the 80 officers had commandeered the children's school as a command centre. From here they planned a series of stealthy raids and arrests to take place at dawn. For many Palm Islanders the experience was one of deja-vu. Indeed, many of those targeted were the descendants of the 1957 strikers.

Yet this was a distinctly twenty-first century conflict — the force included members of the Special Emergency Response Team (SERT), developed to combat threats of terrorism, following the 2001 September 11 attacks upon New York. This team was clad in balaclavas and full riot combat gear — though without identification — and carried automatic weapons, including Taser stun guns. Stun guns send a high voltage electric shock to the body, cause considerable pain and have been associated with 165 deaths in America and Canada as well as two, in 2009, in Australia. A slight increase to voltage can prove fatal. These weapons and the SERT itself were trialled, for the first time in Queensland, upon the unsuspecting Palm community, including women and children, in 5am raids upon the homes of residents.

Under the Premier's declared state of emergency, the SERT took control of the airport, school and hospital, closed roads in and out of the community and waged the first of their 'Gestapo style raids' upon the home of Lex Wotton at 4.30am. Four carloads descended upon the former Palm Island Councillor. Armed police kicked in his door, ran through the house where his partner and children were sleeping and five police aimed rifles at his head. With his hands on his head, he was hit with a Taser weapon, delivering a 50,000 volt shock to his leg. Cecilia Sibley, Wotton's partner, later told the *Townsville Bulletin* that six children were in the house and that her daughter Schanara had a rifle pointed at her head:

> I came out and they (four or five police) were standing around him...next minute we heard this gunshot, like a shotgun. We got a fright and screamed. They hit him on the back of the leg with the stun gun and he went down on his knees and then they hit

him across the legs and he lay down...We were all screaming and crying and they came in and told us to keep quiet and to lie on the floor.

Schanara did not recall for how long the rifle was pointed at her head as she lay down, 'I was frightened and crying.' At another home, fifteen-year-old Kirsten Harvey also had a Taser weapon pointed at her, when she was forced to the ground as police searched for Richard Poynter. 'It had a laser on it. I could see the laser on the fridge...The policeman was standing near the sink, holding the gun on me,' she said. 'I was scared.'[20] At 6.30am Assan Clay, a father of five, woke to the front door being bashed in and leapt from his bed to face shotgun-wielding police who shouted at him to hit the floor. Children aged between five and sixteen were in the lounge room when police searched for Douggie Miller, who was in prison at the time and had been for the past six weeks.[21]

The terrorisation continued over the weekend and into the following week. The school was shut down by the government as unarmed and unresisting Palm Islanders were removed at gunpoint. Nine-year-old Chevez Morton was playing in the backyard on Saturday afternoon when police arrived. 'They told me to lay on the ground and I put my face in the dirt. It made me sad,' he said.

William Blackman, son of the author Renata Prior, and grandson of the late Peter Prior, had fled to the hills when he heard that police were hunting him. (Blackman's grandfather had been directed to halt a rampage by Palm Island's Superintendent in 1930 and, as detailed in Chapter Five, had paid a hefty price.) When Blackman decided to surrender to police, his mother begged photographers from The *Australian* to photograph him, 'so he is not shot'. When he refused to sign a statement, he was charged with 'riotous behaviour'.[22] Like his grandfather before him, he was sent to Townsville 'for summary justice'.

In the midst of the raids and in a mode reminiscent of the Bjelke-Petersen years, police and government made much of the fact that a 'high powered rifle' had apparently gone missing from station. This later became, according to Premier Peter Beattie 'a weapons cache that included stolen fuel' and from Police Minister Judy Spence, 'weapons and a lot of alcohol'. (The rifle was acknowledged as relocated some three months later, found in the police station).[23] Mayor Erykah Kyle pleaded that the community wanted the opportunity to talk to young Palm Islanders, and that some parents were prepared to bring the children in. 'We don't need police breaking down doors,' she said. 'Our old people were waking up in the night terrified...It really traumatised our people in Butler Bay.'[24]

Approximately 50 houses were raided over the days following the riot, with 28 Palm Islanders — including children and a 65-year-old grandmother — charged with 64 serious offences. In keeping with Palm's history, some who were charged and removed at gunpoint (by unidentifiable men in balaclavas bearing Taser weapons) were to be charged with 'going armed in public to cause fear'. Their armaments, for the most part, consisted of stones.

Many were held in the back of police vehicles for hours without access to food, water or medical supplies. Journalist Chris Graham would later comment:

> By the time Palm Islanders set fire to the police watch house Mulrunji had lay dying...while Snr Sgt Hurley allegedly ignored closed circuit video footage of him 'writhing in pain'...by the time Palm Islanders set fire to the police watch house, Queensland Police had well and truly begun to seriously pervert the course of justice...After the riot, the death of Mulrunji Doomadgee was big news. It remains that way today solely because of the Palm Island riots.[25]

Much of the press coverage in the following weeks was sensationalist, some of it blatantly biased and presenting Hurley as an exceptionally good Queensland cop. Less than a month after Mulrunji died while in his custody, the police service exhibited a photograph of Hurley seated on some steps with Aboriginal children on his lap. The image was displayed at a Reconciliation Exhibition on Thursday Island in the Torres Strait and was also printed in the *Courier Mail*. What the exhibition and the press coverage did not disclose was that Hurley's career history also included several complaints against his name that had been lodged in the recent past on Palm Island, all alleging excessive force causing injury.[26]

When questioned by the ABC concerning the use of 'heavily armed police with semi-automatic weapons' who 'stormed' the homes of Palm Islanders, the Premier defended their actions as appropriate — 'There wasn't a Sunday picnic going on.' Denis Fitzpatrick, acting General President of the Queensland Police Service Union (QPSU) argued that 'there had been an operational need to enter homes...this had been done as tactfully and sensitively as possible.'[27] Police also argued that Mulrunji had been involved in a car accident the day before his arrest, where he may have sustained his injuries — an event not recognised by any of Mulrunji's family members.

When the initial CMC team witnessed the 'riot' on the island on 26 November, they were relieved of their duties to investigate the death, and replaced by Detective Ken Webster and Detective Sergeant Britton and Ms Lisa Florence as Aboriginal liaison. It was only then that Aboriginal witnesses were provided with support. State Coroner Christine Clements later noted, 'a support person, independent of both police and the local community might well have elicited more information at an early stage.' She described the initial investigation as 'wilfully blind' and 'reprehensible'.

The Palm Island Aboriginal Council advised the government that if they had been presented with a list of names of people wanted for questioning, that they would have ensured these people were brought in to speak with police. They would have no access to legal support, however, since the state government had banned Aboriginal Legal Aid from the island. Community calls for those on charges associated with the protest to be dealt with by community delivered punishments (via Palm Island's traditional court) were denied, despite extensive evidence that these systems are extremely effective at curbing recidivism in Indigenous communities. Palm Island's leaders were left to run voluntary night patrols to keep their young people calm.

On 27 November, Police Minister Spence argued that police were only acting out of 'a duty to protect everyone' and that the riot was 'no message to show the children of the island'.[28] One can only speculate as to whether she thought pointing guns at their heads was more appropriate. On Sunday 28 November, Premier Beattie and Police Minister Spence were met by a convoy of three vehicles of SERT officers at Palm Island airport and were escorted by them around the island for a four-hour visit.

In a context in which a 65-year-old grandmother was already facing a possible life sentence over charges of demolishing of a building, Spence noted at this point that she had not ruled out a police union demand for attempted murder charges against those involved in the riot. Beattie presented a 'five point plan' that focused on re-establishing 'law and order', rebuilding the police headquarters and imposing tighter alcohol restrictions. He also raised the possibility of withholding funding to the Palm Island Council if it did not cooperate closely with the government.

On the same day the Palm Island Aboriginal Council presented a letter to the Premier. 'Our people are feeling under siege,' it read. No fresh bread or milk was being delivered to the island due to government cessation of supplies, three people were on suicide watch, services at the school and hospital had been removed and the state of emergency had left three Councillors and 50 other people stranded in Townsville. The council had been given no notice of the state of emergency and no certificate had been issued. The letter stressed that the council had been seeking to communicate with the Beattie government but were unable to communicate directly. Children were 'feeling terrorised'. It was requested that no police attend the forthcoming funeral of Mulrunji.[29]

Over the following days Palm Island bore the brunt of maligning by Police Minister Spence that it was a 'dysfunctional community…where few people have any sense of social obligation', while the Premier accused Mayor Kyle, of 'a failure of leadership'. It took nine days for the Premier to finally offer his condolences to the family.[30] Much was made by Beattie of the 'waste of money' that occurred when buildings were burnt. Two of these had already been scheduled for demolition and $2.33 million allocated in 2001 for a new police station.

A second autopsy on 30 November was 'inconclusive but raised doubts about the police version of events'. The report noted that Mulrunji's injuries were 'almost certainly sustained during his arrest' with 'a degree of force applied to Mr Doomadgee's body'. His blood alcohol reading was 0.20 — hardly suggesting that he could have put up a 'fair fight'. He had been placed in the police cell injured and with no medical assistance.

By the time the funeral was approaching, 43 local men, one woman and several children had been arrested for alleged involvement in the riot and or fires. Most were refused bail. Police 'vehemently opposed' those arrested being allowed to return to their homes. A few weeks later the Chief Magistrate David Glasgow granted bail on strict conditions, including prohibition from returning to Palm, daily reporting and abiding by curfews in Townsville and a ban on their participation in any public rallies, meetings 'or other events' about the death. Scores of people were thus denied the right to attend the funeral and many were in prisons throughout Queensland on the day of Mulrunji's burial.

David Shepherd, 27-year-old cross-dresser identified by his 'frock', moved to Cairns while on bail because as a black, gay man he 'feared the rednecks and prejudices' of Townsville. His fears were based on evidence — a government building in Thuringowa was spray painted with the words NOT WELCOME — GO BACK TO PALM ISLAND. Reports circulated of groups of 30 or more 'skinhead' white men appearing late at night to abuse Aboriginal residents of Happy Valley, yelling out that they were members of the KKK, 'go back to Palm Island' or 'we'll bash youse up'. Shepherd was jailed for one month for three counts of breaching bail and for a 'nuisance' offence.

Bail conditions denied David Bulsey, President of the Palm Island's men's group, access to Palm to care for his eight children, including infant twins, leaving his wife, Yvette Lenoy, without support from the income he would have earned on the island. She was seven months pregnant and had gone into premature labour when police smashed in the door of their home. In shock and suffering high blood pressure, she was rushed to Townsville hospital where she gave birth to a daughter named Cameron in honour of Mulrunji. The girl was later diagnosed as suffering from a heart condition as a complication of premature birth. David Bulsey was eventually cleared of riot charges when video footage revealed that his role was to calm people down and to attempt to stop the riot.

Prior to the funeral service, family viewings of the body of Mulrunji triggered further shock headlines, with Elizabeth Doomadgee noting that her brother had a black eye, while Murrandoo Yanner told the press, 'his jaw was swollen and disfigured and there was a heel size lump of skin off his forehead. I tell you, the brother was unrecognisable.'[31] On the day of the funeral, 11 December 2004, a minute's silence was held at rallies in Brisbane and Townsville, with marches nationwide. While 1200 marched in Townsville — others who would have joined were it not for bail conditions — watched from the sidelines. The community was relieved when police stayed away from the funeral procession on Palm. Andrew Boe later noted:

> Not one of the non-Indigenous teachers, nurses, doctors or other service providers thought it appropriate to attend this funeral which attracted about 3000 Aboriginal people from the island as well as from the mainland. The divide spoke volumes about how far true reconciliation is out of the grasp of this community and why in many respects the situation is about race and colour, fear and loathing.[32]

Christmas on the island was affected by the refusal of access to their families for those imprisoned on the mainland. On New Years' Eve after some weeks of calm, a peaceful bonfire was raided at gunpoint by police and closed down. Parents reported that children were now terrified of police. Some had taken to running at the sight of them. A couple of months after the death, it was rumoured amongst Aboriginal residents of Townsville that Chris Hurley (supposedly on holidays on the Gold Coast) was 'cruising' around Townsville with Detective Sergeant Robinson. Their car had allegedly been seen circumnavigating the hospital in which Patrick Bramwell had received medical treatment.[33]

Patrick Bramwell (Roy's nephew) was due to be released from that institution on the day in question. Patrick was expected to testify at any future trial that might be brought against Hurley and had reportedly been warned by police not to talk about what he had witnessed on the day Mulrunji died. The Aboriginal Legal Service was advised that Hurley was 'looking for Patrick' and so arranged to collect Bramwell, sending him by plane to Palm Island where it was believed that he would be safer, being surrounded by his community.

The state government's appointment of Michael Barnes as coroner for the inquest drew sharp criticism from Palm, as it was Barnes who had released the results of the first autopsy before the family had achieved their goal of acquiring a second opinion. On 8 February 2005, the coronial inquest into Mulrunji's death finally commenced in the makeshift courthouse established in the Police Citizens Youth Club (PCYC) building in response to community requests, so that Aboriginal witnesses, especially old people, could testify without the added burden of travel. (Some sessions would later be held in Townsville, in keeping with police requests.)

Seventeen lawyers lined up at the bar table, and all except Andrew Boe, Burmese lawyer for the Palm Island Aboriginal Council (PIAC), were white, while 200 Palm Islanders attended, most sitting at the back. Palm Island witnesses were cross-examined in 'complicated legalese' and became distressed by intense questioning about timing and other details of events. Roy Bramwell stood up without prompting, to show what he had witnessed, mimicking Hurley resting his knees on the ground and swinging punches. Patrick Bramwell retracted his statement that he had seen Hurley assault Mulrunji, and then retracted the retraction. Police accused him of lying. The court was adjourned. That night Bramwell went home and tried to set himself alight.

On 17 February 2005, Premier Beattie flew to the island during a period of mourning — despite being asked by a unanimous council resolution not to do so — in order to open a PCYC building. Beattie's entourage and the trail of journalists visited the local school and asked the Principal if the children could be taken to the centre to sing 'Advance Australia Fair'. The Principal refused — parental consent would be required. Stone-faced protestors with placards demanding justice and jobs, gathered near the Centre, while of the 30 locals who were present, a half dozen were there to be presented with toolboxes for their work on the centre.

The Premier demanded that police run the centre and became subject to bribery allegations, when he offered to cancel a council debt of $770,000 in exchange for public council support for the opening. The debt was incurred as a result of the payment of a government-appointed administrator when the government dismissed the council in 2003. It was being deducted from payments to council at a rate of $178,651 per month. Beattie admitted to offering to waive the debt but denied it was an inducement. The CMC cleared Beattie of the allegation. 'I just cannot believe they (Palm's Councillors) would spit in the eye...of the goodwill I've demonstrated,' he said. 'The government will need to examine whether this council can continue.'[34]

The coronial inquest reconvened on 28 February, but on 4 March State Coroner Michael Barnes stood down amid claims of bias, as he had previously presided over and dismissed complaints against Hurley, in his capacity with the CMC. Discovery of this history did much to foster suspicions of an ongoing official conspiracy in the handling of the death. The Queensland Police Union also called for Barnes to be removed for the indiscretion of having 'beer and a chat' with a lawyer involved with the case. Coroner Christine Clements was appointed to replace him.

The second inquest began on 30 March 2005, but delays were incurred when police challenged the admissibility of evidence regarding Hurley's past and Andrew Boe raised issues of miscommunication with witnesses in previous proceedings due to cultural misunderstandings. Boe noted the adoption of written statements from Aboriginal witnesses who could not read, the use of long-winded questions providing multiple choices and involving double negatives, and the indulgence in sarcasm by counsel assisting the inquiry. Coroner Clements was provided with insights into Aboriginal communication strategies and methods for facilitating clarity, while Erykah Kyle submitted the need for the Coroner to examine documentation of Palm Island's history 'to provide a context to the interaction between the Indigenous community and police'.

This book aims to place that history in the public domain, before exploring the findings of the coronial inquiry and their impacts. The Palm Island people have an extraordinary past. It is a rich, staggeringly brave, stoic and humorous, tragic and inspiring history to which these words can never do justice.

Chapter 2

Out from 'the Big Swag'

The shock headlines in 2004 marked the first time most non-Indigenous Australians had been alerted to the existence of Australia's largest Aboriginal community, Palm Island. Yet amongst Indigenous Australians, the island has a longstanding and widespread recognition as 'the Australian version of Alcatraz'. The Murri[1] artist, Hope Neill, who grew up on Cherbourg reserve has stated:

> Many of our stories were secreted away and went underground, while many also became lost because of the fear of being imprisoned for life on Palm Island if we broke the law. We lived in terror of imprisonment on Palm Island.[2]

Visitors to Palm are generally mesmerised by the island's stunning physical beauty — its aqua seas, postcard perfect skies, lush tropical rainforests and white sandy beaches. Most soon discover that this beauty is belied by the chronic poverty that is endemic across the community. For while events in 2004 drew media attention, the situation on Palm Island has been critical for decades.

Basic amenities that most Australians take for granted are not available. A population of more than 2,000 people is squeezed into 200 homes, many in poor condition. Regularly described as 'Third World', Palm's waiting list for housing consists of 300 families. Of 308 dwellings recently surveyed, more than one third were in urgent need of repair. With an average of close to twenty people in many homes, current funding allows for the building of three to four homes per year. In the 'Socio-Economic Index of Areas' (2008) across the nation, the Australian Bureau of Statistics recorded Palm as the fourth worst-off area in Australia. The three faring no better than Palm were also Indigenous communities.[3]

State government funding to Palm Island of $3,030, 465 — allocated in August 2009 — comprises general financial aid, an environmental health worker program and revenue replacement of $150,200 to cover the government's acquisition of profits from the alcohol canteen. This move was designed to break the nexus between the council's functioning and the supply of alcohol to residents. In this same month the Bligh government made preparations to secure tenure over Indigenous community lands and to negotiate 40-year land leases, so that land can be sub-leased to residents and home ownership encouraged. This has lead to protests from communities, concerned about the failure to address issues of compensation and community control. Palm Island Mayor Alf Lacey responded, 'We understand that there is a chronic shortage of housing in our communities, but I believe very strongly that slipping land away from under Aboriginal people's feet is not the way of doing things.'[4]

Aboriginal councils in Queensland are responsible for up to 59 functional operations compared to 34 for other local governments. On Palm Island this includes responsibility for administering a community housing program, employment and the provision of human services.

Available services on the island are suitable for a population of 500 — while at peak periods numbers are six times that figure. Only two per cent of that population are over the age of 65 — average life expectancy being 50 years.[5] Waves of self-destruction and violence erupt in the context of appalling social conditions. In 1990, an outbreak of elder abuse claimed the lives of some of the people I had interviewed for this research. In 1997, young people who had suicided were being buried on a monthly basis and while for a brief period the statistics improved, in 2003 sixteen young people took their own lives.

For people on isolated Palm Island, lives are built on the depressing assumption of mainstream indifference, because that has so frequently been their experience of history. Following the events in November 2004, members of the community would later speak of how they 'had been cryin' out for help but no one had listened.'[6]

Unresolved historical issues were opened like gaping wounds in the wake of the trauma caused by the death in custody. Much of that history has been hidden or distorted. Established in 1918 as a prison camp for Aboriginal and Torres Strait Islander people, it became the receiving centre for survivors of bitter clashes between colonisers and Indigenous people on the Queensland frontier.

Officially proclaimed 'a penitentiary for troublesome cases', the island detained survivors of the Kalkadoon Wars in the state's northwest, of the brutal massacres of the Cardwell region, and of the Tully River area, where one informant who was a child at the time stated that the people 'were killed without cover in the open river and the water ran red with their blood'.[7]

Throughout the 1920s and 1930s, Palm became the receiving centre for more than half the people removed to government reserves in Queensland, largely for trivial offences. Written records provide such scant explanations as: 'causing trouble', 'for their own protection', 'for the good of other aborigines' and 'to give the Superintendent authority over him'. Others were simply labelled: 'a troublesome character', 'incorrigible', 'very dangerous', 'destitute', 'a larrikin', 'a wanderer' and 'a communist'. Les Malezer has aptly described how the island became 'for our people the "end of the road"…the end point of our "trail of tears"'.[8]

The results have been paradoxical. Palm Island was the government's ultimate punitive destination for those who resisted colonisation — the backbone of a policy of containment and control. It was, in this sense, a detention centre for political prisoners. For more than half a century in this role, it produced generations of outstanding Indigenous leaders whose inspiring courage and fortitude I have attempted to document in these pages.

In keeping with other communities that endure third world conditions, Palm Island is a maligned community, its people accused even recently, by the then Queensland Premier, Peter Beattie, of housing lazy and 'dysfunctional' people who 'should get off their bums' and 'perform'. Yet Palm Islanders have survived decades of working conditions akin to slavery. The island has produced some of the first tertiary-qualified Murri nurses, teachers, visual and performing artists, outstanding sportsmen and women and community workers in this state.

Even recent reports, unfolding around the death of Mulrunji, have provided an obscuring misreading of history, silencing the story of Palm Island as Queensland's 'tropical gulag'. While some have misnamed the reserve as a church run 'mission' and 'a leper colony', still others have ascribed its inception to legislation to eliminate 'blackbirding' and, in extraordinary journalistic licence, have argued that 'There is no Dreamtime story to tell how Palm Island was created, a rarity in Aboriginal culture.'[10]

Yet the Traditional Owners of Palm Island, the Manbarra people, recently signed an Indigenous Land Use Agreement to develop a sponge farm at Coolgaree Bay. The Manbarra are the custodians of the story of Gubbal — the Carpet Snake or Big Snake — which explains the origins of the island. So, too, the people who take the name Bwgcolman are custodians of Palm Island history. The Bwgcolman are the people who have lived and died on Palm Island, and whose ancestors were deported there from all over Queensland, following its inception as a penitentiary.

The voices of 'the other side of the frontier' speak of the 'protectors' as the 'persecutors', the 'pioneers' were 'invaders' and 'glorified thieves', the police were the 'bulliman', Aboriginal 'guerilla leaders' were 'strategists' and 'clever men', and the 'sanctuary' of Palm Island was 'that punishment place'.

It is no accident that later chapters detail a series of nervous breakdowns on the part of the white elite minority dictating life on the island. While Palm's superintendents operated from assumptions of almost absolute power, they did so, over decades, in a context of extreme government neglect of even bare essentials on reserves. Placed in positions as 'benevolent dictators', they lived the enormous contradictions that this term implies. The events detailed in the opening chapter suggest that this model continues to apply to government influence on Palm Island today.

Despite consistently adverse conditions of institutional control and isolation, Palm Islanders have engaged in a history of political resistance that at times erupts with extraordinary ferocity. For almost 40 years, the options available were severely curtailed by the use of police brutality and the island's prison cells, with escape through shark-infested waters regarded as worth the risk by those most desperate to be free. When some of the isolation is broken down by contact with people on the mainland and with visiting Afro-American troops during the Second World War, a more collective and open revolt culminated in the most significant industrial action by Indigenous people in Queensland, with the Palm Island strike of 1957.

In the 50 years since the strike, Palm Islanders have played an important role in the development of Queensland's Foundation for Aboriginal and Islander Research and Action (FAIRA) — a crucial organisation, since the 1970s, in the exposure of race relations in the state — and in struggles for Indigenous models of governance, for land rights and for wage justice. Moreover, in the past two years Palm Islanders have taken action, in a volatile environment, to force the first legal action in Queensland history against a serving police officer in relation to a death in custody.

I have written this book as a conduit to a history not my own, but gleaned from friends and acquaintances from childhood through to the present. I grew up in a housing commission area on the south side of Brisbane where, in the 1960s, my cousins, sisters and I used to sing the song 'Little Boxes', with great derision for our 'ticky tacky' homes. My cousin Jan Hamilton introduced us to Rachael Wilson — later known as Rachael Cummins — who had become a friend at Cavendish Road High School. Having come to Brisbane from Palm Island,

Rachael spoke of how she had grown up in a fibro shed. The floor was cement and the internal walls were a single sheet of masonite.

We took running water and electricity for granted. Our parents were paid in wages for their labour; we kids had not been separated from our families and we could walk down the street whenever we chose. Our parents decided what food we would eat. None of them had ever been arrested for being late for work. Yet scores of Palm Islanders had. As an adult I was able to pursue my interest in Palm Island with the privilege of a university scholarship and invaluable assistance from Rachael Cummins, Leonie Daisy and Renee McBride in the process of meeting and engaging with the community and its representative bodies.

When I first flew over to Palm Island in 1989, I had no real grasp of how deeply Palm Islanders care for their history. Almost everyone I spoke with knew who I should talk to and about which events. With their ancestors exiled from all over Queensland, Palm Islanders carry great maps of genealogies and social histories in their heads. Historical commemorations are an inherent part of cultural practices on the island, history is a part of the air people breathe. As I write, on the wall beside me the Bwgcolman calendar states, 'If you deny the past, forget the future.'

This aspect of the research was in stark contrast to the days spent wading through unkempt boxes of government archives, stored haphazardly in a hostel at Aitkenvale, on the outskirts of Townsville. There I examined documents, some in boxes turned upside down with contents spilling onto the floor — a great mix up of records from Yarrabah, Mona Mona, Palm Island, Cooktown and elsewhere — that were covered in dust and dirt. It was a salutary lesson in Queensland government attitudes towards Aboriginal histories.

Shortly after completing what felt like a dusty, archaeological dig, I began visiting the island on a regular basis into the early 1990s. Father Mick Peters kindly invited me into the premises of the Catholic Church, where elders regularly got together. Paintings of Jesus Christ lined the walls and as I spoke with people over tea and biscuits, Jesus looked back at us with jet black eyes and dark brown skin.

Aboriginal art was being painted onto many of the buildings and elders were working at the schools to share their knowledge of culture and history. At the 'top end', I met the late Johnnie Jumbo who was busy making spears for the outstation at Casement Bay. It was a haven for those wanting to reinvigorate cultural traditions and seeking respite from the alcohol at the centre of town, where the canteen was the social hub and the site of much disorder and distress.

Kippy and the late Silas Prior invited me into their home at the top of a hill near the convent, where their small tin shed provided a view from the cliff of a sweeping panorama of sky, sand and emerald green hills. They gave generously of their time and offered me what I remember as one of the most peaceful days of my life. At the 'bottom end', the late Ivy Sam, gave up her morning to recount a history that she had told and retold in radio interviews and in speeches to public forums, with not a hint of impatience with this stranger, a white girl from the city who had arrived at her doorstep unannounced. Elizabeth Doomadgee and Donnie Currie offered me conversation over turtle stew and while we talked about Palm, Elizabeth's daughters brushed and stroked my hair with their tiny gentle hands.

That 'hellhole' the journalists called Palm Island was the home of a diverse people, all intricately connected, concerned about the welfare of their young and grappling with the issues of addiction and violence that affect so many communities of all kinds. They were doing so in the context of a battle with basic questions of survival — land, water, housing, jobs, health care and education — and with a determination to pursue a process of community ownership known as 'the Bwgcolman way'.

My experience of Palm in this period anchors itself upon one memory in particular. It is 1989 and I have brought a friend who is seeking possible blood relatives on the island. We are directed to Leonie Daisy and Abe Johnson's house, because 'Leonie knows everyone'. The house is directly behind a vacant block that was the site of the Curry tragedy. Having done some homework, I cannot help looking out the window and imagining February 1930. I consider how different the outcome would have been if some of the Murris had removed the Curry children from their home 'for their own safety'. Then I picture the scandal as black people take the white children away.

But Leonie distracts me. She is charismatic and energetic, strong and proud of her Bwgcolman identity and we share a love of history. Daughter of Jimmy Daisy and a niece to Iris Clay, she knows the stories of the island, its culture, people and politics. Opening her linen cupboard one evening, she shows me her 'history shelf', full of photographs, books and memorabilia. We talk until late. The next day Leonie and Abe take us out on their boat to circumnavigate the island.

We visit Eclipse or 'Punishment Island', where we are shown the poisonous red and black berries which people, exiled under punishment, would eat when the choice was suicide over a slow death from starvation. We steer past Turtle Rock, a sacred place that is a giant turtle rising out of the sea. Finding a spot to land, we picnic beside a crystal clear, freshwater creek at North East Bay.

Back on the boat the men dive into the ocean, disappearing under water for impossibly long times, before shooting up into the air, enormous clam shells under their arms and crayfish on the ends of their spears. There is lots of laughter, we eat beautiful fresh, clean food and the weather is a delight. Returning home we distribute fish across the community.

Back at the house that evening, while we help Leonie cook and Abe plays electric guitar, I notice that a movie is running through my mind, like a warm, visual stream that will not let me go. It is the ocean, wave after wave of aqua blue sea, the smell of salt water, the rainforest, the white sandy beaches, but most of all the sea. It is as though the ocean is inside me.

I have not felt this connection with nature since childhood and it is exhilarating. I am mesmerised. And I begin to understand how deep and fundamental is the Bwgcolman attachment to land and to history and not just why, but how, despite all the problems, people stay in this place that is paradise – why they call Palm Island home.

Chapter 3

Kenny's Time
From Carpet Snake Country to Hull River Reserve

> We call upon the government, then, in the name of common justice, to do their duty. The squatter has made Australia what it is, and he and the men in his employ are entitled to the protection for which they contribute.
>
> *Brisbane Courier*, 8 December 1864

> ... the white man was developing out there and the old blackfella was in the road, so they lifted 'em away.
>
> Bill Congoo, *Palm Island — A Punishment Place, Part II*
> (ABC Social History Unit, 1989)

In the Aboriginal histories of Magnetic Island and Palm Island, all are linked to the mainland through the journey of the Dreamtime Snake — called Carpet Snake or Big Snake. Virginnia Wyles recorded her family's knowledge of Magnetic Island: 'The Big Snake came down the Herbert River, went out to sea, and broke up leaving parts of his backbone which are the Palm Islands, and his head which is Magnetic Island.'[1] Reg Palm Island, who spoke of himself as belonging to the Manbarra language group of Palm Island, was interviewed in 1975:

> Young girls at Palm Island were told not to go near this big lagoon, but they wouldn't listen. The Snake swallowed one girl, and when her father came looking for her and couldn't find her he followed the Snake's track, back of this hill here...there is a place around the back of the hill called Carpet Snake Creek.
>
> The father walked down the creek and came to a little island, now called Cordelia Rock, which is Small Carpet Snake. The Small Carpet Snake told the father that the Big Carpet Snake had the little girl, and that he had gone to West Point, Magnetic Island. You can see where he was, on the beach at West Point.

> So the Snake asked the girl's father not to condemn him, because the girl was all right, he could take her out...Then he took all the evil spirits out of the girl, cleaned her up, and then took her back to Palm Island. The girl was sick, but still alive... There are rocks now from the shelter where they lived. The father was a clever man, and when he took the girl out of the Snake, he didn't hurt the Snake. The Snake kept on going; he went toward the mainland and made the Ross River. He kept on going toward the south.[2]

Reg Palm Island's father Dick, his mother Biddy, and his grandfather Mick, passed on to him their knowledge of Palm Island. While Reg's language was Manbarra, Buluguyban was another language used on the island, and speakers of the two groups understood each other. He stated that the original Palm Islanders could understand the language of Murris on the coast from Halifax to Magnetic Island.[3]

Reg recorded that the people travelled from island to island, then to Townsville for large gatherings, using bark canoes which seated six people. Palm Islanders also visited the mainland at Halifax, Ingham and Cape Pallarenda. Mainland groups similarly travelled to Palm by canoe. People of the offshore islands were linked to each other and the mainland linguistically, socially, through trade and travel and through movements occurring for large gatherings. Marriage patterns also linked local groups of the Magnetic/Palm Island/Townsville region predominantly with groups to the north — coastwards to Ingham and northwest to the areas of Mareeba, Dimbulah and Chillagoe. These connections would later serve as networks for sharing information and responses to the arrival of the Europeans.

Reg Palm Island spoke of the various forms of response and adaptation to the invasion of the colonisers in the early twentieth century which he witnessed as a young man. His ancestors had passed down the story that Manbarra people had watched Captain Cook's men land on their country late in the afternoon, but did not approach them. This information is in keeping with the journal kept by Cook when he anchored HMS *Endeavour* opposite Halifax Bay on 7 June, 1770. He recorded of the visit to the island by Hicks, Banks and Solander: 'They met with nothing worth observing.'[4] It is ventured that his perspective on the land was somewhat clouded.

Where, in Manbarra history, the vibrant origin myth of the Carpet Snake explains the creation and shaping of the land, the waters and the elements through the spirit ancestors of the region, and links the people spiritually to that land, the first British colonial records of Palm

Island perceived through European eyes a 'landscape'. It was something separate and alien, an object for criticism and even contempt.

Banks' journal of the episode describes how 'At noon the Islands had mended their appearance and people were seen upon them.' Palm Island is recorded as 'rocky and barren'. On steering closer he noted 'several fires upon it, one vastly large'. Banks added that their boat:

> put off from the shore when an Indian came very near it and shouted to us very loud...we...turned towards the shore by way of seeing what he wanted with us, but he I suppose ran away or hid himself immediately for we could not get sight of him.[5]

The men of the *Endeavour* had seen little visible human population along the whole eastern coastline and their gaze had generally been avoided. Phillip Parker King also met evasions when he surveyed the North Queensland coast in 1819 in the *Mermaid*. On 18 June, he landed on one of the Palm Islands and noted the presence of 'natives' huts and two canoes', the 'snug habitations' being 'of circular shape, and very ingeneously [sic] constructed' with twigs and grass thatch.[6]

In 1839, J Lort Stokes of the *Beagle* noted of the Palm Islands: 'Although a number of fires being once seen is not always a sign in Australia of a densely populated part of the country, yet when they are constantly visible, it is fair to infer, that the inhabitants are numerous and the soil fertile.'[7] The *Will O' the Wisp* carried sandalwood traders who intruded into the Palm Islands in 1845. During their stay, a well-planned attack was made by the island's Indigenous owners. Five or six canoes had surrounded the vessel at half past three in the morning. Six men stationed themselves over the hatchways. John MacGillivray of the *Rattlesnake* recorded: 'Their first act was to throw into the cabin and down the fore hatchway some lighted bark, and when the master and one of the crew rushed on deck in a state of confusion, they were instantly knocked on the head with boomerangs and rendered insensible.'

One of the crew came on deck with a sword, and the Palm Islanders retreated: 'the survivors retired in confusion', increased by the discharge of 'a swivel gun, mounted on a pivot amidships'.[8] Archibald Meston later wrote: 'The cause of the conflict and the number of blacks killed are facts not related by the *Will O' the Wisp* historian. As a matter of course, all subsequent white men visiting the Palms had an unpleasant reception.'[9] And so began a history of cultural and political collision between Indigenous land owners and European invaders which would be marked by conflict and increasing violence on the part of the merchants, now able to navigate a passage through the Great Barrier Reef.

James Morrill was a carpenter's mate of the *Peruvian* which was wrecked on Horseshoe Reef in 1846. Morrill came ashore with other survivors at Cape Cleveland, where he was incorporated into Murri society and lived in the Cleveland Bay area for seventeen years.

He later recorded that large ceremonial gatherings were held in the region, attended by 'considerably over a thousand souls' from ten different tribes of the North Queensland coast.[10] Large gatherings facilitated the conduct of a campaign of defence which was successful in holding back colonisation in many areas, and by 1860 was the prime anxiety of colonial Queensland.

The frontier became what Henry Reynolds has described as 'a finishing school for white arrogance and brutality'.[11] North Queensland Murris were perceived by Europeans as pests in the way of an inevitable and a sacred duty of the British to colonise in the name of 'progress'. The *Courier* argued that 'Nothing will prevent our native tribes acknowledging us as the superior race,' and that 'There is no need to argue in favour of our right to occupy this country — we take this to be for granted.'[12]

Pressure for the confinement and isolation of Murris into segregated reserves increased steadily from the 1860s. It heightened with the establishment of the Cardwell township to service the Valley of Lagoons from 1864, and European sojourns into Townsville, which was soon to follow as a sea port. The region was described by the Cardwell Police Magistrate in this period as 'a country much infested with blacks', and he organised for a gun to be fired to rally the Europeans together should Murris approach at night.[13] Situated at the foot of the Sea View Range, white residents lived in fear of attack for almost twenty years.

European weaponry gave North Queensland whites a strong advantage in the conduct of warfare, but coastal Murris continued to exploit the terrain with its rainforests, rugged mountain ranges and escape routes via the sea. On 12 January 1863 the police officer in Bowen had advised the Colonial Secretary that from the Burdekin to Halifax Bay 'The reports of murders and depredations committed by the blacks are so frequent and the panic in the district so great' as to make the need for 'additional detachments of Native Police'.[14]

The introduction of this force — a response to panic in the Cardwell region — was a crucial alteration to frontier conflict which now became marked with frequent punitive expeditions. It operated as a colonial army, with extermination squads of six to twelve people. In 1865, when Halifax was first occupied by whites, the Murri population was reported as numbering 500. Fifteen years later it was reported to total only 22.[15] WRO Hill, Acting Sub-Inspector under Police Commissioner

Seymour in the late 1860s, believed that: 'the only wise thing to do on seeing a black was to shoot and shoot straight, otherwise he would certainly spear you.'[16]

Women in particular were targeted. Native Police were 'usually encouraged' to shoot the women, seen to be 'agents and abettors' in hampering colonial conquest. George Carrington wrote of contemporary opinion in this period: 'There is another argument, which is obvious, as I have often heard it openly avowed, that the country will never be what it ought until the blacks are exterminated, why, the more women are shot, the better.'[17]

Examinations by Queensland historians of the dispersed records of Native Police activities indicate that the Cardwell to Port Douglas region was a site where their impact was most destructive. Native Police were recruited from distant areas and according to Hill, 'were as easy to manage as children' if the officers used 'a bob, a nip of whisky or a flogging'. Yet the fact that many absconded was a regular complaint of officers.[18]

In 1865, a detachment of this small colonial army arrived in Cardwell in response to local pressure. The Police Magistrate had written to the Colonial Secretary, reporting the killing of a German at the Valley of Lagoons and advising that Murris had become 'unusually numerous all around the town'. A 'great uneasiness' had developed amongst the white population and large numbers of Murris had arrived by canoes from Hinchinbrook Island, 'for what purpose I cannot tell'.[19]

On 23 March 1867 the *Cleveland Bay Express* recorded an 'almost unbroken line of smoke and fires around Halifax Bay...also numerous on the Coast Range, and to be seen on several of the Palm Islands'. Large gatherings were noted as taking place 'all along the coast'. The following year Police Commissioner Seymour of Townsville advised the Colonial Secretary that 'The coast country all along from Townsville to Mackay is inhabited by blacks of the most hostile character.'[20]

In the Murray and Tully River areas, the tactics of the colonisers were increasingly those of arsenic-laced flour and massacre. By the 1870s and 1880s most believed, like George Carrington, that there were two 'classes' of Murris— the 'tame blacks' of the south and the 'wild blacks' of the north, and that 'the best way of "civilising" them is to shoot them'.[21] The Colonial Secretary drew the attention of parliament to an article in the *Central Australasian* which alleged that Sub-Inspector Johnstone, leader of Native Troopers in the Cardwell region:

> ...spoke of killing whole camps – not merely men but girls and piccaninnies – with the greatest coolness. Further experience of

this man and other residents in these parts ...have convinced me that the policy of the Queensland government towards the blacks is simply, though not unavowedly, one of extermination.[22]

One such camp that fell victim to Johnstone's dawn raids was at Tom O'Shanter Point. In 1872, in retaliation for a Dijiri killing of gold prospectors of the *Maria* — shipwrecked on Bramble Reef — Johnstone and his troopers cornered a group before daylight, and massacred almost an entire tribe. The group was driven to the sea and women and children shot as they leapt into the water. In 1875, the killing of the Conns, who were farming south of Cardwell, inspired further random reprisals.

Hunger enticed survivors to move into stations from the 1860s. Fringe camps became an escape from the terrorism of the towns and curfews were imposed. While Murris continued to reside in and around the Townsville region, their movements were restricted by police, and their numbers reduced to approximately one-quarter or less of their pre-contact numbers. Removals occurred upon farmers' requests. Forced removals and food distribution centres would eventually reach their logical extension in the establishment of reserves. Half-hearted and under-funded attempts to develop reserves on Hinchinbrook Island, the Tully River, Cardwell and Townsville occurred in the 1870s and 1880s. Coastal fisheries, especially the harvesting of bêche-de-mer (sea cucumber) and pearl shell, also took their toll, with frequent kidnappings and violence.

Further kidnappings occurred when, at the turn of the century, European perceptions of Indigenous people as 'exotic strangers' became important to the success of tourist ventures in North Queensland. In 1883 Barnum, Bailey and Hutchinson's 'Greatest Show on Earth' circus visited North Queensland, luring away a group of six Manbarra people — three men and two of their wives, as well as a child — and another three people from Hinchinbrook Island to perform overseas as spectacles for audiences in Europe and America. In European zoos the troupes performed as human specimens and grew ill from the cold weather, tuberculosis and other infectious diseases. By 1885 only three members of the troupe were still alive.[23]

On Palm Island a resident tourist industry became entrenched with the construction of a Harry Butler's Guest House at Butler Bay to service colonial travellers. The Butlers had settled at Picnic Point, Magnetic Island, in 1877 and helped to staff stations at Hawkins Point and Nobby Point to accommodate English settlers to Australia. Government records specify that Butler held a private lease of 320 acres (130 hectares) in Butler Bay with accommodation for forty visitors. Another 320 acres were leased by Thos Francis at Coolgaree Bay.[24]

Reg Palm Island said that his father Dick worked for Butler, gathering oysters and peat for manure, while also hunting for fish and turtle to support his family. Both Butler and Francis developed pig farms on the island, causing serious interference with Aboriginal lifestyles. On 14 June 1913 Sweetman, as the Townsville Inspector and Protector of Aboriginals, wrote to the Chief Protector that the pigs 'of which they have a large number' were allowed 'to roam all over the Island, rooting up the whole place': 'The Aboriginals' dogs in hunting wallabies must come across the pigs and naturally hunt them as well. It is hard indeed if under the circumstances the blacks get their best dogs shot.'

Sweetman attached a letter from Reg Palm Island's father, Dick:

> Please Sair,
>
> I am just taking the pleasure of writing a line to ask you about how far Mr Francis and Mr Butler had paid rend for grown in here ...we want to know if they pay rent for this place please Sair....Mr Francis and Mr Butler they are shooting all our Best dog we had just because our dog been bit a pig near our place.... Butlar and Francis told us that if we do kill pig near our place or anywhere else outside this Island they going to Report us ...we want you to come so we can tell you how they Treat us on this Island ...these boys had no blanket they are all at home now and that is all I have to say.[25]

The surviving Manbarra and Buluguyban peoples managed to acquire European dinghies and cutters to the benefit of hunting practices. Reg Palm Island stated that his grandfather Mick would work for half of a year at Halifax on bêche-de-mer boats, and for the other half lived his own lifestyle on the island. He said that many Palm Islanders worked for fishermen at Cooktown (650 kilometres north of Townsville) and died there. His grandmother continued to live in the bush, getting food from the island supplied by two or three people in canoes.

In 1910, the Chief Protector, Richard B Howard, expressed his frustration that attempts to introduce agricultural cultivation had been 'without any result'. Throughout its post-contact history, the official European attitude was one of increasing intervention. Regular government visits with provisions of food and tobacco occurred throughout the early twentieth century, despite official acknowledgment that these were a people 'making a good living and well able to look after themselves'.[26]

Throughout the conflict which colonisation wrought, the Manbarra and Buluguyban at no stage ceded their lands. They were eventually forcibly removed to the mainland. Demands for the segregation of Murris in the Townsville/Palm Island region were made with increasing urgency. Isaac Henry voiced the opinions of many in North Queensland when in 1885 he contacted the Colonial Secretary seeking action. 'It is now,' he wrote, 'a matter of white or black on the Tully.'[27]

With the growing acknowledgment by Europeans of the futility of outright warfare and the strength of Aboriginal resistance came pressure to harness Indigenous labour by force. This process received sanction with the introduction of the *Aboriginals Protection and Restriction of the Sale of Opium Act 1897* which became known simply as the Queensland Act. The rationale for the legislation was provided by Archibald Meston.

A former member of state parliament and sugar planter, Meston had not spoken out concerning the abuse of Murris or proposals to alleviate distress until the 1890s, while others expressed concern, especially over the actions of the Native Police, from the 1850s. Influenced by the eugenic theories of Karl Pearson, Meston abhorred 'the breeding of half-castes'. Author of the 1896 'Report on the Aboriginals of Queensland', Meston advised the government that 'the law of the strongest' dictated that Murris accept 'enforced residence in one locality'. They 'could be collected,' he argued, and 'made to produce their own food by hunting, fishing and cultivation'. He supported the 'principle of isolation on reserves' in response to the 'perpetual warfare' of the colony.[28]

Though proclaimed a 'benevolent' procedure, the process of removal was conducted by armed police who enforced submission using handcuffs and the chaining of feet. Round-ups became a significant feature of people's lives in North Queensland. Police would patrol an area for several days, 'mustering' those who worked without exemption tickets. Warning systems were developed by Murris to signal the need to move camp or to hide in the rainforest to avoid detection between round-ups.

The use of white law to sanction herding people to reserves began in Queensland, lasted in this colony for the longest period of time, affected the greatest number of people and served as a prototype for reserve systems in other colonies. Where in the late nineteenth-century frontier period Aboriginal people in Queensland were treated as animals, by the early twentieth century they were increasingly regarded as children.

Using the familiar model of relations between father and child, paternalism operated ideologically to facilitate institutional rule. But while the father-child relationship is generally tempered by love, the rule of Protectors and Superintendents was motivated by concerns of productivity, indoctrination and social control. In 1905, Roth as Northern Protector expressed the official white attitude to Murris on reserves: 'They are and will always remain children, and therefore must be protected, even sometimes against their will.'[29]

Yet control on reserves was never absolute and by 1916 Chief Protector of Aborigines J W Bleakley, reported to the Under-Secretary of Home Affairs that 'a serious strike had occurred amongst the paid workers at Taroom over objections to monthly banking'.[30] Bleakley, the son of an Ipswich boiler maker, held a clerk's position from 1905 on Thursday Island before his promotion to Chief Protector in 1914. A committed segregationist, the year that he commenced the role he had overseen the gazettal of Palm reserve, as part of his efforts to ensure the establishment of institutions for the maintenance of 'racial purity'. While Bleakley would write frankly of his dissatisfaction over cases of cruelty and injustice towards Aboriginal people, he did so from a mindset committed to the ideas of his epoch in relation to removal of 'the half-caste problem' and 'keeping the breed pure'.

Abscondings from reserves became one of his constant concerns and specifically punitive reserves were soon perceived as necessary. Situated north of Cardwell at South Mission Beach, Hull River reserve was used for the confinement of those who escaped other institutions, and settlers in the region can recall Murris being driven there in handcuffs and chains.[31] Others had been waging an effective armed defence of their homelands in North Queensland — burning sugarcane, stealing cattle and occasionally spearing lone settlers.

Peter Prior recounted:

> In 1916 they picked up my whole family and a few other dark people off Strathmore Station around Collinsville and sent us to Yarrabah Mission first. According to my father they wanted to get rid of all dark people on the mainland. 1917 all the old people didn't like how we were getting fed at Yarrabah, we were only living on cooked banana and potato. More than anyone else, those old people wanted to go back to their homes where they came from...We ran away from there and they picked us up outside of Tully, the whole family, and they kept us at Hull River Mission.[32]

The reserve was run by JM Kenny, an ex-policeman, previously in charge of a Northern Native Police force. Kenny arrived at Hull River on 15 September 1914 and began to establish the site at the northern end of South Mission Beach. Bleakley recorded that despite the fact that Murris had responded with 'great alarm' to the development of the reserve, it had by 1915 'absorbed practically the whole of the native population of that and neighbouring districts'.[33]

Established during the peak of Queensland's removal orders, Hull River was soon overcrowded, with women and children sent to the reserve from camps and towns, following the introduction of government policy that children be removed from 'the aboriginal atmosphere'. Their labour, used to establish plantations, was under duress and without reward. Bleakley complained of 'the disinclination on the part of the inmates to work without pay, even for their own benefit' and noted that under Kenny's rule, 'Loafers and malingerers are punished by the stoppage of rations.'

The housing situation soon affected people's health due to Kenny's poor selection of a site. In February 1917, he reported an outbreak of malaria. Subsequent visits by a government medical officer lead to the removal of the grass huts to higher ground, out of the malarial swamps. Measles, whooping cough and pneumonia took their toll and by the end of that year 200 people had been buried near the beach to the north end of the shelter shed. This amounted to the death of almost 50 per cent of the people removed to Hull River in little more than a three-year period, suggesting that the reserve experience was a very genocidal one indeed.

From its inception, the reserve had a history of turmoil, being troubled with opium addiction, abscondings and the intervention of police to maintain control. On 28 August 1917, Constable Martin reported from Cairns Police Station that he had four men in custody who were sentenced to two months jail after having absconded from Hull River. The old people would crawl out of the windows at night and attempt to return to their lands.[34]

It was in this context that Bleakley recommended the prompt establishment of a reserve on Palm Island. The concept of using the geographical features of an island to form a closed institution was not new. In Queensland, a Select Committee on the Condition of the Aborigines in 1846 had recommended the use of Fraser Island and proposed that 'martial law' and 'captivity' could provide the means of establishing 'penal settlements' on other islands off the Queensland coast.[35] The 'Report of the Commissioners' in 1874 had also favoured the use of islands for penal purposes, noting: 'It would scarcely be practicable to have a prison on the mainland ...but there are several islands off the coast which meet the requirements of isolation combined with ample area of land adapted for agriculture.'[36]

The European strategy of exiling outcasts to offshore islands met with favourable conditions along Queensland's east coast. By the 1880s, a vast array of punitive institutions were used to confine the poor, incapacitated and infirm. Those who did not fit comfortably within the grand colonial framework of work, development, and self-sufficiency were simply 'whisked away'. By the 1890s, even the wildlife was being imprisoned, with Rattlesnake Island, south of Palm off the coast at Kurukon, defined as 'a penal settlement for town goats'![37]

From 1897, the development of a punitive reserve on Badjala land at Fraser Island would serve as a prototype to the later institution on Palm. Murri ex-prisoners were sent to Fraser Island from Brisbane, Rockhampton, Roma, Townsville and Cardwell. The island was under the surveillance of the armed physical presence of the Mestons and a lock-up and police force soon established. Those removed from their homelands developed an earth-eating disease as a result of nutritional deprivation. Before its closure in 1905, the reserve had become 'a vast burial ground' where those who fell ill believed they were destined to die.

By 1916, Chief Protector Bleakley complained to the Under-Secretary that neither Hull, Taroom nor Barambah could cope with the growing numbers under the Act, and that a reserve was needed 'suitable for use as a penitentiary', to confine 'the individuals we desire to punish'. Bleakley decided to take advantage of Kenny's removal of Palm Island people to Hull River, to carry out an inspection of the island.[38]

Bleakley's plans for Palm were soon realised when a cyclone demolished Hull River reserve in 1918. Annie Tallis, a young Murri resident at the time, recalled swimming with a group of girls on 10 March when the blow began late in the afternoon, the sand spinning 'like pins and needles' around their legs: 'We tried to run for cover but the wind was blowing that much we were rolling in the mud. We couldn't walk so we had to crawl on our bellies...It was real slippery and we couldn't stand.'[39]

One of the worst cyclones in living memory to hit the coast, it took the lives of at least fifteen Murri residents, the Superintendent and his daughter. The *North Queensland Register* reported that 'During the storm the surges raged for 100 yards [90 metres] beyond the high water mark and the blacks were wading to their armpits in the tidal wave.' Huge seas swept the frontal ridge, demolishing most of the huts and humpies and scooping out the gravesite. The 'terrified shrieks of the living' mingled with 'the savage outcries of the storm',[40] while distressed birds and millions of insects from the demolished plantations 'cast themselves on the hospitality of human beings to their dismay and discomfort'.

Mr and Mrs Kenny, their daughter and son huddled from the violent gusts of wind under their house, but a heavy piece of timber pierced through their bodies. A girl by the name of Maud had tried to rescue Mr Kenny when he asked her to lift him out, but he fell from her grasp and died. Two Murri residents sheltered beneath the Assistant Superintendent's residence, but when the Hazeldine house collapsed both were crushed to death.

When the wind subsided, rain fell in torrents and a wailing was heard all around the ruined settlement. It was not until the following day that police arrived from Cardwell in response to a notice of the tragedy sent by Banfield of Dunk Island. The steamer *Lass O'Gowrie* arrived on 14 March with Captain Stuart who gave priority to transferring the injured Mrs Kenny to hospital. The government ship *Melbidir* did not arrive for the remaining people until 31 March, more than two weeks later.[41]

Following the arrival of Bleakley from Brisbane, the *Kurandah* transferred the surviving boys and girls to Palm Island, while the *Tully* took the older people, who were forced to leave over 100 dogs which they owned, barking their mourning cries on the beach. Some of the Palm Islanders who had been sent to Hull River found they had come full circle.

Later press reports of the tragedy noted that local residents had been surprised at the outset by the location of a reserve 200 feet (180 metres) high from sea level and 600 yards (550 metres) from the beach, facing due east on the weather-exposed crest of a hill. Despite Kenny's previous experience of two cyclones, argued the *North Queensland Register*, 'the unfair' task of selecting a site should not have been placed in his hands, for 'It was a fatal blunder on the part of the authorities to put such responsibility on the shoulders of a single individual.' Yet, the article concluded, 'how needless and ill-beseeming to discuss the subject'.[42]

If the Hull River experience had seemed to prove the fatal weaknesses of appointing 'lone shepherds' to guide 'whole flocks', the pattern was soon repeated in the subsequent relocation of the reserve to Palm Island. For it was on this isolated island settlement that a 'kindly parental control' was invested in Robert Henry Curry, a returned serviceman, who oversaw the construction of an institution which 'had the appearance of a well run military establishment'. Initially known as 'Uncle Boss', Curry's later actions would earn him the reputation of 'Mad Dog'.

Chapter 4

Curry's Time
'A State of Constant Apprehension'

Our parents were first taken there like refugees, taken by shiploads...My father was sent to Palm in handcuffs because he wanted five shillings when he worked on a cattle station. He died on Palm Island and never saw his parents again.

Thelma McAvoy[1]

Any Aborigines who kicked up a row outside, that's where they'd send you. I can tell you we were frightened of it.

Mo Dallachy[2]

While initially Palm Island operated as the receiving centre for the survivors of the demolished Hull River reserve, the island's population soon expanded as new arrivals became residents of the penitentiary first envisaged by Chief Protector Bleakley in 1916. Throughout the 1920s, Murris and Torres Strait Islanders were shipped to the island 'like cattle' and by truckloads, some following sentencing by white courts, others after release from prison, or from other reserves where they had refused to show deference to white authorities. Others were simply 'whisked away' in periodic government round-ups on the mainland. Fears of being removed to Palm Island, from which there was little chance of escape, were passed down through generations of Indigenous people in Queensland.

The island became a key instrument in the operations of the punitive Queensland Act, playing the dual role of dispossessing and controlling Murris on and near outback stations, while facilitating control of those already confined on mainland reserves. Interviewed by Bill Rosser, Peggy James of the Boulia region in the west recalled that police used the threat of removal to Palm as a successful method of control: 'They had only to mention Palm Island and we were quiet.' Ruby De Satge of Djarra recorded of station labourers: 'They just had to take a flogging and that was it. If they fought back, well, they'd get sent off to Palm Island.'

The reserve also enhanced the government's strategy of cultural genocide. The term 'uncontrollable' in removal orders commonly meant simply being found 'trespassing' on cattle stations which had been built on their lands, disobeying work orders, or practising culture. In addition, Murris were sent to the island for speaking out against the 'protection' laws, so that a growing number of political prisoners were congregated on the reserve. Joe McGinness recalled police 'mustering Aborigines' throughout western Queensland in the 1920s and wrote:

> Both Aborigines and Torres Strait Islanders feared being sent there. The threat was often made by those in authority as intimidation against people whenever they looked like stepping out of line to 'behave yourself or you will be sent to Palm Island'.[3]

In 1923, the stockman Albert Hippi was removed from Saxby Downs Station to Palm Island, the order sanctioned on the basis that 'He frightens women and tries to get liquor.' What the removal order did not record was that Hippi had organised a petition amongst his fellow workers, which he forwarded to the Minister for Justice, J Mullan, seeking greater control over their wages through access to their bank accounts.[4] Removal orders in 1924 sent Paddy Brooks from Millaa Millaa to the island on the basis that he 'causes discontent', Herbert from Camooweal because he 'leaves employers', Martin Joe from Cairns because he 'will not work', Jimmy Rutherford of Charters Towers who was 'too old to work', Emma from Cloncurry labelled 'uncontrollable' and 'immoral', Jimmy from Croydon because he was 'unable to obtain employment', Reilly from Townsville 'upon discharge from jail', Frank from Cairns, labelled an 'agitator' and Billy, Louie and Arrauman from the Kendall River for being 'leaders of three fighting tribes'.[5]

Previous convictions, unemployment, resignation from work and old age thus became punishable offences for Aboriginal people. Women were sent to the island for the 'crime' of having children to white men, others for being 'vagrant' or 'destitute'. In 1919 a series of removals were ordered from Turn Off Lagoon near Burketown because Murris in the area were considered a threat by the station manager. Others in the region were taken, according to government records, 'to be made an example of'. In 1930 *Truth* newspaper reported allegations that police had accepted monetary bribes from station owners to 'bundle' Murris off 'to the obscurity of Palm Island'.[6]

Large numbers of North Queensland Murris and Torres Strait Islanders in coastal regions were also sent to Palm. For some it was an extension onto a sentence for which time had already been served —

the sentence to Palm in some ways more severe, since the time frame was indefinite. Fred Fulford recalled of his removal to Palm in 1924:

> They rounded up all the blacks they thought were troublemakers around the towns at Bowen, Innisfail, Tully and the rest. I did three months in jail in Cairns for helping a man steal a horse. When I came out they put me on a boat.[7]

Chief Protector Bleakley promoted the confinement of children in reserve dormitories, and during his reign parents were sometimes illegally threatened by police that they had either to let go of their children or be sent to Palm Island. Historian Mark Copland's examination and database of removals in Queensland records the removal of 7,198 Indigenous people across Queensland between the years of 1911 and 1940. Many were marched in leg irons, in neck chains, or in both, and often at gunpoint. Some were forced to travel hundreds of miles on foot, sometimes on horseback, or loaded into the back of trucks.

Copland estimated that at least 13,076 Queensland Aboriginal children were separated from country and kin.[8] Conducting oral history in southwestern Queensland in the 1990s, I was told by longstanding residents that in some towns you could hear the wailing as the trucks ran through the back streets at night. Between 1918 and 1971 almost 4,000 people were removed to Palm Island.

It could take several weeks for prisoners to reach the Burns Philp jetty to be taken by launch, under armed police escort, to the island. Older residents of Palm speak of the heartbreak and loneliness they felt when torn from their families. None of the available evidence suggests that Murris attributed any legitimacy to these efforts to annihilate Aboriginal sovereignty over lands. Open revolt occurred at times, some absconding individually, others assaulting police.

In 1924, a group described by police as 'ringleaders' and 'undesirables' were chained together at Normanton and due to be removed to Palm Island, when they staged a planned and concerted attempt at escape. The *North Queensland Register* reported:

> All hands were turned out for the night's camp, the prisoners were all chained together and tied to trees, each man having leg-irons and handcuffs on. The Sergeant picking his way among the chains, feeding the men, leant down to give one his issue, the move nearly cost him his life. One bad character...pushed up close to the boy next to him, gathered up the loose chain and caught the Sergeant around the neck. It was arranged also, that

the other officer of the Patrol be caught in the same way, but the men missed their mark.[9]

Evasions were frequent. Joe McGinness recorded that he and Tom Sullivan had moved from western Queensland to the Northern Territory in order to avoid 'the dragnet' taking people to Palm Island in the late 1920s. Avoiding capture or escape during removal by police were the only means available for resisting the process, since the Act made no provision for a tribunal to hear removal cases, and provided no appeal against the Protector's orders.

By 1930, the population of Palm Island had grown to over one thousand. In this same year the *North Queensland Register* reported that: 'Many bushmen can tell you of old blacks, who for years have evaded capture. Blacks who live in perpetual fear of being rounded up and sent to the island.' While removal from homelands to any of the 'settlements' was described as the source of fear, the spectre of Palm Island had instilled a particular 'dread', and instances were recorded of Murris preferring to live with starvation and in complete isolation than to face 'the so-called glories of an island home'.[10]

Palm Island reserve played a crucial role in repressing Aboriginal political activity in Queensland well into the 1930s, while other states witnessed the formation of organisations like the Australian Aborigines' League and the Australian Aboriginal Progressive Association.[11] Residents of reserves were subjected to levels of bureaucratic control which have 'never applied to persons in Australia outside of jails and asylums'.[12] An alien work ethic became the guiding principle with residents compelled to work a minimum of 24 hours each week without pay, under threat of imprisonment or further banishment to neighbouring Eclipse Island. While white workers were receiving wages with automatic adjustments regulated by the Arbitration Court, Palm Islanders queued for rations of tea, sugar and flour, an experience described by Iris Clay as 'terrible' and 'degrading'. Clothes were provided, but were made from hessian sugar bags — material hardly designed for comfort in a tropical climate.

Epidemics of introduced diseases rapidly took hold on the reserve, and by 1924 the death rate had reached more than sixteen per cent of the population, at a time when the general Queensland death rate was less than nine per cent. Yet official government reports on the reserve spoke of the 'happy appearance of the people' and of a 'general atmosphere of industry and contentment', while the island was promoted as a 'model settlement' for visiting tourists. Following tightly controlled tours of inspection, visitors left the island to record 'there is nothing to grieve about, for a more happy and contented lot of human beings cannot be found anywhere' and that the island was a 'holiday home', with an administration both 'fair and popular'.[13]

When Superintendent Curry first arrived with the Hull River residents in April of 1918 he had erected a tent for himself on the beach, while Murris camped in gunyahs of blade grass, scrap iron and kerosene tins.

Their labour was soon put to use for the construction of roads, the planting of palm trees and vegetables, and for a building program which gave priority to homes for the white staff. A few grass huts would later be built for Murri residents, and a flat-roofed hospital shed for those recovering from the cyclone. They killed pigs and caught fish to obtain food supplies.

Reg Palm Island stated that some of the Traditional Owners were still resident on the island when the reserve was constructed, but they were not hostile towards the institution's residents. As the receiving centre of prisoners and casualties from frontier relations, the reserve soon expanded, with the dominant groups formed by the Kandju, Kuku Yalanji, Yidangi, Kongkanji, Birri Gubba and Kokoimudji of northeast Queensland and the Kalkadoon of the northwest. These groups then camped in specific areas chosen by the older residents, but under Curry's supervision, with tribes from close localities forming joint camps.

Some were sent from mainland reserves as punishment and because of overcrowding. Bessie Lymburner's mother and auntie were sent from overpopulated Mapoon. Though she had committed no crime, her mother's feet were put in chains and she was taken by horseback to Coen and Laura, then by mailtrain from Cooktown, then onto the steamer.[14] By the end of Curry's reign in 1930, Palm Island had acquired representatives of more than forty different language groups.

In a short period, Curry had used his role as a confident and dogmatic overseer to organise the almost complete clearing of the country fronting Challenger Bay, back towards the hills. The institution cost little in government funding. Cyclone salvage brought from Hull River was soon complemented by timber from a mill which was built and worked by Murri labourers. By 1919, three homes had been constructed for white officials and a store, office and nurses' quarters were erected using materials from Hull reserve.

The Works Department valued Curry's home as worth £1,000; that of his assistant was valued at £850.[15] Following the excavation and construction of Mango Avenue by the Hull River people, it was subsequently declared 'out of bounds' to all who were not white, with gates at each end of the road barring access.

Facing Mango Avenue were the homes of nurse Ellen Hazeldine, schoolteacher Eric Davison, storekeeper Leonard Ballard, launch attendant Joseph Hamilton, Assistant Superintendent Thomas Hoffman and Superintendent Robert Curry. The office was situated 50 yards (45 metres) from Curry's house, on the opposite side of the road and at the centre of the settlement. The senior girls' dormitory was built next door to Curry's residence, and a women's jail constructed in Curry's backyard — a mere six yards (5.5 metres) from the house.

The 'native school' and the 'white school' were in two separate buildings on opposite sides of the road. The entire compound was fenced in, with an access gate at the end of Mango Avenue and another at the road leading to the bridge. An additional tall wire fence surrounded both the junior and senior girls' dormitories. By the late 1920s, Palm Island had been landscaped to a design with two key principles — segregation akin to apartheid, and containment akin to a prison.

The lives of Palm Islanders in the camps were strictly supervised by the Superintendent who was frequently armed and by constant patrols of the Native Police appointed by Curry. A visiting reporter from the *North Queensland Register* reported: 'It was remarkable to me how the Superintendent controlled everything, and everybody, without any restraints, and with very few words. He has subordinates among the blacks — and these got the few words of instruction.'[16]

The relationship between the Superintendent and his police was similar to those of military establishments. From a pastoral family background in Malanda, North Queensland, Curry had enlisted in the Australian Imperial Force in 1915 and served in the Remounts Unit until his return to Australia less than twelve months later. He was appointed to the position of Assistant Superintendent at Barambah reserve (renamed Cherbourg in 1931) from June 1917 until the middle of the following year when he was posted as Superintendent to Palm Island, accompanied by his wife Agnes, as matron. Curry adhered to rigid and authoritarian notions of control, and in the latter half of his reign became preoccupied with the extent of his command.

A curfew was established during Curry's time, the bell rang at 9.30 each evening, and residents found outside their homes after 10pm were promptly arrested. By 1919, a lock-up operated to confine those who breached the stringent reserve regulations. Meetings of Murri inmates were taboo on the island, the argument being that 'these gatherings in the early days were nothing more than war councils'. Fear seemed to dominate the conduct of white officials generally, and all kept arms on their premises.

Palm Island people answered to Curry's roll call in the mornings, before working at making roads using their hands, shovels, mattocks and picks. They carried heavy bags of stone from the hills and ground coral to lime in order to whitewash the rocks which lined the streets. Murri labour was used to drain, clear, till and plant in areas designated by Curry as suitable for farming or plantations. Others were employed as butchers, bakers, cleaners, domestics and yardsmen for white households, jailers, carpenters, hygiene workers and plumbers, while others were appointed as Native Police in charge of work gangs.

The number of older residents with complaints today of back and shoulder problems bears testimony to the lack of capital equipment provided for these endeavours. 'We had no horse,' Cappy Smith recalls of the early years, 'we had no dray, we had no plough.' When the dray did arrive it was pulled by Murri labourers in the absence of a horse. As Joe Garbutt put it: 'Well those days we had no bullocks. We were the bullocks ourselves.'[17]

Curry selected those to receive a minimal and sub-standard wage, although most workers were what he referred to as 'half-time boys' who 'cost us nothing', many of whom did the heavy work of making roads and hauling timber. Others received rations for carting cargo from the boats which anchored about a mile out to sea due to fringing coral reefs. The men scaled the reefs barefoot, carrying goods from the steamers which might not arrive until 11pm. Murris had also to carry white tourists and visitors from boat to shoreline, on their back, so that they would not get their feet wet. Boat owners in the trochus shell trade used Palm as a source of diving labour in the 1920s, taking people to sea at meagre rates of £3 or £4 per month.[18]

While Murri labourers built Palm Island reserve, it was the white staff on the island who took the credit. In 1929, for example, the Queensland Public Service Commissioner was advised that Mr Hoffman had built the settlement store, and that Mr Bond had built the hospital on neighbouring Fantome Island. Murri labourers had not only built Fantome's facilities, but also carried cargo to and from the island by hand and shoulder.

Murris on reserves became dependent upon rations and material goods for sustenance and were pressured to adapt to the Western economic system and its protestant work ethic. The Queensland Act facilitated the process. Marnie Kennedy grew up on Palm Island during Curry's time and was sent to work on cattle stations. In *Born a Half-Caste* she wrote:

> We were under the Act which means we must obey, work hard, do as you are told, and be used in any way the white man wishes.

You were not to answer back. You were to do your job be it right or wrong. If you were signed on for twelve months then you had to do twelve months however you hated it.

The changing use of Palm Island in the 1920s was determined by the development of the North Queensland sugar cane fields, the fishing industry, the trochus shell trade and the expansion of the pastoral frontier where Murris became indispensable as stockmen. People were drafted out to mainland employers on contracts which could be neither broken nor even negotiated. The separation of children to dormitories ensured that the women, too, were available as a source of cheap, transportable labour.

The reserve subsidised pastoralists by providing cheap labour. Marnie Kennedy stated that she married a head stockman to escape the Act: 'Some of the girls got married to be free from the chains around our necks and free from the penal settlement.'[19]

Bleakley denied applications for exemption where the appellants were considered 'ineligible or unfit to be given control of their own affairs' or were regarded as not committed to assimilation 'because of being married to, living or associating with aboriginals, lack of education or business ability'. Fewer exemptions than requested were ever granted, and an exempted person could be returned to the reserve and placed again under the Act, at the direction of employers, police and government officials. In 1925, only nineteen of a total of 107 applications were granted. And while the exemption system operated the number of removals continued to grow, Palm Island's official population approaching 900 by 1929.[20]

A compulsory banking system allowed police stations control over money earned and its distribution. The 1897 Act and subsequent legislation enabled the establishment of a 'Provident Fund', which allowed the government to deprive Queensland's Indigenous workers of their wages for over eighty years. Archival research by historian Rosalind Kidd suggests that at least $500 million – 'and it could be several times that' — was taken by successive Queensland governments from Aboriginal earnings — a figure that is ten times the amount offered by the Beattie government as reparation.[21]

The spending of personal money was also highly controlled, and Palm Island's isolation made access to goods especially restricted. Thelma McAvoy recalled: 'My mother used to have like a dog tag to come over [to Townsville] for a day's shopping.' If staying overnight in Townsville, Palm Islanders were required to reside in the town's watch house.

While shortages of funds added to the problems on reserves, state collections of revenue from these institutions were consistently much larger than expenditure. Maintenance expenses were considered covered by the use of deductions from collected Murri wages. Profits from retail stores were derived almost entirely from the earning of Murri inmates, which were also used to fund development and extensions. Other sources of income were derived from the residents' activities. Palm Island footballers earned proceeds of over £800 in 1929 — more than £300 in excess of their expenses — when they displayed their skills at the Brisbane Exhibition Grounds. Yet Palm Islanders did not see this money as it remained within the 'Aboriginal Protection Property Account'.

Before the construction of the jails on Palm Island, people were handcuffed to trees and make to work in chain gangs clearing scrub by hand. Curry operated as prosecutor, clerk of court and judge with no system for appeal. Court was held in the strict privacy of Curry's office.

Curry justified the severity of his punitive procedures with the argument that a 'certain amount of firmness must be shown to the blacks otherwise it would be impossible to control them'.[22] Women who were imprisoned had their heads shaved, were put on a diet of bread and water, and were made to sweep the white street of Mango Avenue. Children were also imprisoned. Marnie Kennedy wrote of her days in the dormitory:

> The matron was a white woman. She knew how to dish out punishment for the least little thing. I was thrown in jail for singing a song called 'Who said I was a bum?'... All she said was 'come with me' and she shoved me in jail for the night. I was given a bag of beans to crack until nine o'clock and no supper. I tried eating the beans but they were hard and dry. I was very frightened and hungry and cried myself to sleep.

Curry used both Curacoa and Eclipse Islands as further penal outposts. During his reign those whom he defined as 'uncontrollable' — often those caught speaking their own languages or gambling — were sent to these islands of exile with rations of bread and water, for a duration which sometimes lasted several weeks. Exiles would try to catch fish with their bare hands.

By the late 1920s, a series of allegations of floggings on Palm Island received public attention. Letters had been sent by residents to newspapers and politicians. In the course of the government's investigation of the complaints, inmates would testify of their fears of Curry and of their experiences of reprisals for attempting to seek redress through official channels. In February 1929, the Home Department's Under-Secretary, WJ Gall, recommended that a police magistrate's inquiry be conducted into allegations that Curry had assaulted the resident Rene Harvey in April of the previous year.

It was alleged that Curry had used a cat o'nine tails-like-whip called a strap, beating the girl until she 'fell senseless to the ground'. The attention of government officials had been drawn to the incident by an anonymous letter from 'a Townsville citizen' and 'as the matter had been the subject of much adverse comment in the North'. Polly Tippo stated that she had found Rene crying on her bed in the dormitory and that: 'Rene Harvey then showed me her legs, they were all bruised and swollen and Rene could not walk that day and when she wanted to walk I put my arms around her and helped her along.'

The strap used was reported by Mary Palm Island to have usually been kept in Curry's house where she worked. Hoffman had made the strap on Curry's request several months before the incident. It was about two feet long and one and a half inches wide, cut into six strands, with knots tied in the ends. Two female residents testified that the strap had been hung on a wall of the senior girls' dormitory on a number of occasions. Curry's statement to the inquiry argued that he had used this device to beat the girl because she had run away with a male inmate, before her return to the dormitory the following day.

The Superintendent recounted that he 'took her by the left arm and gave her two cuts with the strap'. He stated that she had 'pulled away from me and ran out the gate', shouting, 'I'll let no man hit me'. At the gate Rene was wrestled with by a Native Policeman who stopped her. Curry stated: 'I took her by one arm and said "Now you come back to the quarters"... I said, "You still defy me eh?"' and I gave her about nine more straps — across the buttocks and the shoulders.'

Curry denied that the woman had fallen senseless to the ground and justified the beating and the imprisonment of her male companion on the grounds that 'otherwise my authority on the island would have been weakened'. He believed, he said, 'that my prompt action on that occasion had a good effect on the rest of the community'. Curry's attention was drawn to his breach of reserve regulations when questioned by Magistrate Cameron:

> Q: You know that according to the regulations corporal punishment must not be given to girls over sixteen years of age?
> A: Yes.
> Q: Why did you do it in this case?

> A: The case so unusual, so serious and so widely known that I considered it demanded prompt measures to act as a deterrent to others. At the time I overlooked the regulation ...
> Q: Did you report the matter to Mr Bleakley?
> A: I overlooked that too.

Curry stated that he had previously requested the removal of Rene's male companion, Bob Malcolm, whom he described as 'cheeky' and 'brazen'. Curry perceived himself as in a power struggle with Malcolm, and he was determined to win. He told the inquiry:

> Malcolm had often boasted in the camp that he would beat the migaloe, meaning the white man, the boss. By stealing the girl it appeared to me that he was carrying out what he boasted he would do.

During the course of events in April, two of Curry's policemen had rushed Bob Malcolm and thrown him to the ground, allegedly on the assumption that he may have possessed a weapon. Malcolm had subsequently escaped from the jail by punching out a wooden slab. He later returned to the settlement to serve fourteen days. Curry admitted that in the period of Malcolm's absence he had fired a revolver from outside his home, before beginning his search and that he had attempted to set fire to the island in an effort 'to burn him out'. He would later see that Malcolm was transferred to Barambah reserve.

On 18 April, 1929 Curry was advised by Gall of the outcome of the inquiry:

> ...the evidence tendered discloses that Rene Harvey was flogged by you and that the flogging was serve and produced marks on the arm. In so flogging Rene Harvey you committed a breach of the regulation...You are reprimanded...and you are cautioned to comply strictly with the regulations in the future.

Curry was not the only white official to have beaten Murri residents. In 1928, resident Archie Blue complained to Curry that he had been beaten by Doctor Pattison of Palm Island hospital while he was a patient. An inquiry in January the following year concluded that the doctor had struck Blue across the jaw. Ballard stated, 'Doctor Pattison punched the native up the steps and into the hospital,' and he claimed that the doctor was 'very drunk' at the time. Pattison was officially cautioned.

Not all such incidents were reported. Marnie Kennedy recorded of her youth in the dormitory:

> ...we were belted out of bed at five in the morning by the headmistress, and believe me, she could lay the stick on...One of the many beltings I remember well: I did some small wrong and was cuffed over the ears so hard that it dropped me. My ears rang all night and I cried all night. Most of us kids copped this kind of treatment.[23]

Despite the difficulties of escape, abscondings were frequent. In 1924, Bleakley noted that the employment of Palm Islanders on fishing luggers had 'proved unsatisfactory' since half of the 40 men signed on had escaped. Others used passing vessels for transport. Those who were captured were forced to serve time in Stewart's Creek Penal Establishment in Townsville, or were alternatively imprisoned back on the island. One resident who had been banished to Eclipse Island managed to find his way back to Palm by floating on a log — no mean feat in what was then a dangerous channel — landing at Pencil Bay before being recaptured.[24]

People risked their lives to flee Palm Island, some travelling in small boats and even attempting to swim from one island to another. Nineteen of these attempts were made in 1932. The Chief Protector dismissed such incidents as a reflection of 'the native instinct for wanderlust'.[25] When I questioned Bill Congoo as to the history of abscondings and the apparent fearlessness of the people regarding sharks, the answer was simple: 'No one worried too much. There were too many sharks on the shores here.'[26]

The island's isolation from the mainland had a major effect on lifestyles on the reserve. Boats took four or five hours to reach Palm. Rations of tea, sugar, flour and occasionally meat arrived on weekly government boats, but an inquiry in 1930 found that supplies were sometimes less than ordered, quantities having disappeared on route.[27] The availability of seafoods provided an advantage over many mainland reserves, and bush tucker was also hunted. Children would look for fish around the reef to supplement the often scant provisions in dormitories.

Despite the environmental advantages, Palm Island shared a high death rate with other reserves. Construction of housing lagged in comparison to demand. While the island's isolation and quarantine measures meant that only a few deaths resulted from the influenza epidemic of 1919, a 1921 government medical survey found over 70 per cent of the population were infected by an epidemic of hookworm.

Epidemics of measles and fever swept the island in 1922, influenza and dysentery in 1923 and 1926. The loss of 122 lives in 1924 was attributed to venereal diseases, hookworm and scabies.

Medical inspections were compulsory on reserves. Marnie Kennedy described the process:

> Saturday, too, was our medicine day. We were taken to the hospital and given a cup of Epsom salts or a big dose of castor oil...Whoever sent us there thought we needed a good clean-out: inside and out. Once a year we were treated for hookworm. You have to take this medicine on an empty stomach... Everywhere there would be kids rolling or laying on the ground too sick to care what happened to them.[28]

Children were segregated from adults, a system alien to Murri cultural practices, as was the structured gender segregation applied to both young and adult. Boys found in the farm area were punished with fourteen days on bread and water. Wire fence enclosures surrounded the dormitories.

Curry exerted zealous control over sexual relations. Police were instructed to report any knowledge of liaisons not officially sanctioned. Superintendents were required to implement Bleakley's policy of controlling sexual relations as part of his wider program of controlled 'breeding' to 'combat the half-caste evil'. This was the cause of much resentment on the island. Curry could approve or deny requests to marry, and ignore traditional Murri laws on inter-tribal marriage.

The influence of missionaries in the latter half of the decade also disrupted cultural practices. Christian records indicate that they saw their role on the island as primarily to combat what they labelled as 'sorcery'. Murri spirituality, poorly understood and perceived as inferior to the Christian 'faith', was the target of a missionary eradication program.

Father Patrick Moloney of the Catholic Church worked from the premise that Palm Islanders needed 'civilising' — 'he knew that stray sheep had to be rounded up and yarded,' said his fellow churchmen, 'before anything could be done for them.' While Christian missionaries on the reserve were not motivated by wealth — they lived on a bare sustenance — they assumed authority and control over residents and sought to impose the European values of the work ethic, the nuclear family, thrift, abstinence and piety. Yet despite official sanctions and the efforts of authorities and missionaries, traditional rites were carried out in places Palm Islanders declared taboo to all but a few specific people.

Dormitory children who spoke their parents' languages would be whipped. On the veranda of the dormitory the first schooling was conducted, based primarily on the bible. Mrs Agnes Curry, a Catholic, supervised teachings. An Anglican Church survey in 1925 recorded that only Murris on government reserves and missions were receiving any education in North Queensland — this was terminated at the middle primary years. Girls were taught domestic tasks and boys industrial chores.

In 1923, Willie Solomon and Charlie Simian built the grass school. Two years later, the Chief Protector wrote to the Under-Secretary of the Home Secretary's Office seeking aid to establish a separate school for the children of white officials. He used the situation at Taroom as a model whereby Murri children would be taught at a 'special school' controlled by the department, while white children attended a 'provisional school' belonging to the Department of Public Instruction.

The colonial mentality which governed the structure of reserves was based on the premise that whites, being superior, were naturally suited to dominate; that Murris had no culture of their own — merely 'barbarous' and 'savage' practices — and should therefore be compelled to assimilate to European cultural mores. As a consequence, while Murris learnt much about white people on reserves, the whites learnt little about them. As part of the assimilation program, Curry introduced garden competitions between streets, European dancing and a movie theatre.

Ellison Obah of Yarrabah pressured Curry to initiate a brass band on the island, based on his experience of music at his former reserve. The band was eventually funded by collections made on the island, and members were trained in jazz and marching tunes. Those who failed to attend for practice were sent to jail.[29] Curry also organised Christmas celebrations and Joe Garbutt recalled that on New Years Eve 'Curry would fire them shots to wake us all up. We had cups of tea, Christmas cake... go from place to place.'[30]

Curry's willingness to organise entertainments, sports and celebrations, and his preparedness to work hard alongside Murri residents, were the two aspects of his reign on the island which earned him respect from many Palm Islanders. The corroborees are fondly remembered by older residents, providing the setting where men and women were most visible to each other, and where young onlookers gained some degree of socialisation from their parents.

Spear throwing was encouraged on a competitive basis, as was football. The Palm Island football team competed in sports on the mainland and soon gained a reputation for its sporting acumen. But

Brisbane spectators who watched the team play at the Exhibition grounds in 1929, were not privy to the many inter-tribal feuds which took place at football practices on the island.[31]

It was in this area of inter-group conflicts that uneasiness pervaded the island. Joe Garbutt has stated: 'You couldn't walk around after dark here. A bloke would spear you. They'd war with one another if anything went wrong...If someone'd done anything to them they'd take revenge.' One resident found responsible for what white authorities called a 'tribal killing' was sentenced by a white court to the Townsville jail.[32] Alf Palmer has recorded: 'In those days tribes stayed in different places. Otherwise you wouldn't be safe. It might be all right if you stayed awake all night, right to day break. They used to kill one another in those days.'[33]

As early as 1876, Duncan McNab warned the Colonial Secretary that 'hostile tribes cannot be congregated on a reserve'.[34] In 1912, the Chief Protector had advised parliament that 'The grouping of many tribes in one area would mean continual warfare amongst themselves and practically survival of the fittest.'[35] Yet this was the very system adopted on Palm Island and on reserves at Yarrabah, Mapoon and later at Mona Mona and Weipa South. By the late twentieth century, these sites had the highest rates of violence in the Western world.

A visitor on the ship *Chances* later recorded of his sojourn to Palm in 1929:

> C- (Curry) explained the reason why only a handful of white people was able to control several hundred utter savages. Since there were many different tribes represented on Palm Island, he said that if there was to be any letting off of steam, they would go for each other.[36]

The much smaller, more comfortable group of whites holding power on the island also found it impossible to live harmoniously together. The consumption of alcohol often fuelled tempers in their rivalries and disputes, rumours increased ill-feelings and large amounts of government time and money were spent on the investigation of complaints.

In 1919, a complaint by Tedman, clerk on the island, led to an inquiry by the Police Magistrate from Ingham whose findings were that Curry had assaulted the clerk over Tedman's attempt to take Murris to Butler's Guest House against Curry's wishes. Storekeeper Ballard would later advise that he had been assaulted by Curry about one week after his arrival in 1925, over the issue of the accounts.[37]

Disputes also erupted between Palm Island officials and those of the Home Office. In the mid-1920s, Bleakley visited Palm Island accompanied by Under-Secretary Gall. Gall would later report that in their return to Curry's home after dinner at Hamilton's residence, Curry had been 'in a most excited state' and argued that 'He had made the place, nobody would sleep at his house, anybody who tried to get his job would be dealt with and that he would burn the place down.' Gall also alleged to department officials that a few days prior to this Curry had 'a serious difference' with Hoffman and Ballard over gambling which had occurred amongst Aboriginal residents while Curry was away. 'I do not know what happened to Hoffman,' wrote Gall, 'but the two black eyes which Ballard was carrying about with him were ample evidence of the fact that he had been assaulted.'[38]

In February 1927, Hamilton accompanied Curry to a meeting in Townsville's Lowth's Hotel with Gall and Stopford of the Under-Secretary's office. Inspector James Farrell later stated that he encountered Curry and Hamilton approaching the hotel and advised Curry not to confront Gall until the morning. Farrell said his advice was ignored and that the two men 'staggered along the footpath' in an intoxicated state.

Gall later provided his own version of events, claiming that Curry and Hamilton had 'pushed themselves in' and both were intoxicated. In response to 'a simple question' concerning Palm Island, Curry had delivered 'a tirade':

> He asserted that he had read private letters I had sent to the Doctor. I confess I lost my temper and spoke to him as I should not have done. Then Hamilton became insulting, dared me to sack him & C. I ordered Curry and Hamilton to go back to the boat and get back to the Island as quickly as they could, or I might be forced to deal with them.

Curry's account differed. He asserted that he had come to Townsville to report damage to buildings caused by a cyclone, and found Stopford and Gall in the hotel parlour, 'a bottle of whisky in front of them':

> I asked for an interview at 2pm but was not admitted until 7pm and I must admit I had whisky with them while in the parlour. Mr Gall was just about as full as he could be, and he asked me how was things, and I replied good only for the private letters going down to him by certain officials. He then called me a — liar, and I called him one back. In the meantime my launch

driver came in and threatened to pour a glass of beer over his baldy head to make his hair grow.

Tensions between staff on the island mounted as the decade unfolded, the reserve becoming a veritable battlefield of both verbal and physical exchanges. In 1926, Dr Charles Maitland Pattison, formerly of the British Colonial Service in Fiji, was appointed Medical Superintendent to Palm. Curry and Pattison clashed in 1928 and 'came to blows' and on another occasion, alleged Gall, Curry 'assaulted the Doctor, by hitting him on the head with a spanner and laying him aside for nearly a fortnight'. Both men were reprimanded.

In April 1929, Magistrate GA Cameron was instructed to conduct an inquiry in Townsville into allegations that the doctor and Ballard had been feuding. Evidence tendered suggested Pattison had insulted Mrs Ballard. Kornmann, a carpenter on the island, stated that Mrs Ballard 'twice punched the doctor who used some very strong language, after which Mrs Ballard struck him on the jaw'. During the dispute the doctor allegedly accused Mr Ballard of having been 'a VD [venereal disease] case in the Shankers' ward at Edmonton hospital' and that he had 'never seen a day's service in the war'. Curry, Hoffman and the Ballards stated the doctor had been 'full of drink' at the time. These events took place at 7pm on a Sunday night, in the main streets of the settlement, as the officials walked towards the doctor's house, where more abuse and insults were exchanged. The doctor was officially cautioned and 'advised to be more circumspect in future'.

An inquiry in 1930 investigated a further dispute between the doctor and the Superintendent, over the doctor's supply of alcohol to both the nurse and a female Murri resident. Curry had found both women drunk on Christmas Day in 1929, and confronted the doctor, whom he claimed became abusive: 'I then smacked him with my open hand!' continued Curry...'This is the second time I have struck him for that word and in respect to my mother I allow no man to call me that.'[39]

The inquiry by visiting Justice Nevitt concluded that both Curry and Pattison had consumed alcohol on the morning of the altercation and that there was 'ample evidence to prove that the Superintendent, the medical officer, and Mrs Hazeldine...had given alcoholic drinks to the natives. Drink, in his opinion, was at the bottom of the trouble.'[40] Curry grew to deeply resent the doctor and later the Assistant Superintendent, for his Germanic origin and because of his belief that Hoffman was out to usurp his role. A complaint lodged by Curry accused Hoffman of having stolen funds from gate receipts at a football match at Halifax attended by the Palm Island team. Gall later insisted that the £14 be refunded to the Home Office.[41]

Ironically, while theft, drunkenness and violence were exhibited, often publicly, by white overseers with few repercussions, these were the very transgressions which had led to the exile of many Murri residents to Palm Island. And while whites had been invested with control over the conduct of Palm Islanders, it became increasingly evident that these very officials were unable to regulate their own. Breaches of public service rules of conduct were frequent and an atmosphere of jealousy, resentment and distrust increasingly apparent.

Until the close of the decade mainstream society had little insight into the bitter conflicts erupting on the island. What the *Truth* described as 'secret, hole-in-corner enquires' ensured that the public remained unaware, while visitations by tourists were organised to promote the notion that this was a model settlement. The 'sight-seeing' of visitors became fetishised in the 1920s, tourists arriving from as far away as Fremantle and from European countries, in search of the 'exotic'. Curry ensured their movements were thoroughly supervised, and as the owner of the only motorcar on Palm he drove them around 'at breakneck speed'.

The process was akin to people visiting a zoo. Tourists threw lollies at the children and watched them grab for them in the dirt. They tossed money to adults from their boats, making them dive for it in the ocean. For Palm Islanders these visits were amongst those rare occasions when ample food was provided. Older residents of Palm speak appreciatively of the visits with revenue made through the sale of goods on stalls. The tourists themselves were a source of some amusement. Tourists purchased artefacts and paid residents to climb trees for coconuts. Their boats left 'literally bristling' with their acquisitions. Joe Garbutt recalled:

> ...back in Curry's time...We had plenty of entertainment of our own. Got people here in hundreds. All of us what we made, spears, boomerangs, and all that, shields and shells, we sold all that to the tourists...he [Curry] liked to see us make the money for ourselves and we did too. He said 'that's your own'.[42]

Early tourist reports spoke of Curry as 'the right man for the job' and of the administration's high level of efficiency. But later in the decade, as tensions surfaced, Curry had begun advising tourist with candour that white officials were living in a 'constant state of apprehension', that some soothed their fear and sense of isolation through alcohol, and that his own existence on the island was 'like living on the rim of a volcano'. While earlier departmental inquires had dealt with bickering between whites, the Nevitt investigation of 1930 considered allegations of a more serious nature.

Nevitt's visit had been prompted by a letter to Brisbane officials which read:

> Dear Sir — I am sending you a report about our Protector, RH Curry. He is still flogging our people. He belted one of our people and also punched his wife and knocked her down...we want you to look into this matter, as this man is going too far. Also there is other things he is doing to our young girls. He is committing serious offences with them.[43]

In the course of the inquiry a male inmate charged that Curry had interfered with his wife, and the woman confirmed the allegation, stating this had occurred when she worked at Curry's home. Nevitt reported that Curry admitted to having beaten two married inmates. His justification was that the couple had told other Murris that he was interfering with women on the reserve. Some of the older residents of Palm Island believe that Curry was guilty of these allegations.

Despite the seriousness of these charges and further evidence provided to Nevitt of bitter feuding amongst white staff, his report argued that 'he found a high state of efficiency, both externally and internally, in the administration of the settlement', and that the management reflected the greatest credit on all concerned'.[44] This must have been one of the grimmest ironies in the history of Queensland, for on the very day that this report reached the Home Office, Curry ran 'amok'.

Curry's motives and his condition at the time are considered in the following chapter. Equally worthy of examination, however, is the role played by those in higher positions of authority who chose to ignore the mounting evidence that all was not well on Palm Island. The decision to hold secret inquires, to settle with the official caution or reprimand in the face of apparent brutalities, to ignore the growing conflict on the reserve, and to present to the public the image of a glowing state of affairs were in this context actions of striking neglect.

Chapter 5

The 1930 Rampage:
'As Straight as a Gun Barrel'

> I promise you I will clean Palm Island up this time and for good.
> RH Curry, Letter to JW Bleakley, 2 February 1930

On Sunday, 2 February 1930, Superintendent Curry called at the home of his neighbour and assistant at midnight. Thomas Hoffman had retired at 8pm, but was woken by Curry's voice calling out that he was going down to the farm to find Charles Alley. Alley had been sentenced to jail by Curry the day before and was serving his sentence at the barn. Curry had since received notice that Alley was directed to Townsville by Doctor Pattison for medical treatment. 'Aren't you going rather early?' asked Hoffman, to which Curry replied, 'I can't sleep and I'll go down and get it over.'[1] This dialogue marked the beginning of a night of rampage by the Palm Island Superintendent.

Carrying a rifle and revolver, he drove to the lock-up at the farm, where he found both the prisoners, Charles Alley and Dan Kyle, had escaped. Curry then drove to the doctor's residence, about halfway between the farm area and the main settlement. He stopped the car, fired his rifle and rushed up to the house. The Superintendent stood in the doorway, from where he woke Charles and Ethel Pattison 'with the smash of a porcelain jug and a tornado of shots' fired into their bedroom.[2]

The doctor leapt from the bed and moved towards the veranda in search of his gun, when the bullets hit him from behind and he fell to the floor in a pool of blood. Mrs Pattison ran onto the veranda, clutching at wounds to her neck. Curry followed and struck the woman's head and heart with the butt of his rifle. The blows were so severe that the woman's skull was fractured and he shattered the stock of the rifle. Mrs Pattison fell to the floor and Curry jumped from the veranda to the ground below. He then drove recklessly back to the settlement.[3]

Fifteen minutes after the conversation with Curry, the Assistant Superintendent heard Curry's car return. Unaware of events on the north end of the island, Hoffman again fell asleep. Half an hour later the entire settlement experienced a violent awakening. At close to 1am, a loud explosion shattered the still evening air. Residents leapt from their beds in consternation. The air smelt of smoke and kerosene and they could hear the crackle of flames. White staff near the scene soon saw that Curry's home had been blown to pieces and that the Superintendent stood before it, contemplating the sight of the flames.

Hoffman made a belated attempt to rescue the two Curry children. He later testified:

> I rushed round to Curry's place and broke the front door to get in but could not enter as the whole internal part was afire and I could smell kerosene strongly. I ran round the back of Curry's and as I was doing so I heard the report of a shot and the ping ping of a bullet pass me and I went and assisted Hamilton to release two girl prisoner[s] in the cells at the rear of Curry's house.

In the meantime, storekeeper Len Ballard had rushed onto the street in his pyjamas. He heard Mrs Hoffman screaming at her husband to free the women in the jail. While Hoffman and the launch driver, Joseph Hamilton, forced an opening to the jail, Ballard approached Curry. 'He was practically in front of his house,' Ballard later stated:

> The reflection of the fire showed a bright light all around. I said to him, 'Good God. What's all this?' He said, 'I am just looking at it.' I said, 'What's the matter?' He said, 'Oh I have killed the doctor and the matron and had a shot at Hoffman and missed him and you had better get to bloody hell too.'

Curry's threat sent Ballard running back to his home. The white staff and their children began to gather on the avenue behind the shelter of the mango trees. Curry had now broken the window of Hoffman's adjoining home and dashed kerosene into the room. The owner heard one of the staff shout, 'Your house is on fire, Mr Hoffman.' Hoffman later reported: 'I rushed over to my place and met my wife, who said "This man is mad"...I pushed her aside and went in to endeavour to save something but couldn't as the whole place was on fire.'

Curry then traversed to Main Street to continue his rampage. One resident, a ten-year-old child at the time, recalled: 'He was walking around in circles, wailing, unsettling everyone.'[4] Curry's rifle continued to crack and building after building soon burst into flames. While the Superintendent ignited the office, school and general store in succession, the children in the dormitories screamed in terror and their parents ran to release them from the compound. Marnie Kennedy wrote:

> We had just settled down (in the dormitory) when we heard two big bangs and we kids got up screaming and rushed out onto the veranda but the wire netting stopped us from getting out...there were about two or three hundred kids running around screaming and crying in panic and terror and afraid we were next to be burnt....The whole island was lit up bright as day.[5]

Residents now operated on the knowledge that the island was under siege and that the saboteur was the Superintendent who had gone mad. While some Murri residents took their families up into the hills, using what sheets and tarpaulins they could find as cover from the rain, Hoffman hid in the darkness in Mango Avenue. Others reported to the Assistant that they had seen Curry in Main Street and he had told those who got near him 'to get away or he would give them a bit of lead'.

Jack Wondai and Frank Pickles told Hoffman that they had seen Curry standing in front of the general store while it was burning and that he had told them to leave, 'that he was doing the job'. Another resident ran up to Hoffman to state that Curry had said he would burn the hospital down. The patients — one of them wrapped in a sheet and carrying a one-day-old baby, another with a child only a few days old — were removed from the premises into the bush, under a steady downpour of rain.[6]

News that the doctor had been shot finally reached Hoffman and he sent Ballard to Pattison's residence, took up a rifle belonging to schoolteacher Eric Davison, and stood at the hedge in front of the hospital. Eight or nine Murris now gathered around him, while others began to group at the doctor's house.

After the shooting, the doctor and Ethel Pattison had crawled across the floor towards each other. The doctor tied a handkerchief around his wife's neck to try to stop the bleeding. Mrs Pattison then blew a whistle as a cry for help. Pattison's medical assistant, Murri resident Smith, responded, locating forceps which the injured doctor used to tie his own arteries. Smith reported that Curry was now at the beach, seated on a kerosene case, that he was drinking from a bottle, and had a rifle on his knee and a revolver in his hand.[7]

The Palm Islander, Jack Campbell, was sleeping in the boatshed when Henry Pedro called out: 'Boss wants you awake.' Compelling Campbell to accompany him, Curry boarded the launch *Esme*. Jack Campbell later testified:

> Mr Curry and I lay down on launch and went to sleep. When he woke up he told me to go ashore looking for Henry. He was quiet. He said, 'Don't go far. You come back.' He told me he was going to shoot me if I don't come back. [Unable to find

> Henry] I came back to the boat when he told me that. I woke up at daylight.

As the sun rose, residents on the island saw Curry transhipping goods from the *Esme* onto the *Rita*, a smaller launch nearby. Still accompanied by Campbell, Curry stood some distance off in the *Rita* when smoke began rising from the *Esme*. Flames appeared and residents witnessed another explosion, as the benzine tank on the larger launch was detonated by fire. Curry now stood on the turtle-back of the *Rita* where, as if engaged in an orchestrated military campaign, he waved a white calico cloth back towards the shore. The increasingly bizarre events of February 1930 were, however, far from over.

The island settlement was now in ruins. As Curry headed for Fantome Island, Hoffman took the chance to send Jimmy Puttaburra, Albie Kyle and Arthur Murdock, to Rollingstone on a sailing cutter, so that they could get word through to Townsville police. He gave them the written message:

> To the Captain, Dear Sir — We are in sore straits and distress, being without rations. A doctor is needed at once to save life. The stores, the Superintendent's house, the assistant superintendent's house and the offices have burnt to the ground, and the doctor and matron have been shot. Police are urgently required — T. Hoffman, Assistant Superintendent.[8]

Between 7am and 8am, a crowd of Murris gathered around Hoffman in front of Davison's residence in Mango Avenue. Some had come from the doctor's house, others from the camps. Hoffman issued them with four rounds of .22 ammunition and several guns. Elizabeth Ballard later described the scene as 'panic stricken':

> The other whites went away and Mr Hoffman was talking to the boys. He said to them all, 'Go and get Mr Curry [when he returns] do not let him pass, either shoot him or spear him.' Some of the boys asked, 'How will we get on if we do that?' Mr Hoffman said, 'It's quite all right, I will be responsible.'

While Hoffman paced the island in trepidation, the wardsman Albert Morecombe was stationed on Fantome Island, almost five miles across from Palm, when three Murris arrived in a dinghy, carrying a letter from the Assistant Superintendent. Morecombe read that the doctor and matron had been shot and that he was urgently required for medical aid. While dressing to leave for Palm, he heard the reports of the *Esme's* destruction and someone shouted, 'The *Rita* is coming.'

Morecombe, convinced that Hoffman had sent the launch to enable him to get over to Palm, waited for the *Rita* to approach. He soon saw through field glasses that Curry was on board.

Morecombe told patients, staff and the three Palm Islanders to stay at the hospital. When Curry arrived in a dinghy from the *Rita*, he left his house to meet the Superintendent at the beach. His subsequently testified:

> I said 'Good morning Mr Curry.' He said, 'I have finished the fucking doctor and bloody matron, I bet they're dead by now'... He then said, 'I had a go at Hoffman but missed him; the only thing I am sorry for is my own kids.' I said, 'Good heavens, what's happened to them?' He said, 'I gave them an injection of morphia and dynamited them.'

Curry told Morecombe that he was going to nearby Curacoa Island to 'lie off there for the day' — 'Tonight,' he said, 'I am going to finish them off. Then I am going to wait and have a go at the police...If I see any boat leaving the island I'll chase them on the *Rita* and stop them.' The Superintendent had at this stage changed out of his shirt and trousers and was clad in a red bathing suit. Morecombe later told Detective Maloney: 'I had never seen him in this dress before and his speech was intermingled with bursts of laughter and I saw that he was not normal.'

Curry requested a kerosene tin full of water and then left, eight minutes after his arrival, in the direction of Curacoa. He was still accompanied by the unwilling escort Jack Campbell, who later said of the Curacoa sojourn: 'Mr Curry boil rice and have feed. Mr Curry go up hill and look over to Palm Island...Mr Curry sleep and I sleep too.'

Having seen the *Rita* disappear into a shower of rain about a quarter of a mile from Fantome, Morecombe made his way over to the doctor's residence. It took the wardsman and three Palm Islanders more than two hours to reach the reserve in the dinghy. At around 9am, Morecombe went to the aid of the doctor, finding bullet wounds to the abdomen had extended through to the thigh. He also rendered aid to Mrs Pattison, who was wounded in the neck and on the scalp, as well as suffering multiple bruising. At this stage there were '20 or 30 Aboriginals about the place'.

Murri residents, Jimmy Harvey, Peter Prior, Clive Beckett, Ellison Obah and Bruce Mitchell, had gathered around the doctor. Pattison told the matron to 'take those boys into the office' where they were given possession of guns and cartridges. Jimmy Harvey later testified that the doctor said of Curry: 'If you get anywhere near him, try and get him,' while both Peter Prior and the white sawmiller, Ralph Matthews, would report that Pattison had told them: 'Shoot him in the guts, where he shot me.'[9]

At close to midday, Hoffman arrived at the Pattison residence, where he advised the doctor that he had stationed men with firearms from the farm to the beach, and that the patrol would continue until Curry returned. Hoffman then walked around the main settlement throughout the afternoon. At around 4pm, he was advised by Peter Prior that the *Rita* had left Curacoa and was heading towards Palm Island. The Assistant Superintendent told Prior to 'go down to the band house and shoot' if Curry had 'any firearms about him'.

Hoffman then went with Mr and Mrs Ballard, Mr Davison, Mr Hamilton and the other white residents up into the bush out of the range of Curry's .303 rifle. 'I was then aware,' he later stated, 'that the boys were patrolling the beach with rifles awaiting Curry's return. There were no white officials with the aboriginals while they were patrolling the beach.' Davison would later report that he 'heard Mr Hoffman say it was all right — that he had posted natives along the beach' to wait for Curry's return: 'When I heard that the cutter was leaving Curacoa I brought my wife and family into the avenue and with the white officials we went up into the bush. I remained there with the women folk.'

Murri residents had now taken full responsibility for protecting the community while the 'white men lay skulking and quaking in the bush'.[10] Jimmy Harvey stationed himself behind the bandroom, which was eighteen yards to the rear and left of the boatshed. He carried Dr Pattison's .32 automatic pistol. Ellison Obah also waited behind the bandroom with a revolver. Others positioned themselves inside the bandroom, where they could watch Curry's approach through the windows and prepare an ambush. Peter Prior held a magazine shotgun, Clive Beckett a pea rifle, Caesar Anning a rifle, and Billy Donaldson a shotgun. Willie Barambah stationed himself up a palm tree. All would later report of their grave apprehensions when, at close to 4.30pm, Curry and Jack Campbell quit the *Rita* in Challenger Bay and rowed towards the beach in a flattie.[11]

Caesar Anning observed:

> Mr Curry come round the corner of the boatshed coming towards the bandroom. He had a rifle in his left hand and a revolver in his right hand...He was dressed in a bathing costume. He had a red calico round his waist. He was pointing the revolver towards where Peter Prior and I were at the window.[12]

Peter Prior corroborated, stating that on sighting the men in the back of the bandroom Curry had pointed his revolver 'straight to where we were':

> [Curry] was raising his hand with the revolver as if to take a shot when I fired my shot gun and he fell and as I fired I heard another report outside... I am certain that my shot hit him first and that caused him to fall. I was afraid that he would have shot us all if I had not shot first.

In the midst of extreme anxiety and tension, several shots were fired at this time. Ellison Obah recalled:

> I heard shots when Curry landed, and after they went off I don't know whether it was nerve or not, but the revolver went off, and I plugged the [water] tank. You'd pull the trigger too, if someone banged a kerosene tin behind you.[13]

Curry was about ten yards (nine metres) from the bandroom when he received a series of shot pellet wounds which would prove fatal. He lay writhing in agony when Clive Beckett ran over and took Curry's weapon from him. Peter Prior called out for the others to come down from the hills. Hoffman had left the bush and heard the shots as he crossed the football field. The first official to arrive, he shifted Curry closer to the boatshed as a crowd began to gather.

According to Hoffman's account of events, Curry then said to him: 'The Murrays [sic] got me...Why didn't you come out and fight me fair?' to which the Assistant replied: 'You fought your children fair and the doctor fair didn't you?' Curry responded:

> Oh yes I done them in. I didn't want people to say their father was a murderer. You can think yourself lucky I had a shot or two at you and missed you. You can take my job now that you were always after.

The Superintendent then addressed Ellison Obah: 'I didn't come over to shoot you murrays [sic] I only wanted the migloes, then I wanted to get back to the boat and get the bloody police.' He then asked, 'How are the doctor and matron?' and was advised 'They are not too good.' Curry's request that the doctor be sent down 'alongside of me' was ignored, and he then asked for Nellie Bly, a Murri resident in charge of the girls' quarters. Nellie was sent for and she shook hands with the Superintendent and the two said goodbye.

Morecombe had now arrived from the doctor's house and administered a dose of morphia at Curry's request. The wardsman observed 40 to 50 gunshot pellet wounds to Curry's abdomen, upper thighs and wrists. Ballard took the dying man by stretcher to the hospital where, according to the storekeeper: 'He looked up at me and said, "Is that you Len?" I said, "Yes...Is there anything I can do for you?" He said, "I have nothing to say. I deserve all I got." I then left him and went to the doctor's house.'[14]

Curry died about 20 minutes later, at 6.15pm, and at 45 years of age. His nineteen-year-old stepdaughter, Edna, and his eleven-year-old son, Robert, were also dead. The doctor and matron were seriously wounded. Two homes, the main buildings of the settlement, the office records and the launch, had all been destroyed, the damage estimated at £7,000.[15]

Palm Island residents had been subjected to sixteen hours of terror and memories of the 'tragic horror' of 3 February would remain with them for the rest of their lives. Some would not survive. In the aftermath of Curry's rampage, two Murri residents died as a result of their exposure to rain. Mary Quinn, who had given birth only a few days earlier and was carried out of the hospital after Curry's threat to burn it down, and Clem Jackson, who contracted pneumonia, joined the list of casualties of the Superintendent's crusade of arson and bloodshed.

These events on Palm Island on 3 February 1930 provide a graphic microcosm of the historical paradox inherent in the operations of Queensland's 'protection' acts. While reserves were heralded as providing 'havens' from the ravages of colonial conquest, in reality Queensland's reserves were the antithesis of all they were purported to be. White staff on Palm Island lived on Murri lands, in homes built by Murri labour, and worked in jobs dependent on the existence of Murri residents who were held hostage within its boundaries. They called these people who provided their sustenance their 'wards' and saw their own roles as custodial.

The ultimate exhibition of this irony unfolded when Palm Island became a war zone, the entire community threatened by the menacing rampage of its primary white 'protector'. For when 'Uncle Boss Curry' murdered his own children, seriously injured the medical staff, destroyed the reserve buildings and posed himself as a threat to all residents, both black and white, it was behind the shelter of their wards' protection that the white officials hid.

Curry's 'maniacal attack' on the island soon became local knowledge in North Queensland, with attention focused on the fact that white staff had issued guns to Murri residents, taken to the hills and 'pushed up the natives to shoot him'.[16] Hoffman advised a subsequent inquest into the Curry deaths: 'We said we would be with the abos [sic] when the boat came. Mr Ballard was with his wife and children, Mr Davison was with his wife and children, and Mr Morecombe was with the doctor'. Hoffman himself and the Hamilton family had also been up in the hills behind Mango Avenue, about half a mile from their homes.

Morecombe told the inquiry that he had been required at Pattison's side for medical reasons. Of Curry's earlier visit to Fantome Island, he stated: 'It would probably have been quicker to have seized Curry' but he had not done so, he said, because 'I did not think of it.' Hoffman justified his absence at the critical moment of Curry's return: 'I would have been with the boys when he arrived only he arrived too quickly.'

Individualism had ruled, with members of staff intently focused on self-preservation. With a longstanding history of disunity behind them, they had even failed to cooperate at a time when their very discord had culminated in dire threats to life and property. Mrs Ballard testified: 'Mr Hoffman did not call a conference to decide what we should do. There was no attempt between the whites as to what steps they should take for their own protection and the protection of the community.'

In the government inquiry which followed, the assumption of responsibility on the part of the Murris and their cooperative efforts in ensuring a halt to Curry's rampage, drew little reward. Moreover, the inquiry's conclusion astounded many in North Queensland with its biting crescendo of retribution against Palm Islanders. Twenty-year-old Peter Prior was to be charged with murder.

Police had finally arrived on Palm on 3 February, approaching the island at midnight, more than six hours after the ambush. Palm Islanders had reached Rollingstone by dinghy in rough seas, arriving at 8pm. Farmer Toogood had sent them on to station master McAllister, who telephoned Townsville police. The government's choice of this isolated outpost for the reserve's setting meant that it would take five hours for emergency help from Townsville to reach the reserve.

Detective Maloney was accompanied by a party of police — Constables Bahr, Raetz, Vidler, Rawlins, McNevin and Daley, the government medical officer, Dr H Taylor, and 'two black trackers'. Though fully armed, the squad apparently shared with white officials on the island great fears for their own safety: 'It was the purpose of the party,' stated Maloney, 'not to go ashore until daylight.'[17] Hoffman went out to the police by dinghy and the following day Maloney began taking sworn statements from witnesses to events of the previous day. Three days after the tragedy, the northern press had begun to call for a 'full' and 'proper' inquiry into happenings on the island.

On 11 February, Curry's father used the *Telegraph* to voice this demand. Acknowledging that his son 'must have been demented', George

Curry said that the question remained to be answered: 'Why did he come to be in that state?' Moreover, the fact that 'blackfellows were made to shoot my son' was, he said, basis enough to 'make an inquiry imperative': 'That aspect of the situation is scandalous and will have a most serious effect on the morale of blacks in other settlements.'[18]

By mid-February, the government had still not announced whether an inquiry would take place, while the Returned Soldiers' League, of which both Robert Curry and his brother were members, had begun to demand a Royal Commission. The *Daily Standard* of 13 February endorsed this suggestion, stating that 'in the interests of justice' the scope of any inquiry should incorporate all events leading up to Curry's death. Despite the terror and destruction Curry had inflicted, the report noted that 'public opinion' was 'not altogether against Curry': 'The fact that he was shot down by natives while the whites apparently skulked in the background, has done much to veer sympathy in his direction.'[19]

On 16 February, the *Truth* ran the headline: WAS CURRY WHOLLY TO BLAME?, noting 'continuous and harassing back-biting' on the island and 'bitter feeling between white officials'. The article reprinted excerpts of the Nevitt inquiry, which was now released to the press by Premier Moore, coupled with notice that the government would conduct a magisterial investigation into the Curry deaths. Both the *Truth* and the *Daily Standard* described this response as inadequate, the former arguing that it was 'the plain duty of the government to go further and appoint something in the nature of a Commission, with full scope to inquiry into every ramification of Palm Island and...the grim horror that shocked a continent.' The *Daily Standard* reported the need for a full investigation which would address the issue: WAS THE HOME DEPARTMENT TO BLAME?[20]

From 27 February to 28 March 1930, Magistrate GA Cameron conducted an inquest into the events in which, the government acknowledged, Peter Prior had shot Curry 'under orders' of 'certain white officials'. Until an adjournment to Townsville on 3 March, the inquiry was conducted in the white children's school shed of the main settlement, with 'torrential rain' at times 'pelting down on the iron roof...making it almost impossible to hear the voices of the witnesses'. Despite the Home Department's decision to restrict the inquiry to 'the cause of death', and the magistrate's opening remarks that 'he did not want to have questions of administration asked in Court', the evidence of the 26 witnesses would disclose a multitude of factors leading to the Superintendent's final breakdown. Reasons would also emerge as to why the Home Department did not want a general inquiry.

Statements revealed that Curry's wife, Agnes, had died in childbirth at Townsville General Hospital in mid-November 1929, and 'a big change came over Mr Currie [sic]' from this time. It was then that the Superintendent had taken to alcohol. His personal bereavement was probably intensified by the pending loss of his son, Robbie, due to leave for the mainland to attend school at Ingham, and his step-daughter, Edna, recently engaged to be married to a man named Morrissey.[21]

Curry's grief unfolded in the context of a dramatic deterioration in relations between white staff. Before her death in November, Agnes Curry had told a friend in Townsville that there was no privacy on the island and they 'had no peace'.[22] The 'harassing back-biting' of previous years had culminated in vicious rumours and a stand-off situation where, in the case of the doctor and the Superintendent, all communication had ceased.

Hoffman described the doctor as 'a difficult man', 'inclined to be insulting...when in drink'; and Palm Island, he said, was 'not a model settlement'. Ballard described the doctor as having 'a very nasty disposition'.[23] Curry was described as bad-tempered, and his health condition meant that he, too, was prone to ill-effects from alcohol. At the Cameron Inquiry of March 1929, Curry had stated that he did not drink spirits because of 'neuralgia of the cranial nerve from which I suffer'. Dr Pattison told the same investigation that he was treating Curry for this condition, administering injections of novocaine to ease the pain in his head. The doctor added that while Curry was supposed to rest after these injections, he would instead go straight back to work.[24]

Twelve months later, at the inquest, Dr Pattison advised that after a feud with Curry on Christmas Day, the two no longer visited each other's homes and that all verbal communication soon ceased. Presumably, then, Curry was without medical treatment by the end of the year. Hoffman stated that after the Nevitt Inquiry of January 1930, Curry was sick for a week and confined to his home.[25]

While the white staff had presented 'a fairly united front' before examining tribunals, by the late 1920s Curry, the Ballards and the doctor had increasingly resorted to physical combat. This tendency reached serious proportions on Christmas Day. In the midst of the dispute over alcohol, Curry's blows had knocked Pattison to the floor of his office, where he lay bleeding from the face and neck. The doctor alleged that Curry stood over him and kicked him in the head and shoulders. Mrs Pattison described her husband as suffering a 'very pronounced nervous condition' as a result.[26] This was the administration which the subsequent Nevitt Inquiry described as displaying 'a high state of efficiency' – a management reflecting 'the greatest credit on all concerned'.

Despite the report's vindication of Curry, the Superintendent had become convinced that he would be transferred following the visit by

Justice Nevitt. On the eve of the inquiry, Curry told Hoffman he was 'going to get the sack' and his manner afterwards was described as 'morose', 'solemn' and 'despondent'.[27] Nevitt had investigated accusations that Curry was interfering with Murri women and supplying alcohol to Murri residents. The report dismissed the former charge but sustained the latter. Witnesses to those charges were Dan Kyle and Charles Alley, the two men Curry subsequently imprisoned and then sought at the outset of his rampage. One of the girls released from the jail by Hoffman had also been imprisoned by Curry for talking about the Superintendent 'carrying on with other girls in the settlement'.

After Nevitt held Court, Curry had taken his revenge. On Saturday, 2 February, police told Alley he had to attend Curry's office at 10am. Alley testified to the inquest:

> When I walked into the office he handed me the Bible and said 'Take an oath.' I said, 'If it concerns my evidence I have already given the magistrate I have no more to say Sir.' He said to me, 'Fourteen days hard labour for contempt of Court'.

Dan Kyle was later advised to attend the office as well. In his own words: 'As soon as I walked in Mr Curry said, "This is a Court of Justice"...and handed me the Bible and said "Take an oath."' Kyle then asked what the charge was:

> With that he put the Bible down and charged me with bringing a bottle of wine onto Palm Island from Townsville when I went to town about two weeks before Christmas. He said, 'If you take the punishment I give you Mr Nevitt cannot punish you because you have been punished already.'

With both Kyle and Alley sentenced to three days in the barn, the Superintendent felt assured of their whereabouts until a messenger with a medical report advised him that Alley was due in Townsville on Sunday night for the treatment of malaria. According to Hoffman, Curry had already been annoyed with the doctor through the course of the week, when Pattison directed Alley be confined to light work. The sawmiller Ralph Matthews was at Curry's house on the evening of 2 February, when a note arrived from the doctor objecting to the imprisonment of one of the girls in the jail behind Curry's home as she was pregnant and under medical treatment.

Curry's fears of being transferred had existed for some time. In April, 1929, *Smith's Weekly* described the flogging of Rene Harvey as 'despicable and revolting' and argued that 'the time has arrived to clean Palm Island up thoroughly'. The report concluded: 'the first step should be Curry's dismissal'.[28] It seems likely that Curry would have at least heard of this report, given the circulation of local news by residents in North Queensland, and Curry's stated intention of 'cleaning up' the island himself.

When Agnes Curry became ill in November 1929, Curry told Ballard that he had been informed by Chief Protector Bleakley that he would have to leave the island 'if anything happened to her'. Curry's fears of removal were also conveyed in a letter his step-daughter wrote to an aunt, and, following the death of his wife Curry advised Hoffman that he had been 'offered a change to Thursday Island' and that 'if he ever got the sack he would clean this place up'.

At the inquest Hoffman testified: 'Mr Curry was absolutely wrapped up in the settlement. He said he would die here,' while Ballard noted: 'Mr Curry practically regarded this settlement as a child of his brain.' Older residents state that Curry wanted to marry a Murri woman on the reserve, that other white officials as well as his own children refused to allow this to happen on racial grounds, and that Curry went 'really mad' as a result. While this aspect of the situation was not raised in the inquiries of 1930, it perhaps explains why some in North Queensland felt that 'none of the real underlying issues came out'.

Curry's actions had undoubtedly been premeditated. Rosie Dinduck, Curry's housekeeper, testified that on the Sunday morning of 2 February, the Superintendent had told her 'that he was going to burn the place down'. Dinduck stated that she then began to cry and Curry told her to 'shut up' – 'If you tell anybody I will soon find out and you will be the first one I get.' Dinduck further stated that in the afternoon Curry began cleaning his gun in the dining room. Edna brought Curry cartridges at his request: 'He said he was going down to the quarters to shoot two cats.'

Matthews then arrived and Curry conversed with him on the veranda. Remaining at Curry's residence from 4pm to 8pm, Matthews testified that Curry 'had seemed to be in his normal senses', though he 'complained of the heat and the pain he had in his side'. 'The girl and boy,' he stated, 'were very happy'. Curry left the house for about twenty minutes. Len Ballard testified that the Superintendent arrived at his home between 2pm and 3pm and told Mrs Ballard he had written a letter to the *Truth* newspaper concerning Palm Island. Mrs Ballard stated that when Curry told her this, she had laughed at him. Curry told Mr Ballard, 'In my own mind I have resigned.'

The Superintendent had in fact drafted two letters — one to Chief Protector Bleakley and another to the *Truth* — both of which he gave to Henry Pedro to post, early on the evening of 2 February. In the letter to the *Truth* the Superintendent alleged that Hoffman had 'robbed the natives' of their football funds, and that after the row in Townsville with 'the Palm Island mob', Gall had sworn to 'certain men in town' that he would 'have his revenge'. 'I am going to explain to you,' wrote Curry, 'he has done so'.

Curry wrote of his conviction that Ballard and Pattison had been spying on him at the request of the Home Secretary. The doctor was an 'Irish cad', wrote Curry, and his position on the island was a political appointment. Curry questioned Pattison's medical competency and wrote with sarcasm: 'Since his reign here he has been assaulted by five of the officials so you will judge by that he is of a quiet nature.'

The Superintendent's feelings of persecution climaxed with the Nevitt Inquiry:

> The latest is some aboriginal wrote the Chief Protector, and a so-called justice was sent up to inquire into these complaints. On arrival no trace could be found of the writer, but I had to stand up with no defence just treated like a dog. If a tram conductor called and told Gall anything he would go to any expense to get me…I am going to get them and cause some worry and expense. I cannot carry on any longer, the odds are against me.

To Bleakley he wrote:

> This will be the last letter that you will receive from me, and I must thank you and the heads of your department for the unjust treatment you have dealt out to me in the past…the attacks that have been made on me have been serious but nothing to the complaints that an aboriginal made and never signed his name, nevertheless it pleased the Home Secretary to have me tried I was not given a chance to defend myself and the man you sent took the abos side all through the case…the Dr deserves all he gets.

The flogging of Rene Harvey and reports of his drinking habits clearly preyed on his mind: 'When you have time go to your mission stations and see how the natives are getting starved. Ask the wowsers if they flog the girls.' Curry's concluding remarks speak of his over-empowerment after a twelve-year reign as Superintendent of dispossessed Aboriginal people in a remote settlement. He writes of his impending retaliation against any who might challenge him:

> I know Gall will miss the Dr [sic] at any rate he can send a wreath along as I am going to revenge those who have injured

me, and I will make them cry for mercy. I am just as sane as you are so don't think other wise.

Kind regards
RH Curry

At the conclusion of Cameron's inquest, the *Truth* argued that 'The magisterial inquiry has disclosed sufficient to make it clear that nothing less than a royal commission can supply the answer to the questions involved' in the Palm Island tragedy.[29] The Police Commissioner's office was advised that the Moore government had instead decided to charge Peter Prior with murder.[30]

While both Hoffman and Pattison were also charged — with procuring to kill — Peter Prior was the first arrested. On 17 April 1930, Detective Maloney escorted Prior to Townsville on the *Magneta* where he advised Prior that Brisbane authorities had decided to charge him with murder, warning 'that anything he said might be later used as evidence against him'. Appearing on Prior's behalf, T Daly interjected: 'You were a bit late with your warning, weren't you?'

Before GA Cameron again, Prior stated that he had woken on the night of 2 February to the screams of children from the dormitory, and on seeing the fire and explosions went to get his mother from the hospital. 'Mr Hoffman told me when I reported to him,' he stated, 'to go down to the bandhouse and to shoot if Curry had any firearms about him.' Prior stated he was 'certain that my shot hit him first'.[31]

Depositions from the inquest were forwarded to the hearings. Amongst them was a statement from sawmiller Matthews concerning events after Curry's departure in the *Rita*: 'Mr Hoffman told a number of boys to spread themselves along the beach. He said, "You have your guns, don't let him land. Make sure of him."' He stated Hoffman told him he had given the Murris firearms and ammunition. Caesar Anning's statement noted of Hoffman: 'He told me to go down to the beach and try and stop Mr Curry from coming in.' Anning reported that the Assistant Superintendent gave him a pea rifle and four bullets: 'He said to shoot him.'

Harold Conway's evidence to the hearings confirmed that Hoffman directed Caesar Anning to shoot Curry and that he would stand responsible. Ellison Obah and Jimmy Harvey corroborated. Hoffman denied these claims: 'I did not give any instruction to shoot deceased in the event of his coming to the island. They said, "We're not going to let him through." I said "All right then."' When questioned by Detective Maloney: 'Peter Prior tells me you told him to shoot if Curry had any firearms,' Hoffman replied, 'No. I told them not to let him through and gave them firearms to protect themselves.' Hoffman would even suggest that Murri residents had been instructing him: 'The boys said give us the rifles and you look after the women and kiddies.'[32]

Elizabeth Ballard told the hearings that Hoffman had ordered the Murris grouped outside Davison's house to shoot or spear Curry and that a short while after she heard him say: 'Look, boys, I'll give one pound to the first one who does it.' Aubrey Walsh confirmed the offer of a reward, as did Ellison Obah, Caesar Anning, Clive Beckett, Colin Stevens and Jimmy Harvey. Hoffman denied these allegations.[33]

Moreover, in what the press described as 'sensational evidence' to the hearings, Stevens told the court that Hoffman had approached him behind the Palm Island store after the inquest had been completed, and had said to him: 'What is this I hear about you're rubbing the dirt into me?...You said I was at the bottom of shooting Curry.' Stevens told the Assistant Superintendent he would answer no questions unless they went before 'the boss'. At Cornelius O'Leary's office, Hoffman repeated his initial claim against Stevens before the Acting Superintendent. Stevens replied:

> You sent the boys down there and told them you would give them a pound each. I am the bloke who asked you what would happen if we did and you said you would stand responsible. Mr Hoffman said, 'I know this but that's all dead and gone.'[34]

Dr Pattison's testimony also contradicted the evidence given by witnesses:

> I did not give a rifle or cartridges to the boys on the morning that I was lying wounded at my house...I have no recollection of telling them where they could get the rifle or cartridges. I have no recollection of instructing the boys.

Questioned by Mr Townley: 'Did you at any time upon that day counsel anybody to shoot Curry?' the doctor replied: 'I did not.' Asked if she saw her husband give guns or had heard him tell the men to shoot Curry, Mrs Pattison replied: 'I prefer not to answer that question.' Acting for Pattison, JP Quinn defended his client, arguing that 'aboriginal witnesses' were 'unworthy, and would say anything they were expected to say.'[35]

Following the hearings, Peter Prior was confined to Stewart's Creek prison on remand until 11 August, on which date he was committed for trial on the charge of murder. Hoffman and Pattison were released on bail. By June the Attorney-General had decided not to file an indictment on the doctor.[36] While white witness, Elizabeth Ballard, was reimbursed for hotel expenses, incurred while in Townsville, Clive Beckett, Caesar Anning, Jimmy Harvey, Keith Walsh, Harold Conway and Colin Stevens, were kept in the Townsville watch house. For a period of three weeks they were treated as virtual prisoners, while Palm Islanders, Elison Obah and Billy Donaldson, were also confined to the watch house for a period of eight days. Peter Prior was imprisoned in Stewart's Creek prison for a period of four months.

Charges against Prior and Hoffman were finally heard in the Supreme Court's criminal sittings on 14 August 1930. The hearing commenced before a crowded gallery and a Crown jury with the court was presided over by Justice RJ Douglas. BA Ross appeared as crown prosecutor. Ross opened the Crown's case with a brief summation of events on 3 February, noting that Hoffman had distributed arms to Murri residents and given instructions to shoot Curry on his return to Palm from Curacoa Island. The shot which proved fatal was from 'the species of weapon' in Prior's possession at the time.[37]

As Ross began to call witnesses, Justice Douglas asked: 'Is that all you are going to prove Mr Ross?' Ross argued that he would divulge 'many more facts' to which the judge replied that he had read the depositions. 'Presuming that Hoffman shot Curry himself,' he asked, 'would he not be justified in doing so?'

> Mr Ross: Well your Honour, is it for me to say?
> His Honour: What is your personal opinion?
> Mr Ross: Personally, I think he would have been justified.
> His Honour: Well, is the prosecution proceeding because Curry was shot down by a black man and not a white man?

Justice Douglas then advised that he would tell the jury: 'that if a man attacked a community such as Curry did, that community would be justified in defending itself'. He noted that 'if the jury convicted', the case 'would be set aside by a Court of Criminal Appeal'. Ross responded 'it would be a waste of time to proceed any further. I'll enter a *nolle prosequi* [proceed no further].' The Judge responded: 'I think it's the best thing you can do; I don't think the bill should have ever been filed.'[38] Hoffman and Prior were subsequently acquitted and discharged.

Following the remarks of Justice Douglas, press reports of the Palm Island court cases turned decidedly against the government's decision to prosecute. The *Townsville Evening Star*'s position shifted from one of apparent neutrality to scathing editorial condemnation, in which the government's legal actions were 'inexplicable' and the prosecution had 'most unfairly harassed innocent people who had already suffered severely', as well as putting 'the country to considerable unnecessary expense'. Where the *Truth* had argued in February that the facts of the events should be 'cleaned up and punishment meted out', by August the *Truth* declared the court hearings a 'Travesty of Judicial Wisdom', a result of the 'Department's Stupid Bungling', a case of 'When Justice Was Blind'.[39]

While some voices raised Curry's war service and suggested he was 'shell shocked', his war records provide no evidence of this. Yet Curry seems to have convinced those around him that he was something of a war hero, with press reports and oral histories arguing that the Superintendent had served as a light-horseman at Gallipoli and in the field artillery in the Sinai, and that he was injured in battle. Curry seems to have constructed a mythical past, since official war archives show that he did not enlist until October 1915, five months after the initial Gallipoli landing, and he served with one of the Remount Units in Egypt, breaking-in difficult horses and training them for military service. His only recorded injury was a 'mildly crushed foot'.[40]

Men selected for the remounts tended to be those who were middle-aged or unfit for active service. Testimonies from Palm Islanders argued that Curry could not bend his right arm. Since he was only 29-years-old at the time of his enlistment, it seems likely that the deformity to his right arm had existed prior to his enrolment with the remounts and had classed him with the unfit. Curry's foot injury occurred in September 1916 and he was returned to Australia in October. The two Australian remount units were reduced to only two squadrons in that same month and Curry was discharged from the Australian Imperial Force on 13 December 1916.[41]

The actual form of his rampage provides more graphic evidence of his delusional condition, for Curry's actions at this time were those of a man at war. Known as a 'crack shooter', his attack was planned and his weaponry compiled in advance. About a fortnight before Curry's explosion of reserve properties, Hoffman had noticed the disappearance of arsenic and two packets of gelignite from the store. When he questioned the Superintendent, Curry returned only one packet of explosives.

On Saturday 1 February, Curry had a case of kerosene sent to his home and on the morning of 2 February he had Henry Pedro assist him to shift two dynamite cases and food supplies to the *Esme*. Curry told launch attendant Hamilton he was getting it ready for Monday, when he would take a dinghy over to Lucinda Point for a man called Stubbs. The same reasoning was given to Hoffman when he inquired about the pile of medical aids, benzine, explosives, rifle and cartridges he saw inside the store on the same Sunday morning.

On the morning after the tragedy, Detective Maloney and Constable Daley accompanied Hoffman to the *Rita*. What they found on board reads like the rations of a soldier engaged in a military campaign, including six cases of benzine, 21 tins of luncheon beef, medicines and dressings, razors, a Winchester rifle, two packets and three plugs of gelignite, one box of detonators, two pieces of fuse, two boxes of Winchester cartridges, four packets of .303 cartridges and 43 loose revolver bullets.

Curry's single-handed attack on the island involved burning out 'the village' — an action somewhat reminiscent of the Second Light Horse Regiment's campaign in Egypt. Some of his body language in the course of the rampage was militaristic — leaping from Pattison's veranda and waving of a white flag from the top of the *Rita*, as if signalling withdrawal. Before returning to Palm, Curry had surveyed his target from the mountain summit of Curacoa Island.

In marching up the beach fully armed and in full view of the Palm Islanders' rifle range, Curry faced an ambush akin to the ANZAC predicament at Gallipoli. Both Bleakley and the Assistant Under-Secretary of the Home Office, CE Chuter, later advised journalist HS Rodie of their mutual opinion that in 'walking up the beach and waiting where he must have realised he was under observation', Curry had 'framed his own execution'.[42] It seems feasible to speculate, given his demented condition at the time, that Curry was positioning himself in the role of the heroic soldier he liked to claim to have been.

His friends had said of Curry that he was 'a rough diamond' and 'as straight as a gun barrel', a description alarmingly appropriate to the conclusion of his reign. He would frequently sit on the steps of his home to clean his rifle, and residents were reportedly used to his 'flashing of firearms'. Curry often went down to the beach with a .303 rifle to shoot at seagulls and sometimes he shot at whales from boats in the island's bays. Len Ballard testified to the inquest that two years before the events of February 1930 Curry told him that he would take Gall and Bleakley 'out in the motorcar and put them over the rocks', and that 'he would shoot anybody that reported him'. In the Christmas period of 1929, he threatened his assistant, 'I was paid to shoot bloody Germans like you, and I'll get you.'

That fact that such threats were considered 'a joke' reflects upon the calibre of recruits to the administration of reserves in Queensland. The department was afforded a low status in the public service generally, and standards of skill or qualification for officialdom seem to have been minimal. An ex-nurse of both Fantome and Palm Islands stated that 'in the main, as far as I could see, it was an easy way of making a living for people who hadn't succeeded on the mainland'.[43]

Curry's sociopathic behaviour seems to have resulted from myriad factors, with his neuralgia and withdrawal from novocaine, after the feud on Christmas Day, of obvious significance. Abdomen pain, muscle ache, insomnia and restlessness, are all symptomatic of withdrawal from narcotic analgesics, were described by witnesses as features of Curry's physical condition in the weeks leading up to the tragedy.[44] This unhealthy physical and mental state was compounded by Curry's excessive alcohol intake.

Curry's familial circumstances, the economic squeeze on reserves induced by the Moore government's austerity measures, frictions between white staff and Curry's belief that he would soon be dismissed, provided the ingredients for his entering the late stages of severe stress breakdown. The experience of a 'territorial' threat was especially significant if Curry was in fact involved with a Murri woman resident on the reserve, and entertaining ideas of marriage.

Yet perhaps of greater significance — although given no apparent attention from any quarter — was the fact that Curry had experienced a twelve-year reign as 'supreme commander' of an isolated island settlement upon which he had almost complete control over the daily lives of more than a thousand Aboriginal residents. Here was a man used to making executive decisions concerning where people lived, where and how they worked, whom they married, even what they ate and challenges to his rule could be easily over-ridden through sleight of hand, which included the power to imprison, humiliate, starve and exile. If power is corrupting, perhaps dehumanising, Curry was provided with supreme power through Queensland's institutionalised racism which had invested such power in the hands of one white man.

Despite the public attention to Curry's rampage in 1930 — the incident was reported even as far afield as the French press — the events of 3 February have remained something of a hidden chapter in Queensland history. Both church and government records would later refer surreptitiously to 'the Palm Island tragedy' without mention of Curry's name or of the events in question. Others would leave somewhat distorted records, relying upon the kinds of unsubstantiated rumours which had helped to infest the island with friction. Alexander Crosby Brown, for example, recorded that a few months after the ship *Chances* left Palm Island in 1929, he and the crew heard the 'gruesome report' that Curry had 'leapt from his bed' one night, 'seized a carving knife' and murdered his wife and children, before rushing out to sea where he drowned himself.[45]

Certainly departmental inaction had resulted in the unnecessary waste of life in February 1930. As the *Daily Standard* reported, the Home

Office was familiar with Curry's 'outbreaks of madness' and 'drinking bouts' as a result of three inquiries in previous years.[46] Indeed, if anyone had been 'protected' by the operations of the department, it had been the Superintendent whose insanity was covered by tardy and secretive responses to reports of abuse.

In the aftermath of the trial in August, the government forced both Dr Pattison and Thomas Hoffman to resign. Len Ballard was transferred to Barambah, Albert Morecombe was suspended for drunkenness and resigned, while Protector Cornelius O'Leary was placed in charge as Acting Superintendent. The post-Curry era on Palm Island would witness a white regime administering control with even greater intensity.

This chapter of Palm Island history should not close without reference to media reports labelling Palm as 'Danger Island' and the 1999 Guinness Book of Records now notorious description of the island as 'the most dangerous place outside a war zone'.[47] For if Palm was ever a dangerous place to be, this was never more so than on 3 February 1930. It is testimony to the depth of understanding and forgiveness in Murri perspectives, that the elders I interviewed voiced their compassion for Robert Curry and acknowledged the intense pressures he was under at the time of his breakdown.

Parallels between these events and the dramatic incidents on the island in 2004 are clear. Almost eighty years after Curry's rampage, complaints and reports that all was not well on Palm Island were again ignored. Moreover, subsequent investigations up to the present time have left many residents feeling, as they did in 1930, that 'none of the underlying issues have come out.'

Chapter 6

Gribble's Time:

'Fiscal Restraint'

We had Ceravite [cereal] every morning...But that Ceravite was all fulla grubs. And this man would come over with a strap over his shoulder, and if we didn't eat that, he'd lash us, 'cross the back. So we used to get this and put it in our mouth...till he got right up the other end...We'd spit it back in the plate. You know, it was really sickening...We were really hungry.

Ivy Sam[1]

On this ideal settlement...the natives are well cared for...They are happy...Smiling faces are everywhere.

National Eucharistic Congress, Melbourne, 1934[2]

The contrast between black and white lives on Palm Island was mirrored in the gulf between official accounts of life on the reserve and oral testimonies from residents. This chasm of realities was at its most stark during the 1930s depression, when the island bore the brunt of the government's policy of stringent 'fiscal restraint'. Most of the ill and elderly were slowly starving to death. Inadequate supplies of rations and medicines combined with poor sanitation and general living conditions. The death rate reached more than six per cent in the early 1930s and numbers of deaths outstripped the birth rate until after the Second World War.[3]

One of its most distinguishing features of the period was the abandonment, abuse and neglect of children. The 'Dormitory Women's Reunion' on Palm Island in June 2007 was both a healing and a sad occasion. And while some contemporary contributions to public debate have fostered a kind of nostalgic reflection upon 'the good old days' of Indigenous communities where there was 'law and order' and 'everyone made a contribution', the overall context in which life was orderly and employment available for some people, some of the time, involved excessive levels of control over people's daily lives.

Removals intensified in this period and in the peak period of 1934 to 1938, 331 removal orders were to the island. Despite the excess of deaths over births up until 1947, the reserve's population expanded steadily throughout this era and was never less than 1,000. By the late 1930s Chief Protector Bleakley had targeted the whole Palm Island group, including Eclipse, Fantome, Esk, Curacoa, Havana, Brisk and Falcon Islands, as possible sites for further institutions. The Townsville Land Commissioner's office subsequently reported that the Palm Island group was 'ideally situated' for detention and punishment purposes and for the separation of 'castes', and in July 1938 the surrounding islands to Palm were gazetted as reserve lands.[4]

Palm Island was assigned multiple roles over the course of the 1930s and 1940s, being used as a detention centre, as an 'industrial school' for Aboriginal children, as an old people's home, as a general health clearing station, a service centre for the infectious diseases hospital established on nearby Fantome Island and as a regional holding centre for the mentally ill.

The very process of removal to Palm threw some of the old people into the illness termed 'longing for, crying for or being sick for country', where symptoms of loss and depression are so severe as to be life-threatening. Yet accusations that removals from homelands and exile to Palm were resulting in deaths seem to have passed unheeded by the Queensland government. In 1933 the island's resident doctor, Thomas L Bancroft, wrote:

> Some of the natives long to return to their own country. One poor chap, a Diamantina native from Julia Creek [250 kilometres east of Mount Isa], wanted to return there...We tried to induce the Home Secretary to allow him to return, but there was a delay and he died of a broken heart. Another wanted to return to Normanton but pined away before permission was granted.[5]

In evidence to the New South Wales inquiry into Aboriginal administration in 1937, North Queensland pastoralist McGregor Watson reported that many station labourers were being sent to Palm Island where

> most of them die, and some have been known to die within five days. Taking them away from their country is a terrible thing. The local policeman, being the protector, can do what he likes with the blacks by threatening to send them to the island.[6]

The process of removal was often physically torturous, compounding the trauma of being wrenched from country. In the 1930s, neck chains were used to arrest and convey elders in the North Queensland region by foot to the coast, then to Palm Island. In 1932, police troopers arrived upriver from Laura to remove two Murri women and three men to Palm, at the behest of a local Superintendent. The three men were chained neck to neck and dragged by police on a 240 mile (385 kilometres) walk to Laura in a midsummer tropical heat. The previous year 'another party' had been removed from the area and one of the men had died on the journey. In 1936, Bleakley reported on 'the combing out of a number of undesirable, old and inefficient natives' from the Normanton and Turn Off Lagoon district, through their deportation to Palm.[7] A non-Indigenous health worker on Palm Island in this period recalled:

> There was a whole group come down in chains from Coen [Far North Queensland]. They'd walked the whole distance. Police would be on horseback...A policeman got one of the native girls pregnant on the way. That was a big scream when she got down here pregnant. He was very indignant about it, the Superintendent. The girl was only fourteen or fifteen.[8]

Removals frequently involved long-term mental and emotional distress caused by separation from families, particularly for children. The late Iris Clay recalled being sent to Palm with her father, who was about to expose an affair between the missionary-manager on Mapoon and a black female resident. Iris's father was council chairman on Mapoon at the time:

> They put handcuffs on my father and we were rowed out to the lugger...As we were being rowed out my two sisters, Elizabeth and Maria, followed us out. They kept walking behind the boat, you know...until the water was up over their heads.[9]

The late Ivy Sam was a child living in Cloncurry (120 kilometres east of Mount Isa) in the 1930s, with her mother and her father, an Englishman and drover, when the police came:

> I was taken to Palm Island when I was four...the police came and sent my mother and us children away...They just ordered us to go...My father was heartbroken. He just stood there crying as the train left the station... I didn't see him again...I didn't know what the sea was, I hadn't seen it before. I thought it was a huge waterhole. It really scared me.

In 1922, Palm had become the first reserve to receive children under the 1911 *State Children's Act*, which sanctioned the committal of Aboriginal children as State wards to 'industrial schools' on reserves. Imprisoned in the Palm Island girls' dormitory, Ivy became one of the victims of the internment of children and their use as free labour that the Act facilitated:

> As children we weren't allowed to play. I remember coming home from school and we used to go near the airport (to Convent School)...we used to walk to school every day and coming back you'd be tired, you know, and maybe you'd want to have a bath. But you weren't allowed on the bed...They'd have these big sacks full of beans and we had to crack them...If it wasn't beans we'd have to sit there and peel mangoes.

By contrast, the white elite minority ruling the island had leisurely lives with Aboriginal servants close to hand:

> They didn't do a thing in those days. European ladies. Girls looked after their babies. Washed their clothes, ironed, cleaned, cooked. So they really lived a ladies' life you know. They couldn't even go down to the boat, collect their mail or carry their parcels up. They had these old Aboriginal men to do all that.[10]

In the post-Curry period the government's practical commitment to its policy that reserves should produce their own funds was questionable. Agriculture was often poorly supervised and milking cows destroyed many personal vegetable gardens. While there is a clear note of demoralisation amongst white staff in this era, wrought by the escalating loss of life, Dr Bancroft was more active in his complaints, advising the press in 1933 that Mauritius beans were being grown for farmers on the mainland 'while the natives are almost starving'. One informant recalled that in the late 1930s dormitory children would often cry themselves to sleep for want of food, and that apart from occasional supplies from parents 'we were scratching around looking for pawpaw seeds, roots, rotten eggs and what not.'[11]

While everyone on Palm Island was required to work a minimum of three and a half days per week — sweeping streets, scrubbing floors, getting timber, planting tobacco and diving for trochus shell — those doing only compulsory work were totally dependent on rations. In the early years of the Depression, rations administered to Murris were approximately half of those made available to unemployed whites, and rates were further reduced as a stringency measure. Meat was issued three times each week, having been conveyed 44 miles [70 kilometres] by launch from Townsville, stored in sacks in the cockpit, where it was 'exposed to the hot tropical sun'.[12]

By contrast, white staff on Palm Island could buy from the general store and received free issues of milk, firewood and vegetables. They were able to order their own food from Townsville which arrived with the steamer vessels each month. Murris would attempt to supplement food supplies through dragnet and spear fishing, finding themselves increasingly competing with visiting fishermen who were collecting hundreds of tons of fish for sale to southern markets.

Management of this system of stark inequality was ensured through the intensification of institutionalised tyranny. In the aftermath of the Curry tragedy, a residue of fear and suspicion pervaded the reserve, contributing to a high turnover of Superintendents. Gall recommended in 1933 that the roll call be more strictly enforced each morning, that parades be conducted by the Superintendent, not the storekeeper, and that 'action be taken to ensure that the men commence work after their dismissal from the parade line'. In this same year Bleakley reported:

> At Palm Island the native police squad was reorganised and strengthened and strict training given, which resulted in marked improvement in discipline all round. A new and effective lock-up was built and also a barracks for the police.[13]

Increasing control was also facilitated by changes to the 'protection' acts in 1934 and 1939, which expanded the powers of Superintendents to subjugate residents. Home Secretary EM Hanlon rationalised the extension of controls in 1934, arguing that new laws were needed 'to protect' Indigenous people 'not only from white people but also from themselves'.[14] This translated for Palm Islanders, as one elder has described it:

> Everything on Palm Island is the idea of the Superintendent...We got to do everything what suit the Superintendent, not us and every super [sic] that go there got the law in his own mouth...What he say is law and the state government allow him to make the rules... If they say go to jail you can't say what for and you don't know when you come out.[15]

New arrivals to the island had to immediately report to the Superintendent's office where their luggage was examined. The autocratic powers of Superintendents allowed wide scope for discrepancies and anomalies in the meting out of punishments. A total of eleven Superintendents were in charge of Palm Island over the course of the 1930s and 1940s. A more consistent presence on the island was provided by the Reverend Ernest Gribble, Anglican Chaplain at Palm Island for the period 1930 to 1957. Gribble had founded the Forrest River Mission in the Kimberleys and served for nine years as Superintendent of Yarrabah (37 kilometres south of Cairns). An authoritarian and a paternalist towards Aboriginal residents of reserves and missions, Gribble was also at times a staunch advocate for their human rights. His campaigning had forced the royal commission into the Forrest River massacre in 1926. On Palm Island he was critical of the reserve's Superintendents and frequently wrote letters to John Feetham, Bishop of North Queensland, protesting unjust treatments of residents. There were, he believed, members of staff on the island who had 'no time for the Aboriginals' and Superintendent EA Cornell, he wrote, 'knew absolutely nothing about the natives or even the handling of men'.[16]

Many of Palm's Superintendents were chosen for their expertise in agricultural pursuits. In January 1931, Cornell filled the vacancy left by O'Leary who became Deputy Chief Protector. The absurdity of Cornell, a prickly pear expert from Gayndah, being placed in charge of Murri lives, has not been lost on the Palm Island elders who regarded his appointment as an insult. Cornell's incessant feuding with the Palm Island doctor and his use of intimidation and violence towards residents were reminiscent of Curry's reign.

Against a backdrop of continued internal staff bickering there was, as the Home Office's Under-Secretary, Gall described it in 1931, 'a general feeling of mistrust' pervading relationships on the island. Gall's comments followed his inquiries into an incident in which Superintendent Cornell had engaged in a physical scuffle with a Murri resident whom he struck on the head with a steel spirit level. The Palm Islander in question had participated in the ambush of Curry in the previous year. Although the Superintendent had been the aggressor, Gall recorded fears that Cornell would 'probably be murdered'.[17] Inspector Loch of Townsville who took the resident into custody advised the local Anglican Bishop of the evident anxiety amongst white staff on Palm Island. They were, he said, 'absurdly nervous and always on their toes'.[18]

Superintendent JE Delaney, who followed Cornell's reign, was promoted from his role as the island's farm foreman. Delaney soon gained a reputation for being 'a hard man to work for', who gave 'no time for a break', and a Superintendent who 'chased black women'. In 1933, one of the residents advised Reverend Gribble that Delaney had imprisoned a young woman and 'was in the lock-up with her with the door closed for a long time'. When Gribble approached Delaney over the issue 'His manner was strange,' wrote Gribble, 'and mentally I registered him as guilty of something.'[19]

Delaney had to cope with administering the reserve in the context of the Depression and stringent economic policies of the Home Office. The wages bill was lowered through a reduction of staff; food and building supplies ran consistently short of demand. The problem of inadequate supplies, combined with allegations of brutality, interference with women and drunkenness on the part of Delaney, present a picture of a re-run of the Curry era. In 1934 several residents, including a policeman, advised Gribble that Delaney had threatened to shoot a male resident in the presence of six policemen. 'We are living in a very strained and pregnant atmosphere,' wrote Gribble, and Delaney 'has every appearance of mental breakdown'.[20]

Delaney resigned in the following year and Tom Pryor was seconded from the Thursday Island office. The next four years would see a rapid turnover of Superintendents. Pryor was replaced by Dr J Grahame Drew in 1936, and Drew by FH Julian in 1937. Dr CA Courtney took charge in 1938. Given the health problems on Palm Island in this period, it is not surprising that the average endurance by these men of the combined role of Superintendent and medical officer was less than twelve months.

Those medical men who served as Superintendents seem to have been no less authoritarian than those with former trade or military experience, with Dr Julian remembered for his insistence that all residents, including those suffering from leprosy, stand and salute him whenever they crossed his path. The reign of Dr Courtney was followed by that of Cecil Foote in 1939, who kept a revolver within arm's reach of his desk, and of GR Roberts, promoted from his position as clerk, who 'shifted from one office to the one next door'.

Roberts was replaced the following year by George Sturgess, who had taken the role of temporary launch driver during Hamilton's absence in 1934 and who became temporary farm overseer in 1936. Sturgess soon gained a reputation for being deaf, and so won the title of 'Binagury' (can't hear). While he is remembered as having sent many people to jail, he is also credited for having respected the older people by not forcing them to work, as others before him had done.

A white health worker described how staff in the 1930s took advantage of widespread illiteracy with the English language: 'There were perks and kick-backs and in some quarters downright dishonesty because most of them could not sign a name.'[21] There were also emerging a small number of white critics who began to speak in these years of how Queensland's reserves had come to resemble 'concentration camps' or 'graveyards.'

Reverend Gribble was one of the most caustic critics. He frequently communicated with the reserve's Superintendents, the Australian Board of Missions, the Chief Protector, and the Association for the Protection of Native Races. He also encouraged Palm Islanders to agitate for their rights using urban political means — petitions, the press and the departmental bureaucracy. From 1935, Gribble was able to cease his continual ferry journeys to and from Townsville and to take up residence on the island. A zealous priest, Gribble had built a congregation of 200 shortly after his arrival and within twelve months the St George's Church had been erected from thatch and palm-tree walls. He started a lending library, gave open-air lectures which drew large crowds and developed the church as the centre of structured social life with dances, scout meetings, a choir and band.

Gribble was committed to the 1930s emphasis upon assimilation to European values. Weekly dances were designed to reduce the attendance at corroborees and he supported the impounding of children to keep them away from 'bush life'.[22] Yet if Gribble's beliefs and practices were at times erratic or contradictory, he did organise substantial contributions to the community, such as the James Noble Fund, designed to finance the secondary education of selected Anglican Palm Island youth – an endowment he organised in commemoration of James Noble who had come from Yarrabah to work as his assistant. Noble had been ordained as an Anglican cleric in 1925.

The Catholic Church also had a presence on the island and gained a lease on Butlervale, an area of Palm Island land excluded from the reserve, in 1927, so that their first permanent priest, Father Maloney, had easy access to Murri residents. From Maloney's arrival in 1931, Gribble faced stiff competition in his attempts to win converts. Father Foster of the Roman Catholic Church is remembered for having broken down the racial segregation of church seating, when in the 1940s he arrived to find all the whites of his congregation seated at the front. Foster told them that everyone was amongst the 'children of God' and that there was 'no certain place' there for anyone. The following Sunday non-Indigenous Roman Catholics were seated throughout the church.[23]

Gribble developed an intense sectarianism towards the Roman Catholic Church, expressing a dislike of the nuns who worked at the school and on Fantome Island and labelling the Missionaries of Mary from Quebec as a group of 'dago disturbers'. His obsessions extended on one occasion, to disinterring one of his congregation who had been buried by the Roman Catholic Priest on account of the need to act in the heat of summer. Roman Catholic staff on Fantome fought strenuously against Gribble's proposal that he also have a presence at the lazaret, a hospital for contagious diseases, especially leprosy, on Fantome. The intensity of this feuding between white authorities over Indigenous residents as 'property' was again reminiscent of the Curry period — in this case a turf war was evolving over Indigenous 'souls'.

Health workers on Palm Island were also beginning to publicly critique government operations on the reserve. Staff shortages, lack of trained health staff, inadequate drug supplies, excessive workloads and overcrowded hospital facilities led to frustration and demoralisation.

It was in 1932 that Dr Thomas L Bancroft defined Palm Island as 'the Black-fellow's Graveyard', reporting conditions of 'filthiness and squalor' and a 'great mortality' amongst residents. Bancroft told the *Courier Mail* that he had spent eighteen months and his own money to have a building erected for health services, and that he was then discharged.[24]

Dr Raphael Cilento later agreed with Bancroft's report, while Dr Elliott Murray, Bancroft's successor, noted that the limited bed capacity of twenty resulted in hospital patients sleeping on mattresses on the floor.[25] Cilento made extensive investigations and reports on Aboriginal health in North Queensland in the 1930s in his role as Director of Tropical Hygiene for the Commonwealth Health Department. He linked substandard housing, poor nutrition, endemic parasitic infections, early ageing, poverty and squalor, all of which he defined as preventable.

In 1932, he inspected Palm at the request of Chief Protector Bleakley, reporting in November that sanitation was poor, inadequate food supplies had resulted in lethargy and depression, there had been a 'stalemate of progress' due to friction amongst white staff and Indigenous residents were withdrawing to camps beyond immediate supervision. This insistence by Murris on moving away from the reserve and its authorities was also a regular complaint of Reverend Gribble.

Cilento's emphasis upon 'material betterment' was matched by an equally strong desire to see increasing segregation based upon a 'card system' of classifying those on Palm into different 'castes', with white, yellow and red cards allocated according to degrees of ill health and age.[26] His perspectives were in keeping with dominant race-based thinking at a time when Australia's 'racial hygiene' movement was peaking in strength, premised upon the concept of Aryan superiority and maintaining 'the purity' of the 'white blood.' Consideration was being given to 'sterilization of the half-caste' by officials, including Under-Secretary Gall of the Home Office.[27]

Cilento likewise urged 'keeping the white blood pure'. He favoured the use of Palm Island as a health clearing station, the exile of residents to specific surrounding islands allocated to separate 'acute cases' from 'chronic' and the segregation of all unwell children to a separate 'compound'. Many of his recommendations were adopted. However, while surrounding islands were gazetted as reserves in 1938, these sites were used, not as health facilities, but as secondary detention centres for punishment. Cilento's 'vision' of a card system was never realised.

In 1946, Bleakley recorded of the 1930s: 'Pre-war it was generally accepted that the rate of earnings and the cost of living of the ordinary aboriginal worker was from one-third to one-half that of the white worker.'[28] In the late 1930s, those working under the Act but on the mainland were generally receiving 30 shillings per week — double the wages paid on the reserve — but were paid in hand only a portion as pocket money. The late Monty Prior has succinctly defined the Trust Fund system: 'They had the fund. We had the trust.'

By the end of the decade young Palm Island men were making furniture for white homes while female child labourers were responsible for sewing and cooking for other inmates and worked as aids and attendants to the hospital, the school and in the homes of white staff. Boys were apprenticed on job sites making sanitary pans, garbage bins, tanks and buckets, shoeing horses, repairing farm implements and fishing vessels. In this way unpaid child labour subsidised the maintenance of the reserve.

Adult Palm Islanders were employed in compulsory timber getting, sawmilling, carpentry, plumbing, road and bridge construction as well as diving for trochus shell, pearl, dugong and bêche-de-mer in the pre-Second World War period. Huge logs were brought down the mountains by bullock teams to the beach, where a small launch or whale boat would take them to the mill for cutting. When cutting timber, gangs would sometimes walk nine miles to Barber Bay. Six or seven logs would have to be shifted at one time, using ropes, for a period of several months, for which workers received tobacco, flour and rice.

Willie Thaiday also worked as a trochus shell diver: 'You pick up the shells all right but the government take them. We get nothing for it. We only get tobacco and we make damper and dumpling.'[29] By 1936, the trochus shell trade from Palm Island was generating income of £530 per annum.

The roll call for compulsory work was announced by bells rung each morning. Fourteen days hard labour was the penalty for those who failed to attend for work. The late Bill Congoo recalled:

> There was no such thing as not working. Everyone worked. Long as you can walk you gotta work. Even if you're just limping along. Old men. They used to come down the beach here, carry the whitefellas' grocery up...They were bloody slaves those poor old men...If the boat happened to come in when the tide's out, well they gotta carry it in. On their shoulders.[30]

Each member of the white staff also received the services of one or two men as 'houseboys' and gardeners. GD Bradbury's inspection report of 1932 noted: 'There is a feeling of antagonism amongst some of the staff of the Settlements to any scheme which will give the aboriginal any official recognition. That such antagonism is borne of jealousy or fear of being supplanted is undoubted.'[31] Police on the reserve continued to operate as the Superintendent's private force. Gribble was critical of the procedures whereby, 'on the word of a policeman' the Superintendent meted out punishments.[32] Gall recorded that in the 1930s those who were 'disobedient' were 'sent to Eclipse Island with a few pounds of flour and a box of matches'. They were, he wrote, 'practically starved'. Tom Morgan Snr was arrested for punching a policeman who accused him of 'cheeking' the Superintendent. He was sent to Eclipse Island by himself for a period of twelve months and three weeks, surviving his exile by virtue of his auntie sending over rations and food by clandestine means.[33]

Escorts of Native Police accompanied children wherever they went and dormitories for females remained enclosed by 'cage-like' wire fences. Christian missionaries recorded that girls were sleeping on the dormitory floors for lack of bed space, and Dr Bancroft reported that overcrowded conditions had lead to this institution receiving the name of 'the Black Hole of Calcutta'.[34] Older residents who grew up in the dormitories speak of these days as 'sad times', with their parents only allowed to visit on Wednesdays and weekends, and then only with permission from the Superintendent or Matron. Ivy Sam recalls crying herself to sleep at nights, and when she later managed the boys' home she looked after children who were 'very lost'. Some she said were unsure if they had parents at all, and their crying in the evenings 'used to remind me of myself'.

Bill Seaton has stated that during Roberts' time children who objected to eating the weevilly porridge supplies faced both starvation and retribution: 'You'd be punished, get locked up...They had a little place there to lock us up...One time there was thirty or forty of us.' These boys had been squeezed into the small confinement room for having run to the hills on hearing rumours that a hairy man was up in the bush. 'We went up to try and have a look, see if it was true...when we came back they were waiting for us,'[35] Fred Clay recalled that his dormitory boss would force the boys to parade single file, around the dormitory if misdemeanours occurred: 'as we passed, he would hand us a rock and tell us to put it on our head and keep walking around.' On one winter's evening the boys were paraded in this way for two hours.[36]

Escaping with boyfriends or girlfriends was a major reason for many of the punishments. Girls who ran away to meet boys would have their heads shaved by the dormitory matron. No contact was allowed between young men and women until the late 1930s, when complaints by Dr Drew, then the Superintendent, led to one-hour visits in the afternoon. No physical touching was permitted between young couples and their interactions were closely patrolled by police. The clearest parallel to this system of visitation is that which occurs in jails.

If little room was available for open confrontation with those running this system, oral histories are peppered with stories of Palm Island's

Aboriginal tricksters and their clever circumvention and subversion of the rules and regulations. Some, for example, involve a man dressed in a white shirt who was out walking after the evening curfew. When the police came along he hid his presence by standing under a clothesline, raising his shoulders and swaying his body so that he looked like a piece of laundry blowing in the wind. Others tell of men who would dress as women, raise their voices several octaves and in this way access their women friends in the dormitories.

Children were more vulnerable. Schooling was segregated and authoritarian and ceased at grade four of primary school. Bleakley's 1933 report reassured the government that the 'practical' training given was designed to make Palm Islanders 'useful members of their own communities', rather 'than to compete with their white cousins in the busy civilised world outside'.[37]

In terms of open rebellion, escape from Palm Island became the method which offered the highest chances of avoiding a punitive backlash. The location of the reserve, surrounded by shark-infested waters, made this a very desperate and brave endeavour. Of the group of nineteen men who absconded in 1932, only eleven were recaptured. All of those caught were sentenced to imprisonment and while some returned to Palm Island, others were sent to mainland reserves. A total of 51 desertions were recorded in that year alone.[38]

Some Palm Islanders did manage to continue attending gatherings in their own lands and to search and locate relations both on Magnetic Island and the mainland. Anthropologist Nancy Williams records that families continued to receive visits from relations at Pallarenda and Kissing Point on the mainland, despite the repressive sanctions of the Palm Island reserve.[39] The *Sydney Morning Herald* reported in March 1932 that a Palm Islander had 'deserted' on an 'improvised raft made from two logs fastened together by light boards' with a blanket as a sail. He had braved cyclonic winds and huge waves to arrive at Forrest Home, near Ingham, 26 hours later. 'Tippo said it was worth the risk to leave the settlement,' the report noted: 'He did not care for it and did not want to go back.'[40]

In 1935, 'Hooligan' led police on a six-month chase after fleeing Palm Island by boat, making his way to the country behind Cardwell, 175 kilometres north of Townsville. Described by local press reports as a 'witch doctor' who 'wields great influence over the tribes of the (Herbert River) station country', Hooligan made his way through the winter to Mt Garnet station, approximately 100 kilometres northwest of Cardwell, where he collected his family. Pursued into the bush by Constable Pratt, Hooligan threw a tomahawk at his stalker, evaded the firing of Pratt's bullets as he crossed the Herbert River, and was not recaptured until December when he was located at an Aboriginal camp in the Cardwell area when he was set upon by Pratt while asleep. Pratt had responded to complaints from a Mrs Collin that he was 'formenting (sic) trouble' at Kirrima station. Hooligan agreed to return to Palm Island on the condition that his family accompany him. Such was the pressure from pastoralists to have 'Hooligan' removed from the area that police, who had his family in custody, agreed.[41]

Anglican missionaries seem to have unwittingly contributed to groups of residents making sojourns back to their traditional lands, with Gribble repeatedly complaining that the church launch had been stolen. Acts of bravery were not confined to adults. Fred Clay escaped at fifteen years of age to the mainland, 'jumping a train' to Ingham, before he was arrested at gunpoint, imprisoned in the town and then deported back to the reserve.

Palm Islanders would swim around the jetty to avoid water police and some swam the mile-wide channel to Brisk Island from Eclipse. Gribble reported that a Palm Islander had returned to his country on the Mitchell River several times: 'once he crossed to the mainland from Palm Island on a log, no mean feat.' By 1938 the Chief Protector's reports would refer simply to 'the usual numbers of escapes having occurred'. Yet in that same year a North Queensland grazier wrote to the first Indigenous newspaper, the *Australian Abo Call* in New South Wales, noting that Aboriginal people were drowning in their attempts to escape the island.[42]

As the twentieth century progressed, Palm Islanders increasingly used political means to seek better conditions on the island and the payment of wages. A 'native council' was established in 1936 and its role was to offer advice regarding resident welfare and to 'make suggestions for the removal of grievances and to act as an official permanent jury in the law courts'. While elected, the taking of positions remained dependent upon superintendent approval.

Some success was achieved by Willie Thaiday, Alby Kyle, Sid Cerico, Fred Brackenbridge, Percy Smallwood and George Ryan in using this body to secure wages for those receiving only rations in 1936, following their negotiations with Deputy Chief Protector O'Leary. While their initial four shillings per fortnight agreement was rescinded after some of the men were caught gambling, it was later regained with an increase to seven shillings. However, by 1937 Reverend Gribble was complaining that Superintendent Julian regarded the council as a 'silly' initiative and that it had ceased to function since the Superintendent refused to call meetings.[43]

Palm Island's history in this area of negotiation and protest was in keeping with the emergence, nationally, of Indigenous organisations acting to bring about social change. Press coverage of reserves was limited, however, and rigid departmental control over who entered or left the reserve ensured that it was difficult for residents to gain access to information and resources that might enable the exercise of civil rights.

Sections of the labour movement became involved, alongside other non-Indigenous supporters, in campaigns for human rights. This support was crucial in a context where the protests in reserve settings were so difficult. In 1938, the *North Queensland Guardian* called for 'the close cooperation of all sympathisers' to the efforts of the Aborigines' Progressive Association and condemned the government's powers to remove Murris to reserves and confiscate wages. Challenging these powers was defined as a labour movement responsibility. Attention was also directed to Palm Island, where 'frightful conditions' were said to exist and calls made for an inquiry into the reserve to expose the fraudulent nature of Hanlon's claims that Palm Islanders lived in a 'demi-paradise'.[44]

The Second World War years witnessed the departure of 'mobile gangs' of reserve Murris for employment in essential industries, with 2,800 Indigenous workers employed in the pastoral industry state-wide by 1943. Palm Islanders found themselves alongside workers from Cherbourg, Yarrabah and Woorabinda reserves, and in the cane fields, maize and corn crops of North Queensland they laboured alongside Italian internees. These settings fostered alliances that would prove to have strategic value in the 1950s and that were influential in the 1957 Palm Island strike.

Those who remained on the reserve were impacted by the pressures to increase production of food and clothing while being affected by wartime shortages. In the first six months of 1943, 58 people died. Poor housing and inadequate clothing had disastrous results in winter with pneumonia sweeping the settlement. Contaminated well-water triggered outbreaks of diarrhoea and infant mortality rates were 7.7 times the Queensland average.[45]

Over the course of the Second World War, Townsville played host to more than 50,000 American and Australian troops when it became the major launching site for battles in the South West Pacific. Palm Island became the site of the Black Cat squadron which flew Catalina flying boats on long range missions.

That a large proportion of troops on Palm were African-American was in keeping with General MacArthur's agreement to a request from the Curtin government's that troops be racially segregated so that contact between white Australian women and black American men was minimised.

Japan's advances into southeast Asia and the takeover of New Guinea created panic in North Queensland, escalated by three, albeit unsuccessful, bombings of the port of Townsville in the years 1942 to 1943. Japanese planes flew over Palm and the reserve practised blackouts in this period.

The American occupation lasted for eighteen months, while the numbers of residents on the reserve declined. Recruitment of white staff became difficult because of the island's vulnerability to attack, and, during the height of panic in 1942, the evacuation of white female staff and their children was ordered. The convent school and St Anne's staff evacuated to Ravenswood, an old gold mining town 130 kilometres south of Townsville near Charters Towers, and others to various parts of the mainland. No such protection was afforded Murri women and children on the island.

Some Palm Islanders tried to join the armed services, but not everyone was accepted. Some of the elders of Palm Island were indignant upon finding that when they cited their residence as the reserve they were immediately rebuffed by recruiting officers. Robert A Hall's *The Black Diggers* notes that while much confusion emerged at recruiting stations because of changing policies, and despite formal bars, more than 3,000 Indigenous people enlisted in Australia's war effort.[46]

Palm Islanders felt the threat of warfare in a more immediate sense than did most resident Australians, being situated in close proximity to the explosive area of the Pacific war. For those confined to the island, the social impact of the presence of American troops provided a high excitement that contrasted sharply with the general austerity of reserve life. Jack (deceased) and Jean Sibley recall the Americans flying acrobatically in their aeroplanes, show-riding their horses up the streets of the reserve and being generally exhibitionist.

Palm Island boys were taken for rides on their seaplanes, cartons of cigarettes were thrown over dormitory fences and food and clothing freely distributed amongst reserve residents. More reaction was created, however, by the willingness of US troops to ignore reserve regulations and enter the female dormitories. If caught during the evenings the men were taken to jail by military police and banned from the reserve area for two-week periods.

Mrs Sibley can recall walking back to the dormitory from the hospital one morning and being followed by American troops, of whom she felt afraid:

> When I looked back I see these two Americans trotting behind me — so I thought I'd gallop too. I did gallop and they were after me. I raced into the dormitory and I said: 'The Americans

are coming.' Everybody starts screamin' and they were right in the dormitory, these Yanks. They couldn't stop 'em – even the manager. They said come on girls, we'll take you out for a walk. We said no, we're not allowed...They opened up all the doors.

Despite sanctions, some of the Americans managed to have affairs with Palm Island women. About two hundred Afro-American troops resided at Cannon Bay where they had a dance hall brightly lit, and football matches were also held with Palm Islanders. Their presence on the island was equated with a sense of security as well as social excitement and access to goods not otherwise available. By February 1944, the Americans were beginning to leave the island, the naval station was closed in May and the last of the Americans went home in August.

Living conditions and general health status improved little over the course of the late 1940s, although schoolteacher FA Krause noted that the construction of fibro and cement homes — postponed during the war years — would resume in the late 1940s.[47] Whooping cough, skin diseases and mumps afflicted children on the reserve in epidemic proportions throughout this era. Gastroenteritis and influenza claimed many lives up into the 1950s.

In 1950, Palm Island's medical officer, Dr Hilyard Smith, reported that the reserve was suffering from a lack of staff, no time was available for training, the matron was 'forced to do the work of four nurses' and 'our hospital has been overcrowded and beds have had to overflow onto the veranda to meet the emergencies.' The following year he reported that for three months the island had no resident medical officer. Probably the most distressing trend in death rates was the loss of infant and child lives. In 1949, Hilyard Smith reported the death of seven babies aged between two hours and fourteen months. The high infant mortality rate remained a feature of Palm Island history up into the late twentieth century.[48]

In the 1950s, the atmosphere on Palm Island would change remarkably with the arrival of ex-policeman Roy Henry Bartlam as Superintendent in 1953. Bartlam's obsession with control would lead to enormous tension on the island as the decade progressed. As the conflict between residents and the Superintendent intensified, Gribble was being ushered from the island by Bishop Shevill in Townsville. Old, frail and in the care of one of the Anglican sisters, Gribble did not want to leave. Shevill announced that Gribble's salary would be terminated and, with a strange foreshadowing of what would happen to those who resisted Bartlam's rule, the air force launch was sent to take him, against his will, to the mainland. Gribble died in October 1957 at Yarrabah.

Chapter 7

Fantome Island, Phantom Welfare

> We have survived the whiteman's world
> And the horror and the torment of the old
> We have survived the whiteman's world
> And you know, you can't change that.
> No Fixed Address[1]

If 'Gribble's Time' had been characterised by high rates of sickness and death on Palm Island, then the struggle for survival in the context of inadequate food, shelter, sanitation and health care was demonstrated in even more exaggerated form only six miles across from Palm, on neighbouring Fantome Island. Here, in 1928, a lock hospital was established for the confinement of victims of venereal diseases. From across Queensland, Aboriginal people were torn from families, institutionalised and subjected to drugs which caused many to faint, vomit, sweat, tremor and literally shrink in size and strength. Until 1973, Fantome Island existed as a hidden fourth-world community in a first-world country.

Like its adjacent counterpart on Palm, the Fantome reserve served many functions over the course of its history. From the 1930s, it became a leprosarium as well as a health screening centre for everyone sent to Palm. The island featured an expanding burial ground, with a death rate that by 1932 had reached almost fourteen per cent of its population. During the years 1935 and 1936, death rates on the island were approximately ten times the crude death rate for Queensland generally. For Fantome Islanders, this translated as the loss of 77 lives over the three years from 1935 to 1937.[2]

The overwhelming majority of patients detained on Fantome were suffering from diseases not known to Indigenous people prior to the arrival of Europeans. Early written colonial records frequently commented on the apparent good health evident in the Aboriginal people they encountered. Small group sizes, lifestyles involving frequent exercise and a nutritious diet discouraged the development of ill-health and the spread of disease. In the pre-invasion period, Indigenous people of the land mass now known as Australia enjoyed much better health, on the whole, than did their English contemporaries.

The introduction of diseases such as smallpox, syphilis, measles and leprosy was responsible for much of the death toll in North Queensland, as it was in other parts of Australia, contributing significantly to white Australia's colonial hegemony. Dispossession from lands was fundamental to this process, since the destruction of Aboriginal economies was a direct cause of ill-health. The loss of any community's ability to feed itself, and the malnutrition which results, lowers resistance to infectious diseases, while parasitic diseases may reduce the ability to absorb nutrition from the food that is available.

Plans for Fantome Island's institutions developed in the context of desires to intensify white settlement in North Queensland and anxious public debate concerning the assurance of 'safe white settlement' in the region. In the 1930s, EM Hanlon, then Minister for Health and Home Affairs, was explicit that the government's goal in confining Murris to reserve institutions was to ensure that 'a very grave danger to our own health can be removed'.[3]

It was in 1925 that Bleakley's report noted the continuing prevalence of venereal disease in the Gulf and eastern coastal region, including Palm reserve, and recorded that a site had been chosen for the construction of a hospital on Fantome. A major consideration was its close proximity to Palm, regarded as useful to government 'economy'. Resident medical staff on the main reserve would be drafted into the additional responsibility. The government's actions, in terms of actual medical attention, were decidedly tokenistic. A Palm Island doctor was to visit twice weekly, and in practice, sometimes not at all, while a wardsman was to be entrusted to administer medications to more than 200 people.[4]

In 1926, Fantome Island building work was delayed when a cyclone demolished the partially erected hospital. The numbers confined to the lock hospital more than doubled each year in the period 1930 to 1933. Two epidemics of influenza struck Fantome Islanders in the twelve months of 1932. Bleakley seemed to accept that the island would function partially as a graveyard. The death rate of 13.65 per cent in this year was, he wrote, 'not surprising' given 'the condition of many of the cases on admission', and so could even be described as 'good under the circumstances'.[5]

The use of Fantome Island from 1936 as a general health 'clearing station' for all those sent to Palm was facilitated by changes to the 'protection' Act in 1934. While the rapid expansion of Fantome's population meant that by 1933 the staff reportedly had 'difficulty coping', the amending legislation of 1934, with its provision for compulsory submission to medical examinations, exacerbated problems of overcrowding by sending people removed to Palm Island via Fantome for health clearances.

Early twentieth-century attitudes to venereal disease were laced with deep-seated fears about the breakdown of late Victorian sexual morality and this anxiety became enmeshed with racial hostilities and stereotypes. Authoritarian moral sanctioning and banishment heavily outweighed concerns for recovery. In 1933, Dr Cilento commented of his visit to the island that while victims of syphilis received medical attention, those suffering from gonorrhoea — 'and almost all have gonorrhoea' — 'simply cannot have any useful attention and remain apparently fixtures'. Up until complaints were made by Deputy Superintendent Julian, in the late 1930s, female patients on Fantome had their feet chained.[6]

The decision in 1939 to expand facilities to include a leprosarium followed official surveys of leprosy in Murri populations and literal hunts by police to 'round up' victims of the disease. The state government received federal assistance for the institution and from 1940 it relinquished administrative responsibility on Fantome to the Australian Sisters of Our Lady of Help, a Roman Catholic organisation of women. In each of the three institutions — the lock hospital, screening centre and leprosarium — the practices of Western medicine were imposed upon Murris without consent.

Murri medicine practices have traditionally involved preventative and holistic approaches, with an emphasis upon self-responsibility to maintain a healthy and balanced physical, emotional and spiritual state. Indigenous medicine is inextricably linked to land-based cultural beliefs and efforts to avoid ill-health are based on laws which govern behaviour. Healers' resources include herbal medicines, diet, use of ochre, smoke, steam and heat and skills in restoring harmonious relations. While records of residents and white health workers on Palm Island in this period have noted the successes of Indigenous medicine men in healing the sick, the process of colonisation and Christianisation increasingly marginalised the community's own healers in favour of the dominance of Western medical practices.

Dr Raphael Cilento became instrumental in the process of removals to Fantome. Accompanied by the police superintendent of Gordonvale, he engaged in attempts to surprise camps in North Queensland in the early 1930s and wrote of how, setting out at 5am, 'We caught and examined most of those we wanted but there were several whom the police themselves have been hunting for months and these got away.' Camps were frequently deserted upon warnings that the doctor and police were approaching; 'The sight of the ambulance,' wrote Cilento, 'was to send them scuttling from any camp into the bush.'

From its inception as an institution, Murris were removed to Fantome Island in chains. Cilento recorded in 1931 that he and Police Superintendent Lidstone caught 'a young and powerful aboriginal' whose 'tell tale heart fluttered the skin like a captive bird'. Having enforced questionnaires and examinations on the men's camp, Cilento wrote: 'I felt a curious little pang of pity and remorse just as I have always felt when I have seen natives charge into rifle fire or some other hopeless opposition.' At the completion of more than 100 miles (160 kilometres) of travel in hunting the sick, Cilento recorded: 'Everything I did was unauthorised, most of it illegal, and it all went along like a song.'[7]

Venereal disease was a devastating affliction amongst Aboriginal groups. Colonisation's disruptions to the economic and personal foundations of family life resulted in the destruction of traditional marital and sexual practices and to survival through prostitution. In addition, there was no traditional mechanism to combat the disease. In Queensland, while no lock hospital was designed specifically for the removal of Murris who had venereal disease until after the First World War, many had already been deported to reserves, particularly Fraser Island. Victims of leprosy were also segregated and sometimes removed from the mainland to Great Lizard and later Fitzroy and Harrett Islands, while Dayman Island became a reception centre from 1899. The 1892 legislation, with its emphasis upon detention and isolation, made no stipulations regarding lazaret conditions to contain contagious diseases and did not require that attendants have any medical knowledge. The Minister could direct examination and confinement of all reported cases.

This history flavoured the nature of the lock hospital and later the lazaret on Fantome Island. Medically, the period was characterised by the dominance of the 'laboratory model' of public health programs.

Fantome's hospital was increasingly regarded by medical experts and administrators as well situated for 'investigation purposes' and as 'practically a closed experiment in health care'. Lack of trained and adequate staff did not hinder the delivery of interventions to this particular section of the public. When Palm Island was without a medical superintendent for several months in 1935, so too was the lock hospital.

One informant recalls that she was sent to Fantome Island in the 1930s as a nurse, arriving to find that there was no doctor, no other nurses and about 150 patients. Home Office funds were saved by having patients put to work including policing, cooking, woodcutting, grounds work, garbage and sanitary jobs.[8]

In 1932, Bleakley noted that while a 'regrettable' number of female children had been admitted to the hospital, discharges appeared small in comparison and there had been 'much wearisome, non-progressive work and many disappointments'. Supplies of food and medical staff from neighbouring Palm were unobtainable during periods of bad weather and in the absence of a suitable launch in the mid 1930s. The government's poor choice of a site for the lock hospital — at the back of Juno Bay, surrounded by coral reef — meant that boats were unable to row the last 100 metres of the journey to the island. In the absence of a jetty until the late 1960s, the task of taking goods to the island was laborious and fraught with danger. Soil condition for growing food was poor.

The 1930s' reports of the Department of Health and Home Affairs note of treatments for venereal disease that 'slipshod methods are altogether too common', and that 'spot diagnosis' of discharges and sores were often 'unsupported by the necessary microscopic and serologic tests and aids' required for adequate diagnosis. Treatment consisted of injections of Salvarsan, an arsenic compound developed by German Nobel laureate Ehrlich, which killed the spirochete, the organism causing syphilis. Although the drug was effective in this task, it was also toxic and required a painful regime of injections for up to two years. No alternative was available until the development of penicillin in 1943, which was not released for civilian use until 1944.[9]

During 1940 to 1941, Public Service Inspectors DW Johnson and CD O'Brien visited the lock hospital and furnished a series of reports to the Department of Health and Home Affairs, noting that state health regulations were not implemented, nor even known to staff on the island. Removals to Fantome were conducted without the necessary paper work, including medical certificates, and hence were illegal. Babies born on the island were immediately taken away to Palm Island's dormitories, causing trauma to new parents and exacerbating health problems.

Despite Fantome Island's status as a state-run hospital, Murri patients, unlike their white counterparts elsewhere, had fees of 2 shillings per day extracted from their bank accounts in payment for their confinement. Yet Johnson and O'Brien reported that food supplies were inadequate, with vitamin contents 'dangerously low', and there was a 'complete absence of fresh or dried fruits and fresh vegetables, except potatoes and onions'. Staff were not adequately trained and some of the patients 'for some not clearly defined reasons' were not being treated.

'Nurse' Brumm had a midwifery certificate but was untrained as a general nurse. She was given the task of intravenous injections with 'no instruction on the subject by any medical man'. Superintendent Julian had never actually witnessed her doing it. Moreover, Julian himself, with no medical training in the area and no instruction on dosages, had been 'compelled to work out his own doses' and complained that he had received 'little or no direction in the treatment of VD'.[10]

The report noted that records were inadequately kept, examinations and diagnoses not recorded, and that visiting Dr Courtney 'admitted he did not make any entries or sign anything during his visits'. Blood tests were infrequently conducted and general treatments for both syphilis and gonorrhoea were 'very unsatisfactory'. Quoting a number of patient history cards to justify their criticisms, Johnson and O'Brien cited of an eighteen-year-old female: 'No action was apparently taken about the positive blood tests, which indicated infection either with syphilis or yaws. There is no record that Dr Courtney ever examined or even saw the patient.' A 30-year-old male admitted for venereal disease had not been smear-tested prior to diagnosis and treatment. Cured and arrested cases were reported to be detained in the lock hospital 'owing largely to "housing difficulties" at Palm Island Settlement'.

The inspectors then described as 'a classic illustration of the bungling administration of the Sub-Department' the case history of a woman and her husband who were removed to Fantome Island from Woorabinda. In the absence of a medical certificate, both were detained despite the male being free of infection, the woman's relations were not informed of her death on 9 August 1940 until 29 September, and it was not officially recorded until 7 October. At the conclusion of their assessment, Johnson and O'Brien recommended that the lock hospital be transferred to Palm Island and reorganised, with staff and relatives of patients to be housed separately — suggestions not enacted for another six years.[11]

With Fantome Island a clearing station for all those destined for Palm from 1936, staff were then charged with attending to tubercular 'and similar cases', and 'waves of admissions' occurred. Two hundred and thirteen patients were admitted to the hospital in 1936, creating a total of 447 patients of whom only 195 were discharged. The death rate remained high and in 1937 about ten per cent of the population of that year died.[12]

In this context Catholic and Anglican missionaries to Fantome Island vied for souls. Those on their death beds could find themselves baptised several times. While the Anglicans wrote fancifully of the island as 'a kind of sanitorium' with 'all the advantages of a seaside resort',[13] the inspection reports of the 1940s condemned the quarantine functions of Fantome as virtually useless in long-term health care.

Johnson and O'Brien commented that the screening 'system is inefficient and inconsistent, and quite useless in preventing the entry of venereal or other infectious disease into Palm Island settlement'. Moreover, medical histories were not obtained from patients and no physical examinations for venereal diseases were made. Remarks from Dr Courtney were cited:

> I do not examine new arrivals as to condition of blood or urine, or conduct any tests for hookworm disease. I do not examine

new arrivals with a stethoscope as a rule. If Julian says they are fit for discharge they are discharged.

Johnson and O'Brien described four categories of inmates, including 'those who were sent for various reasons'. Twenty-nine inmates were recorded as relatives of the ill, sixteen of whom were children, while seven youths were on staff. Five patients were listed as 'mental cases' and four were 'undefined'. It is difficult to imagine the benefits available to these people through confinement to a lock hospital for venereal disease.

Fantome Island Lazaret was constructed in the context of increased detections of leprosy amongst the Queensland Murri population and recommendations from one of the leading figures of this research that a leprosarium be built. In 1934, Raphael Cilento, then Director-General of Health and Medical Services — a eugenicist who supported the White Australia Policy — suggested the design and construction of a 'village community for aboriginals' with the principles of segregation and confinement as its underpinnings. Cilento's suggestion was supported by the 1937/38 reports of the National Health and Medical Research Council. The *Health Act 1937* had given the Director-General of Health and Medical Services powers to detain, examine and confine suspected leprosy sufferers at his discretion.

The establishment of Fantome's lazaret also resolved the problem of where to transfer Murri inmates of Peel Island in Queensland's southeast, so that, according to the Minister EM Hanlon, improvements could be made at Peel 'which obviously could not be made while mixed races were there'. On 10 May 1939, Fantome Island's leprosarium was approved and money allocated by the state's health department for a laboratory.[14] Some of Peel Island's inmates had been previously transferred from Fantome Island, and were now forced to travel a complete circle as a result of the government's decision.

On 8 January 1940, an army landing barge arrived at Peel, taking Murri patients, their goods and chattels, including a piano which 'they had managed to keep from the white patients' grasp'. Forty-nine Murri patients were taken to Brisbane, leaving 26 whites on the island. From Brisbane, they boarded a train to Cardwell, accompanied by Matron Avonia O'Brien and three police. Of the 49 people transferred, a total of 40 had died within their first five years on Fantome Island, not from leprosy, but from tuberculosis, for which they had not been vetted.[15]

While Dr Courtney would argue that there was 'no reason whatsoever for any anxiety' regarding the 'feeding and welfare' of Fantome Islanders, Matron O'Brien lodged a series of complaints, advising the Department in April that the bread supplied to patients was 'unfit to eat', that 'the quality of meat was so bad that I would not think anyone would be allowed to sell such', and that she had given patients her own food supplies in the absence of a response to her protests to Dr Courtney. She had to feed 29 people with 'five corned ox cheeks for the day, ten potatoes and eight onions'. The matron no doubted experienced a contrast to her previous work on Peel, where the government had spent approximately £1,000 per year on each white patient. On Fantome Island the government spent one tenth of that amount.

In 1940, the government relinquished responsibility for nursing duties at Fantome leprosarium, approaching Sisters Catherine, Bernadette and Agnes, as well as Mother Peter of the Sisters of Our Lady of Help, already stationed on Palm.

Until the late 1940s, the medical industry's treatment of leprosy relied upon the use of chaulmoogra oil, a nauseous-tasting vegetable oil from seeds of a Burmese tree, in the form of injections and capsules, which yielded 'disappointing results', and feelings of despondency regarding progress at Fantome are evident in church records from this time.

Missionaries were interested in working in 'curative, hospital-based medicine', since it offered direct personal contact and the notion of healing which carried a 'religious potency'. Unlike preventative, public health activities, this work could be fused with efforts in the 'salvation' of individual souls. Sectarian in-fighting between Roman Catholics and Anglicans on Fantome involved accusations that the Sisters were forcing patients to attend religious services twice daily, and wrangling over who should conduct the rituals associated with birth, death and marriage.

The Sisters' diary notations record severe reactions to medical treatments on the part of patients, including nausea and in one case virtual blindness. One patient was so ill as to be 'almost covered in bandages' while others were described as 'very weak'. The entry for March 1940 recorded the 'very poor state of inmates, insufficient huts and kitchens', and in February the following year 'unrest and agitation' was noted as a frequent occurrence.[16]

The late Cliff Wyles, who worked as 'boat boy' for Father Foster, recalls seeing people who were missing a finger one day, being virtually without a hand the following day. He stated that the disease was so rapid that only milder cases survived. Many of the doctors were unqualified, frequently being students.[17] While the Sub-Department of Native Affairs argued that the leprosarium was 'most satisfactorily conducted' and the inmates 'happy and cooperative...and very grateful' for their treatment, annual reports of the Health and Medical Services branch of Health and Home Affairs show little improvement over this decade.[18]

The Second World War overshadowed the island with fears of invasion and petrol rationing left Fantome Island isolated. Mass was infrequently held and one of the priests had a nervous breakdown.[19] While some of the tensions eased in the post-war period, new developments in leprosy drugs brought problems. Under the regime, dapsone and sulphetrone from the chemical class of sulphone drugs were used successfully to treat leprosy from 1946. However side effects included anaemia, gastro-intestinal complaints and what was referred to as 'dapsone syndrome'. This condition could include dizziness, nausea, swelling of limbs and face, nodules under the skin and shivering attacks. Sulphones were introduced to Peel Island in 1948 and to Fantome in 1949.[20]

From 1948, Peel Island's doctor was also charged with responsibility for Fantome, where he would visit for six-week periods. Dr Morgan Gabriel, Peel Island Superintendent from 1951 to 1959, recorded that while some Fantome Islanders seemed to respond to sulphones more promptly than whites, others had no tolerance for the drugs. Dr Gabriel earned the respect of patients. He was so committed to his belief in the role of nutrition in resistance to the disease that he injected infected blood into himself in an attempt to prove that healthy body systems were able to fight the disease.[21]

In the post-war period, some progress was made with both the use of sulphones at the lazaret, and with penicillin for venereal disease. The first discharge from the leprosarium was in 1950. Others followed and throughout the decade the death rate fell. Yet some patients still found no relief from the disease, while others pined away from the loss of their families. The Office of the Director of Native Affairs report for 1951 noted that 90 per cent of Fantome Islanders had little or no tolerance of sulphetrone.[22]

The late Paddy Tanner recalled of his stay there until 1958, that he experienced severe reactions to experimental drugs. Already sick from dapsone, he was brutally affected by experiments with CIBA. Having taken four tablets on one occasion he was convinced by staff to take a dosage of five and found himself unable to even break a matchstick twelve months later. He lost a great deal of weight, was unable to hold down any food except oranges, and had to crawl on his hands and knees to move around. Fantome Island was, he said, 'a sad proposition' in history.

In 1959, the remaining white patients at Peel Island were transferred to an annex of the Princess Alexandra Hospital in South Brisbane, where they could leave at their will. Fantome Islanders, isolated from families and friends, were aware of this anomaly and resented the double standards. Stephen Hagan recorded how his Uncle Robert 'Bobby' Bismark, removed from Cunnamulla to Fantome in 1959, was denied permission to return to his home town upon release because the Protector at Cunnamulla did not want him to reside with his wife and family who were not wards of the department. He passed away on Palm Island on 23 April, 1969, with a telegram being sent from Palm's manager to the Manager of Woorabinda. Hagan notes, 'Unless his relatives and friends had access to a Lear jet to fly from Woorabinda to Palm Island, Bobby Bismark would not have had a single one attend his funeral.' [23]

In the 1960s and 1970s, Fantome Islanders remained in detention and had to attend compulsory medical examinations upon release. Detailed reports were maintained on all patients, and these included comments on who 'the gamblers' and 'the stirrers' were. Like their fellows and kin on Palm Island, they were treated as virtual prisoners and this continued well into the period after the Second World War.

On 30 June 1973 the hospital closed, and by October the three remaining male patients were transferred to Palm Island hospital. Bishop Faulkner wrote to Pat Killoran, the Director of Aboriginal Affairs, authorising the Department of Aboriginal and Island Affairs to burn the buildings and they were razed to the ground in 1974.

Some former Murri residents of Fantome believe the burning was designed to circumvent claims to the land by former inmates.

Western hospital and laboratory medicine did eventually offer physical relief and recovery to the majority of patients. The path to this point had been a long and painful one, the island the subject of extensive neglect. The cost in human life had been appallingly high.

Chapter 8

Bartlam's Time:
'We Couldn't Tolerate Any More', the 1957 Strike

Joe Geia's song 'Uncle Willie' pays tribute to his uncle, Willie Thaiday, one of the men deported from Palm Island as a result of the strike by Murri workers in 1957. Thaiday provides his own account of these events in his autobiography *Under the Act*. Other participants in the strike have recorded their experiences through an oral history series conducted by the Australian Broadcasting Corporation. Still others participated in the strike's recreation in the film *Protected* (1976) by Alessandro Cavadini and Carolyn Strachan.[1]

Almost 20 years after the events of the strike, some of the original strikers and their close relations re-enacted this little known chapter of resistance to Queensland's punitive Act. Ironically, in the course of this recording, these members of the film's cast were threatened, yet again, with their deportation from the island. More recently, the Palm Island community organised a reunion of the original strikers and their descendants to commemorate the fiftieth anniversary of this significant event in Queensland's history.

History suggests that no strike ever has a single cause and decisions to take industrial action are heavily influenced by broad, historical settings. In the 1950s, Murris were increasingly conscious that they could not partake of Australia's much vaunted post-war prosperity, confined as most were to poor socio-economic conditions on pastoral stations, on the outskirts of towns and within the reserves. While increasing discussion of race relations occurred at a national level, governments were unwilling to modify their policies beyond limited extensions to welfare measures.

Yet the national setting in this period also witnessed the revival of the Aboriginal activism that had begun to bloom in the 1920s and 1930s before it was cut short by the intervention of the Second World War. During the war years, increased access to employment on pastoral stations, farming areas and cane fields had broken down some of the isolation caused by restrictions on movements and Aboriginal people became increasingly conscious of the need for their own political organisations. In addition, the growing trend for Aboriginal people to move towards capital cities for employment and to seek relief from the reserve setting brought significant numbers closer to the sources of political power.

Yet while Aboriginal activism began again to flourish and a pan-Aboriginal movement emerged, for those confined to reserves, expressions of political protest were fraught with dangers. This was particularly so in Queensland, where the Department of Native Affairs was most intransigent and the chances of punitive retribution very high. For people on Palm this period became the most extensively repressive in the history of the island from the time that ex-policeman Roy Bartlam took control as Superintendent in 1953.

Bartlam believed that Murris on reserves were unable to think for themselves and argued that they 'must be controlled for the good not only of themselves, but of the general community'. His interpretation of this control led to the imprisonment of some of the young men on the island in excess of thirty times by the early 1960s, and the use of intimidation and police brutality to cement his reign.

Bartlam cut a tall and imposing figure and his constant patrol of the island gave him a kind of omnipresence of which the children were particularly fearful. They gave him the name of 'Tomato Face' in honour of his red complexion, and the warning that 'Tomato Face' was coming to school sent shivers of fear through the classrooms. In contrast to other Superintendents, I was unable to find anyone on Palm Island with a good word to say for Bartlam. Palm Island elders refer to him as 'the red emperor', a version of 'Hitler', a 'commandant', a Superintendent who 'worked us like slaves' and would 'treat you like a dog', an 'old bastard', 'a street with one way traffic' and a man with 'a heart of stone'.[2]

The late Bill Congoo recalled:

> Even the white man was frightened of him, he was a bastard. I think he was a bit mental, well something was wrong with him... he would only speak to you if he wanted to speak to you. He wanted to be the greatest in supremacy.

Bartlam insisted on a rigid apartheid system and that Murris salute all whites whom they passed in the street. Mrs Sibley has commented: 'You couldn't even stand up and talk to a white man or a white woman in the street — he'd see you, he'd send for you.' Engaging in excessive interventions into people's homes, his own abode was a 'palace' with three or four workers undertaking chores for eight hours each day. These men were paid 'only about two dollar — that's for the week'.

Bartlam maintained his reign through a heavy reliance on the powers of the police, most of whom he recruited from the ranks of Murris sent from the mainland for misdemeanours, and who felt little loyalty to the local community. Referred to as his 'yes men', Bartlam's police operated as something of a private para-military force. While past Superintendents had conducted morning parades with workers answering to a roll call, it was Bartlam who insisted that police strictly enforce it, and anyone who arrived late for parade was immediately imprisoned for a two-week period. Police were also forced to parade. Bill Congoo recalled Bartlam sending police to pick up workers if they were 'a minute behind time': 'He used to catch 'em along the street. They got police stationed at every road...You had to be there — like school, be treated like school kids.'

Bartlam's insistence upon the evening curfew was equally vindictive, and people were at times arrested close to home and only a few minutes after 10pm. People were punished for laughing or whistling after the curfew bell had rung. Seven days jail, without the option of a court hearing, was the sentence for trivial offences. Bells were also rung to signify tea and lunch breaks from work, the time to return to work and the time to cease work. 'Bells, bells, bells,' Qwanji recalled, 'the whole settlement was governed by bells.'

The operations of Palm Island's administration remained largely hidden from mainstream Australia, with tourist visits heavily controlled to present the image of a show-piece reserve. Only a small minority of journalists were prepared to expose real conditions on Palm. In 1957, the Communist Party newspaper, the *Tribune*, wrote of how tourist visitors to the reserve saw 'a beautiful tropical isle dotted with palms', when in fact Palm Island was really the 'prison of our coloured brothers':

> They are not told that a jail sentence awaits a 'free citizen' who is out after 10pm. Nor are they aware that lights sweep the beaches of Palm Island at night and that boats are securely fixed to prevent them being used without a permit.

Bartlam's surveillance procedures were part of a military-like discipline, and police were equipped with batons, one to one and a half metres long and made from hard bloodwood, to assist them in the enforcement of his rule. Palm Island elders state that two residents died on the reserve in this period as a result of police brutality, while

Andrew Obah carried a scar across his forehead as a consequence of having been hit by one of the police batons.

Much of the brutality occurred in the course of arrests for petty misdemeanours. The jail was situated 270 metres from Bartlam's office, and men were confined there for such 'offences' as being 'untidy' and for failing to have a haircut, while women were imprisoned for wearing shorts or dresses above the knee. On one occasion, a group of people was arrested for standing together and laughing, and a man was imprisoned for waving to his wife. The late Bill Congoo recalled being confined to a jail cell for a period of six weeks without even coming out of his cell in that time. Others were imprisoned for as long as 21 weeks. No visitors were allowed to see prisoners in the jail and the men were marched to and from cells in military-style lines.

The jail itself consisted of two cells, each 2.5 metres long and 2.7 metres wide, with room enough for two people but with four to five people usually jammed into each. There was only one sanitary tin for each cell and prisoners would take turns in putting their heads to the windows for air. Prison gangs were put to work on paddocks and in logging the mountains, and were let out into the exercise yard to break truckloads of stones by hammer and by hand and to chop wood for the white staff.

Labour relations outside the jail were equally punitive, and the source of much tension and conflict. Bartlam selected those who would work for wages, usually £2–3 per fortnight — about one-tenth of a white Australian labourer's wage at this time. Most, however, were employed for a compulsory 30 hours labour for which they received only rations. Bartlam insisted that everyone work, including the elderly, obsessed as he was with the government's policy of establishing 'self-sufficiency' on reserves. Anyone who refused to work was threatened with the loss of their rations.

Mrs Sibley recalled: 'The pregnant women had to go up that hill with 'er bag and you know, get a bag of wood and bring it down. Men wasn't allowed to get wood until after 5.' If groups of men were found sitting anywhere, they would be accused of gambling. While many on Palm worked without pay, others were denied their full wages through the 'Trust Fund' system.

Palm Islanders employed in the building trades took the heaviest brunt of Bartlam's regime. In keeping with the state government's emphasis upon housing as 'a very high priority' in programs for the 'ultimate assimilation' of Murris, Bartlam engaged in what he called a 'housing drive' with missionary-like zeal. It was during his reign that the tribal camps were disbanded and people were moved into houses, usually with only two rooms and designed to suit a European, nuclear-family lifestyle. While the old people on Palm did not want to move, they were given no option.

Construction timtables were rigid and Bartlam's inspections regular. Bill Congoo, a carpenter in this period, recalled how everyone would be given one week to complete their section of the house, and if it was not finished on time 'you had to answer to Bartlam for it'. The Superintendent's zealous commitment to assimilation extended beyond Palm Island, and while visiting the mainland in May 1957, he took it upon himself to play the role of a policeman, inspecting camps in Cardwell and the Upper Murray River. Bartlam later reported to the Director of Native Affairs that he had removed nine people to Palm Island from these areas. Despite his report's acknowledgment that 'No sign of any disease or ailment was noticed in the area,' Bartlam claimed that the removals were for 'hygiene reasons'.

On Palm Island men were expected to carry 100 pounds (45 kilograms) on their backs when carting cargo from ships, while sawmilling work required moving logs out over wet, oyster clad rocks to the sea for transportation to other parts of the island. Bartlam had a reputation for refusing to listen to anyone else's opinion on how a job should be done, and those he considered to be not working hard enough were forced to work on Saturdays as well or take a cut in their wages.

The late Willie Thaiday wrote of his work as manager of the banana farm: 'Any small thing that you do wrong he cut your wages. He is never satisfied. I only get ten shillings a week yet he cut my wages — no wages at all for one month.' Even women with small children at home were forced to work. 'I saw with my own eyes, the women who refused to go and scrub the hospital or the houses of the white officials. He shove them in jail.'

While departmental reports in this period boasted that 'the Queensland government provides finance [to reserves] which can fairly be regarded as generous', those receiving only rations on Palm survived on meagre supplies of rice, sugar and flour, while the meat supply, consisting of bones, gristle and fat, was the source of a great deal of dissatisfaction. Ivy Sam recalled:

> The money. The food. The way we were treated by the Europeans. That's what the strike was all about. And the meat...It was just bones. But the staff used to go down and order whatever cuts they wanted. The white staff. The choice cuts. They got all that.

> We just got the leftovers. Sometimes the scraps...I remember when I got married, it was still being issued. All sawdust and everything be in it, you know. Half the time you wouldn't eat it. You'd give it to your dogs.

Bartlam was obsessive about cleanliness and defined 40 per cent of the Welfare Officer's duties as involving visits to residents' homes, 'giving advice and instruction on home affairs'. The Superintendent's insistence upon intensive interference in what, for most Australians, was a person's private life, created strong feelings of resentment amongst the community. His surveillance and control were relentless. He continued inspections of homes when Palm Islanders left the reserve to work, sending police on the mainland to monitor the state of their sleeping quarters.

Recreation was also rigorously scrutinised. While annual shows produced prolific arts and crafts in this period, the work was done under compulsion and threat of punishment, as were evening band practices. Anyone who did not participate in sports or dances was subject to questioning. In all of these areas, the Superintendent demanded stringent racial segregation. Neville Bonner who fourteen years later became the first Indigenous person elected to Federal Parliament, accompanied his wife, Mona, to Palm Island when she was sent under punishment. Bonner recalled: 'Whites could not visit blacks socially or vice versa. The children went to different schools. The white officers weren't allowed to play sport with us in case they got beaten.'

One of the white staff in this period defied the segregation system on Palm and invited Murri residents to her home for tea and cakes. When several people accepted Mrs Swann's invitation, police soon knocked on the door of her home. White residents told the black police officers that there were no Murris in the house, and, ironically, the reserve procedures regarding housing prevented them taking the case any further. 'There was no white sergeant,' recalls Algan Walsh, 'all dark police and they wouldn't dare go into the white man's home. They opened up the back door and we shot up the hill.'

Bartlam's control over sexual relations was also resented. Since visits were confined to an hour from 4pm on weekdays, men who worked until 5pm were unable to visit women confined to dormitories except on Saturdays. Thelma McAvoy recalls the humiliation: 'We sat like myalls [fools] out on the street with our boyfriends.' For those who broke these regulations, punishments were brutal. Bartlam continued the procedures of shaving women's heads and the donning of sack dresses when they fled from the dormitories. The late Bill Congoo escaped with two other men and three women and stayed for a week in the bush past Doctor's Point, where they lived on tea, sugar, flour, wallaby and fish. For this little taste of freedom, Bill paid dearly, being given three consecutive two-week sentences by Bartlam on his return to the reserve.

Requests to visit the mainland for reasons other than work were usually refused during Bartlam's time, and permits were required to go fishing, sailing, swimming, visiting other islands or hunting at night. Bartlam made residents anchor the government boat, 'like jacky boys', when he took visiting magistrates out for a cruise or went fishing on weekends. On his return, he made people scale his fish, under threat of a jail term should they refuse.

Removal from Palm was also used as a punishment. Bill Skuthorp had conflict with Bartlam when he refused to allow Bill's son to leave Palm to attend college. When Skuthorp wrote to the department about the issue, Bartlam promptly responded by sending Bill to the mainland. In these instances the message was directed not only at the scapegoat, but at all residents who were witness to the Superintendent's exhibition of power. It was Bartlam's stubborn inflexibility on all issues that began to turn resentment into anger and a strong desire to act for change to the whole system of operations on the island.

While there had been a series of disturbances on Palm since its inception, no organised, collective and open revolt occurred until 1957. When recording their experiences of the strike, Palm Islanders refer to the work, the wages, the meat rations and the general climate of autocratic control as leading to a situation which, according to Ivy Sam, 'we couldn't tolerate any more.'

Precipitating events provided the trigger. Within the context of simmering tension and resentments, Bartlam ignited a flame to plans for industrial action which were beginning to be made almost four months prior to the work stoppage in June. While the notion of staging a strike was still in discussion stage during Easter 1957, Bartlam put men to work at building a further jail for themselves and their community at Pencil Bay. The Superintendent saw the task as so urgent that he employed the men to work over a weekend as well as on Easter Monday, a practice unusual 'except in emergency'. He also declared the tennis courts and an area of beach 'out of bounds' to Murris, and blocked community activities such as sports and the band sessions.

Bartlam then organised, without consultation, the demolition of a number of Murri homes, as well as their boats. It seems likely that at

Palm Island jetty. Author's private collection

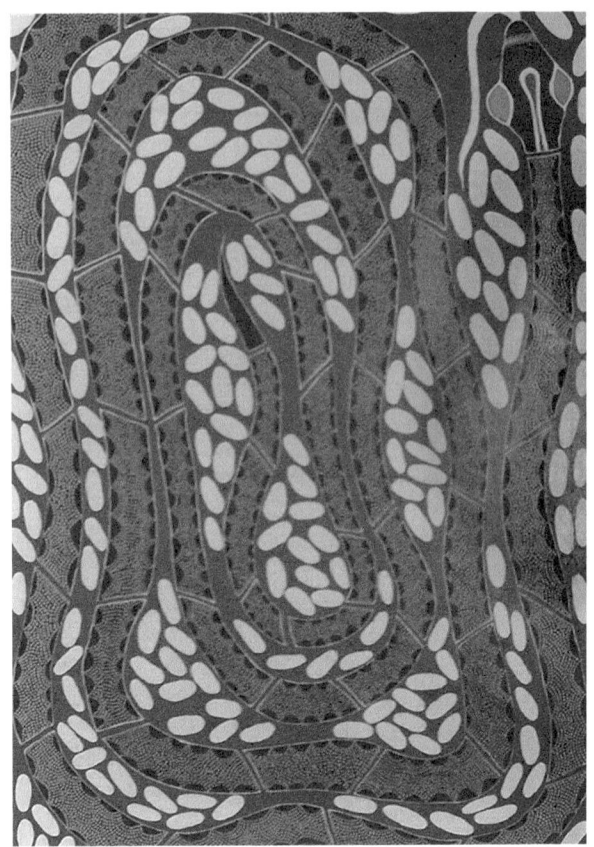

Carpet snake painting. Courtesy and © James McAvoy (artist) with assistance from Joanne Bulmer, Vina Palmer and HJ Wilson. Author's private collection

Bêche-de-mer fishermen, Challenger Bay, 1885. Courtesy of Oxley Memorial Library

Butler's Guest House. Courtesy of Oxley Memorial Library

'Group of inmates — Hull River Settlement' in Queensland. Parliamentary Papers, Vol. III (1916–17). Courtesy of Oxley Memorial Library

'Women and children — removed to Hull River settlement' in Queensland. Parliamentary Papers, Vol. III (1916–17). Courtesy of Oxley Memorial Library

Early Reserve Housing, Palm Island, 1930. Courtesy of Oxley Memorial Library

Henry Wilson and grand-daughters. Author's private collection

This image has been removed from the ebook edition for copyright reasons

Mango Avenue and site of Curry residence. Author's private collection

Administrators with Palm Island children. Courtesy of Oxley Memorial Library

Robert Curry and Palm Island Brass Band. Front row: (l–r) Arthur Brackenridge, Daniel Kyle, Ellison Obah, Jim Harvey, Clive Beckett, Captain Smith. Back row (left to right) Meza, Norm Summers, Ben Rotumah, Alex Locke, Keith Walsh, Jack Andersen (drummer), Delvin. Courtesy of Bwgcolman Community School

Corroborees, 1925. Courtesy of Oxley Memorial Library

Palm Island, 1925. Courtesy of Oxley Memorial Library

Matron Ethel Pattison and Dr Charles Pattison, 1920s. Courtesy of Australian Institute of Aboriginal and Torres Strait Islander Studies

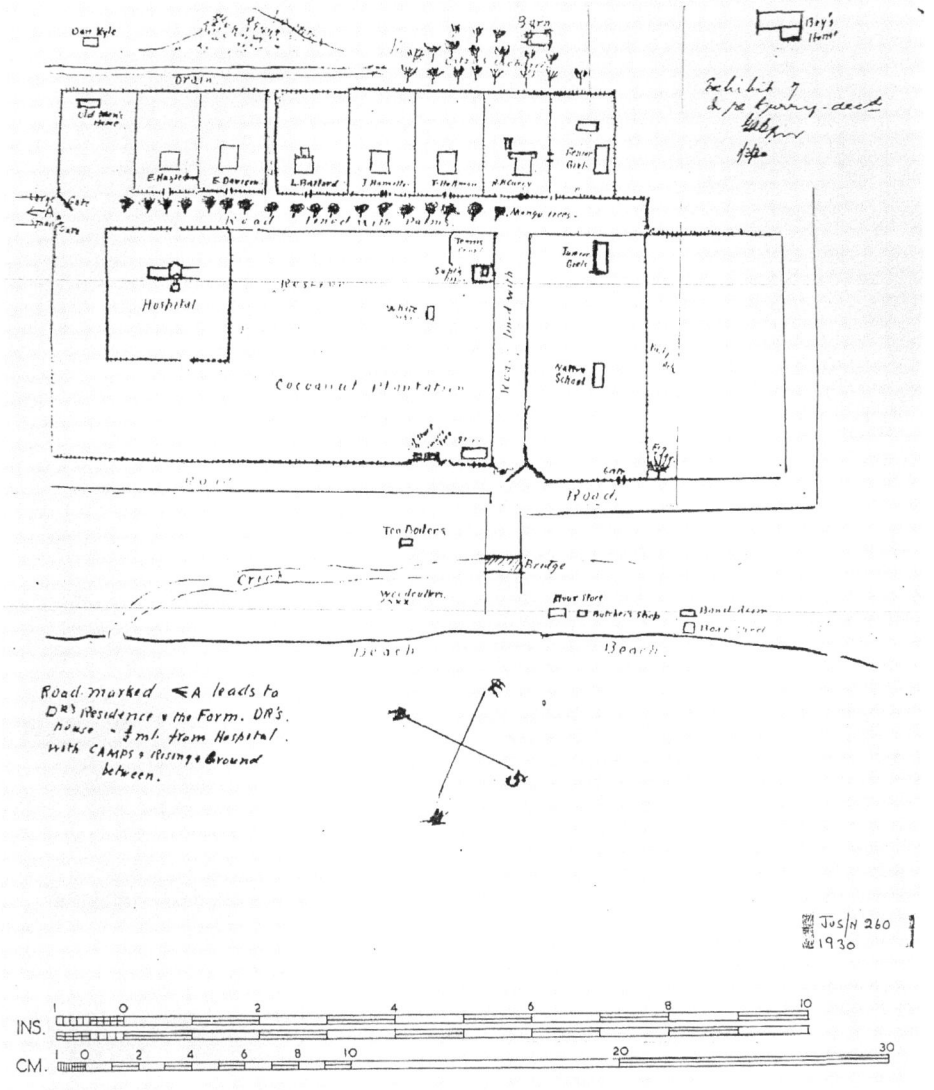

Site where Robert Curry was shot, 1930. Inquest into the deaths of Robert Henry Curry, Robert Curry and Edna Curry, Justices Department, 1930. Courtesy of Queensland State Archives

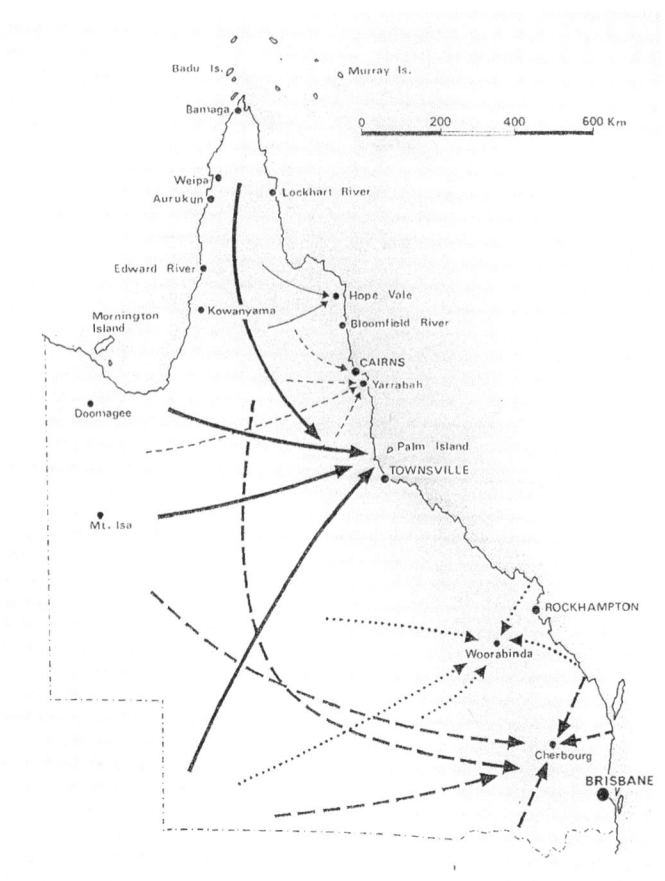

Map of Removals. Christopher Anderson, 'Queensland Aboriginal people Today', JH Holmes (ed.), 'Queensland – a Geographical Interpretation' in *Queensland Geographical Journal*, 4th Series, Vol. 1, 1986

Tom Morgan Snr. Author's private collection

Palm Island football team, 1941. Back row (l–r): George Duncan, Reggie Bligh, Tommy Doyle, Joe Hunter, Jimmy Daisey, Stephen Pickles, Tom Anderson, Kitchener Bligh; Middle row (l–r): Albert Cape-Bedford, Julian Blanket, Phillip Kyle (Sec), Ernie Puttaburra, Willie Thaiday, Albie Kyle (Patron), Tom Prior; Front row (l–r): Tom Ryan (V-Captain), Walla Wilson, George Wilson, George Ryan (Captain), Reg Dodd (C'man), Les Hatfield, Frank Pickles; Mascots: Arnold Ryan and Ralph Dodd. Courtesy of Rachael Cummins

Sister conducting laboratory medicine. Fantome Island Home Secretary's Office, 1927–40. Courtesy of Queensland State Archives

Construction work, Fantome Island, 1940s. Cliff Wyles, Reggie James and Johnny Jumbo. Courtesy of Australian Institute of Aboriginal and Torres Strait Islander Studies

All Souls' Day Mass Fantome Island, 1948. Courtesy of Australian Institute of Aboriginal and Torres Strait Islander Studies

'Taking Their Daily Medicine'.
Courtesy of Australian
Institute of Aboriginal and
Torres Strait Islander Studies

Memorial to strikers. Author's private collection

Lakeisha in the car, Thru the Lens: Palm Island youth photography project, 2009. Photography by Karen Walsh. Courtesy Bwgcolman Future Inc.

Silhouette at sunset, Thru the Lens: Palm Island youth photography project, 2009. Photography by Lakeisha Ryan. Courtesy Bwgcolman Future Inc.

this stage, given the number of reported 'pimps' or 'spies' who kept Bartlam informed of the community's activities, the Superintendent probably had an inkling of the plans to strike and hence was engaging in a show of strength in an effort to deter would-be activists.

While a brief strike had occurred at Taroom reserve (980 kilometres southeast of Townsville) in 1916, Palm Islanders seem to have waged the first major strike on a Queensland reserve in the mid-twentieth century. Meetings to discuss the prospect of strike action were held at Bill Congoo's house and on the streets, and initially these talks involved Sonny Sibley, Fred Clay, Fred Doolan, George Watson, Bill Congoo, Eric Lymburner, Albie Geia and Willie Thaiday, in cautious communications regarding the best action to take 'against Mr Bartlam'. It was in the context of these discussions that the catalyst came with Bartlam's decision to deport Albie Geia as a 'troublemaker'.

Geia was foreman of the hygiene gang and he had been 'chipped' by the overseer, Mr Croker, who was also Bartlam's brother-in-law. Willie Thaiday wrote: 'Mr Croker come from the bush somewhere and start to tell them what to do. They don't pay Albie the right wage so Albie tells them they can stick the money.' Since 'answering back' to a European was an offence, Croker took Geia to Bartlam on Monday 10 June, and the Superintendent instructed the police to hold him in custody.

Bartlam read a telegram from the now Director of Native Affairs, Cornelius O'Leary ordering Geia to leave the island on which he had been born and bred. Geia refused to leave. He walked out of the office and later scuffled with police. The Palm Island community soon rallied behind Geia and threatened Bartlam with a general strike if he was to be removed.[3] Don Brady has commented: 'Albie was a kind of leader. We respected him because there were so many times he'd stuck his neck out for us.'

On Tuesday 11 June, the *Telegraph* described the subsequent strike as an 'Island rebellion', recorded that:

> ...the trouble began when a native who had been charged with threatening the Superintendent and was being removed broke away from the native police and was joined by a crowd of demonstrators. They attacked the native police and abused settlement officers.[4]

This spontaneous protest was indicative of the immediate and widespread support for action on the part of the Murri community. It was no accident that this occurred, since Bartlam had progressively alienated the majority of Palm Island residents, his relentless persecutions eventually leaving few families untouched. Where, during Curry's time, internal relations between white staff had simmered to boiling point, now the tensions in relations between black and white residents had reached a crescendo. Bartlam made a crucial mistake in underestimating the groundswell of support for Geia, while his general attitude in the early months of 1957 had been over-confident. The entire Palm community had begun to organise against him.

When a small group of Palm Islanders decided to begin strike action in June, it was with a view to 'hope for the best'. They soon discovered an unspoken urgency for change. Bartlam attempted to arrest a gathering of eight men planning the strike. When he instructed police to arrest them as gamblers, a fight erupted; the men refused to go to jail and returned to their homes. The Superintendent was increasingly confronted with his loss of control over the island. Bill Congoo recalled that 'at that time the whole island had enough. So we more or less was lucky we hit at the right time...I got a shock myself, to see all the people turn up when the strike was on.'

Following an initial stop-work meeting, building work and deliveries ceased except where goods were going to the hospital or to missionaries. Murris were posted at every corner to ensure that no one worked for the white administration. Even members of the police squad joined the strike, Bill Seaton and Silas Prior both recalled how they were promptly dismissed from the force.

The demands of the strikers were for an adequate meat supply, increased wages, better housing and for Bartlam to leave the island. These demands and notice of the strike were recorded by Albie Geia's brother Tom, in a letter to Director O'Leary, in which it was requested that he come to the island to hear the community's grievances. Palm Islanders subsequently heard nothing of the whereabouts of the letter and O'Leary failed to arrive. Bartlam had now confined himself to his office and was 'not game enough', writes Thaiday, to be anywhere on the reserve without police around him for protection.

While Bartlam was in his office holding a meeting with the remaining members of the police force, the women of Palm began to gather outside from where they engaged in spontaneous acts of protest. The unsavoury rations of meat were thrown at the Superintendent's veranda and handfuls of sand tossed through the windows into the office. The protest later moved to Mango Avenue, where Palm Islanders marched up the street that had been forbidden them for decades. 'It got bigger and bigger,' Mrs Sibley recalled:

> The crowd kept growin'. I saw them all together, I was standin' up at the corner. I said there's something down this office. I

only got halfway when I see the crowd marchin' up the street. They opened up this street [Mango Avenue], they just marched through.

On this, the first day of the strike, Bartlam had clearly lost his authority over the island and events were approaching something of an unarmed insurrection. By nightfall the Superintendent had instructed Police Sergeant Jack Barry to telephone Townsville police. Barry reported that 'the native population had taken a prisoner from his custody' and police reinforcements were needed to quell the 'disturbance'. A squad of twenty police under the charge of Sub-Inspector Cooke rushed to the island by RAAF crash launch that evening.

The settlement bell was used by the strikers to signal the arrival of police. About 250 people then converged on the jetty to watch the rein-forcements come ashore. Bill Congoo and Sonny Sibley led residents up to the picture theatre where a large meeting was held before the crowd dispersed. Bartlam and the police had kept away, but the officers from Townsville were patrolling the island early the following morning. Their departure from Townsville by crash launch had summoned the attention of the press, which now ran headlines on the 'native revolt' and the 'Palm Island Riot'.

Throughout the course of this dispute the mainstream media proved consistently unwilling to give the events on Palm Island the status of a strike, and the only hints of any underlying cause of the 'disturbance' were fleeting references to the Superintendent's attempt to deport Albie Geia.

The strikers held meetings every day while the atmosphere grew volatile. On the second day of the strike, with residents no longer subjected to the ringing of bells for parades and work schedules, a deceptive quiet pervaded the island. Unbeknown to other strikers, Bartlam now located his first target, taking Fred Doolan, who had been instrumental in the initiation of industrial action, into police custody and deporting him to the mainland as a 'troublemaker'. Because this removal was stealthily conducted, Bartlam had carried it out successfully, but he soon discovered that Doolan's deportation had failed to break the strike.

White residents were now confined to their homes and for the first time in the history of the island, were apparently united. While seven Murri residents had signed a petition disassociating themselves from the strike, in a population of almost 1,400 their numbers were insignificant. Murri involvement in the Palm Island strike was characterised by an overwhelming unity, while the deep division in the population of the reserve was clearly along racial lines, associated as this was with inequalities of wealth and power.

On Tuesday 11 June, as a squad of six more police and another Sub-Inspector arrived on Palm from Townsville, so too did the reserve's rations and supplies for white residents. Despite the forbidding presence of armed police patrolling Palm, Murri residents took control of the distribution of these goods, temporarily reversing the social roles on the island. They carried the meat to the butcher shop, where they carved and distributed it to the Murri community, leaving none for the white staff, and they smashed the bottles of alcohol which had been destined for white households. Yet, while the tide had most decidedly turned, the government was unwilling to acknowledge that its control over Palm Island residents had capsized.

On the very day that the distribution of supplies was taken over by the community, and only two days into what would become a five-day strike, the Director of Native Affairs advised the press that the situation on Palm was 'under control'. The continued presence of mainland police on Palm was explained as merely 'a precaution'.

While police continued patrols and, with Bartlam's assistance, located the homes of leading figures in the strike, white officials were unable to move on their targets to conduct arrests since the entire island would have been inflamed. With this knowledge, born of events earlier in the week, Bartlam once again opted for stealth. For the organisers of the strike, this was a period of being diligently alert. Bill Congoo recalled: 'We knew they were gonna pick us up but we didn't know what day or night.'

At 4am on Thursday 13 June, Bartlam and the police made their move. 'They swooped on the sleeping men' and arrests began. The door to Albie Geia's home was broken down with a telegraph pole, while Bill Congoo's door was smashed to pieces with an axe. Meanwhile, the homes of Sonny Sibley, George Watson, Willie Thaiday, Eric Lymburner and Gordon Tapau were also invaded and women and children looked on while the men were arrested and placed in handcuffs.

Bill Congoo said of his arrest:

> That's where they come [my home, where meetings were held] and break down the door. Tried to get me out. I tried to get out the window, I had a revolver in me back...I had no shirt on. Never even had a belt. I had to walk down the street with my hands cuffed holding my trousers up — till my wife came along later on.

Willie Thaiday wrote:

> Early in the morning, about four o'clock they strike my place — Detective Sergeant Cronin, Inspector Cooke and Greg Barry [sic], Senior Sergeant of Police. Mr Cronin say:
> 'Don't move Willie or you gonna get hurt...' They shove me, make me go forward. Detective Cronin say: 'Don't try any dirty tricks or else you get hurt.' They slam handcuffs on my hands and we come down to the beach. There is another five coming too and we all seem to reach that boat together.

A machine gun was pointed towards the beach from the boat while the men walked on board. Through the course of the week, strike meetings had decided that 'runners' would use the siren at the power house as a signal of alarm in the event of arrests. Charlie Warner ran to blow the siren. Mrs Sibley recalled: 'Somebody out of that mob [at the meetings] was a pimp...'Cause when he got down there he got a flogging for it — kicked 'im, they belted him with batten [sic] and everything – the white police.' This act of brutality effectively quashed the planned rallying of the community to the aid of the deportees.

At this stage, even some of the wives of these men were unaware that their husbands were about to be brutally deported from the island. Bessie Lymburner, whose husband Eric was on board the boat, had to tell Madge Thaiday that her husband Bill was not in the local island watch house as many believed. A great deal of distress was caused by the confusion and as news of the impending deportation spread, people began to clang pots and pans together to express their anger and to signal their protest.

Some of the families of the strikers were now forced to board the boat as well. Madge Thaiday and eight Thaiday children, some of whom were toddlers, now joined the men, their destinations unknown to them. Bessie Lymburner recalls: 'They just pushed them on the boat, that's how cruel they were.'

Residents awoke that morning to the sight of these members of their community standing on the launch out to sea and now manacled in leg irons. The irony of being banished from the very place to which his parents had been exiled was clear to Bill Congoo, who said of these events: 'The only time we stood up for ourselves we were stood down on for doing it.'

It is testimony to the incredible resilience of the Palm Island people that even in the face of these overwhelming odds, imprisoned in a military patrol boat, surrounded by armed police, exiled from their homes and bound for destinations over which they had no control, the group refused to let their spirits wane. 'I felt great,' Bill Congoo recalled, 'at least someone was taking notice, no fear.' Willie Thaiday wrote:

> Soon as we pull out a bit I strike out a big song — island song about our home. The captain, fellow called Mr Whiting, hear us and say, 'Who them boys? They can't be going to prison in handcuffs. They seem so happy.'
>
> We sing like anything in the military patrol boat...The policemen are on top and machine gun is pointed down to us but while we are in front of machine gun we sing like anything... The walky talky is going all the time.... 'They singing like hell here.' Mr Whiting can't get over it.

The journey to Townsville involved rough seas with winds running at thirty or forty knots. Even with people soaking wet and vomiting, police kept the strikers in handcuffs, except for Willie Thaiday who had to hold his small children together. Bill Congoo recalled that at the time they were conscious that if the boat overturned they would all be likely to drown. 'It was as if they'd killed someone,' comment's Bessie Lymburner, while Willie Thaiday wrote of the police: 'All them got guns at their sides. Just like we do a big murder.'

On arrival in Townsville the strikers had expected to attend a hearing, but instead were imprisoned in the watch house for three days before being removed to other reserves. During the imprisonment, no charges were laid against them and no legal advice was provided. Other members of the community were to follow the strike leaders as further scapegoats in the aftermath of these initial deportations. Bessie Lymburner's community came to her aid with £300 to assist her financially, and with tears expressing their grief at her departure. Seven members of the Watson family were deported two days later, alongside eight members of the Sibley family and ten Geias.[5] Forty-seven Palm Island residents had now been exiled to confinement on the mainland.

The *Townsville Daily Bulletin* provided coverage of these events, commenting blandly that in a 'dawn raid' Palm Islanders had been removed and, in something of an understatement, 'The operation passed off quietly before 5 o'clock.'[6] The *Telegraph* was a little more sensational, citing Director O'Leary's references to 'troublemakers and agitators'. Moreover, aligning itself with the government's stance, it portrayed those imprisoned in Townsville's watch house as both criminal and violent. 'Several who had records of violence and trouble, and jail sentences,' wrote the *Telegraph* on 13 June, 'had threatened to bash other natives on the island who wanted to work.' No reference was made to the nature of Bartlam's regime, nor to the violent methods by which the strikers had been removed.[7]

By contrast, the left-wing press condemned the state Gair Labor government, with the *Tribune* referring to Palm Island as a 'penal settlement' and the so-called 'rebellion' as a 'thoroughly justified 'strike' to 'secure better wages'. Both government and police were reproached for their arresting procedures and for the subsequent exile of Palm families to other reserves 'without their having any choice in the matter'. The *Tribune's* call for a public inquiry into these events fell upon deaf ears.[8]

On 14 June, O'Leary wrote to the Superintendents at Woorabinda and Cherbourg reserves to confirm advice that they would soon receive the Palm Island strikers from Townsville 'as a means of breaking up a gang of malcontents'.[9] Albie Geia, Sonny Sibley and Willie Thaiday were to be confined to Woorabinda, Bill Congoo, George Watson and Eric Lymburner to Cherbourg, while Gordon Tapau would be removed to Bamaga on the northern tip of Cape York. Their wives and children would accompany them, wrote O'Leary, but he was not certain when this would happen 'due to the urgency of removal of the men'.

The government's perspective was that their exile from Palm would be permanent. On 19 June 1957, 25 Palm Islanders left Townsville, under police escort on the Brisbane mailtrain. Bessie Lymburner recalled how Murris in the Townsville region, aware of their plight, had gathered at the station to see them off. On Cherbourg, Bessie and her husband, who had been told they would have a home, found themselves forced to reside with another family. They were offered a 'slum house' but rejected it. Like their fellow Palm Islanders on these inland southern reserves, they felt the impact of the cold winter most severely, as well as being homesick for Palm, and Eric grew so ill that he almost died.

Willie Thaiday and his family were put in Rockhampton jail on their way to Woorabinda, carrying only a few summer clothes. On the drive from Fargo, with Willie still wearing handcuffs, they were 'jammed up like fish in a tin'. While on Palm, Thaiday had won the 'good home' competition. Now he found himself at Woorabinda being offered a dilapidated bark shack which was 'proper filthy'. Refusing to enter it, the Thaidays were forced to reside in the boys' home, with 'no saucepan, no plate, no spoon, nothing' and ten in the family. Madge Thaiday's relations later offered assistance, while Bill was given a farm labourer's job for which he was paid with tobacco.

Fred Doolan, who had lost touch with the strikers since his deportation very early in the dispute, now made contact with Sonny Sibley at Rockhampton train station. Doolan was on his way to a boxing tournament when he caught a glimpse of Sibley, in handcuffs and with a police escort, and through the windows of their two separate trains they exchanged conversation. Sonny Sibley's removal to Woorabinda would later prove to be legally questionable since he had been exempted from the Act. However, his wife Alice, pregnant at the time of her deportation, *was* subject to the regulations of the Act, and she and her children were forcibly separated from Sonny when the department decided that he was not allowed to live with them. Sonny left Woorabinda with his permit and sought the aid of the trade union movement. The *Tribune* reported in October that while O'Leary would not allow Sonny Sibley to rejoin his wife on the reserve, 'following representations by Col Maxwell, AMIEU Central District Secretary, [he] agreed to allow the families to rendezvous at Douringa'. Rockhampton trade unions supplied a truck, food and tents to enable the brief reunion to occur.

Director O'Leary would later deny, on a subsequent morning parade on Palm, that anyone had been forced to leave the reserve.[10] This was possibly true in one case. Charlie Warner, who had been severely beaten by police when he tried to sound the alarm that arrests were under way, was granted an exemption from the Act and allowed to move to Townsville. It was common knowledge, however, that the strike organisers and their families had been forcibly deported, and their exile left behind a great deal of sadness, anger and fear in the hearts of the remaining community.

On the day that the group were deported, Superintendent Bartlam had issued a threat that if all Palm Island Murris did not return to work immediately no supplies would be brought over, effectively starving them out. Six of the Townsville police remained stationed on the island. A meeting of workers gathered at the store resolved that they had little option but to return to their jobs. It was felt that a stand had been made; the strike had proved that conditions needed examining and the Director had promised to come to the island, although he would do so 'in his own time'.

When O'Leary did finally arrive on Palm in July, he confined himself to Bartlam's office, and for a long period spoke only to white witnesses of events in the recent strike. On the following day Henry Noble, the Minister for Health and Home Affairs, and Tom Aikens, an Independent Member for Townsville, also visited Palm. Neville Bonner described his discussions with these Queensland politicians as disillusioning:

> I put to him [the Minister] that Aborigines who were prepared to work for the betterment of the community should be trained to take their place as staff officers and perhaps eventually there could be Aboriginal superintendents too. I was told, very firmly, that this was not the aim of his department or the government. As Aborigines became competent to manage their own affairs, they would be moved off the settlements...There was no question of self-government or self-determination.[11]

In its internal departmental correspondence in July, the department congratulated itself for taking 'prompt action' in the dispute and for 'removing the ringleaders', an action it blithely described as having a 'salutory effect'.[12] The Minister Noble, advised Queensland Parliament in November that his inspection of the island had proven that complaints regarding Palm were 'unfounded' and that the reserve 'was being conducted efficiently and well, in the interests of its native residents'. Allegations to the contrary were, he said, merely complaints by a few coloured people whose records were such as to make them not very dependable sources of information'.[13] If that was true and the government had nothing to hide concerning affairs on Palm Island, it is difficult to explain why delegates from the Trades and Labour Councils of both Cairns and Townsville had been blocked from visiting the reserve in October.

In the aftermath of the strike, Bartlam intensified his control. At the morning parade of 3 July 1957, Palm Islanders were advised that if they wished to remain on the island they were required 'not only to abide by the rules of the settlement', but to be 'loyal to the Administration'.[14] Those who failed to comply were confronted with what became an increasingly fanatical resort to deportations.

About one week after the strike, Michael Seaton was deported from the island following a confrontation with Bartlam at a building site. Seaton grew angry and asked Bartlam if he wanted the men to 'slave our guts out'. The Superintendent left, but the following day Seaton was taken by police to Bartlam's office where he was told he was a 'bad influence' and would be leaving the island and his family on the following Monday. A spate of removals occurred in the following weeks.

Two people were removed to Cherbourg on 9 July, a further seven on 16 July, and ten adults and three children followed one week later. Seven family members and another individual were sent to Woorabinda on 16 July. Two families and another Palm Islander were subsequently deported there on 23 July, while on the same day one family was removed to Hopevale, on the Cape York peninsula and another to Mona Mona Mission which was 30 kilometres northwest of Cairns, near Kuranda. This amounted to the removal of a further 50 Palm Islanders in little more than a month. The banishments continued, with nine men sent to Bamaga, on the Cape York peninsula in August, for reasons, wrote Bartlam, of their being 'troublemakers', 'larrikins' and a 'bad influence on the reserve'.

Some of these people had been chosen for their involvement in protest activities and were receiving delayed punishments. Others on the island were rewarded for having opted to align themselves with Bartlam. The seven men who had signed the petition against the strike were all provided with jobs afterwards, although one of the police officers, who conducted the arrest of Willie Thaiday, left Palm Island because of community ill-feeling towards him.

Despite the continuation of scapegoating during 1957, Palm Islanders state that many gains had been made as a result of the strike and that, as Bill Skuthorp put it, 'people seemed to get more freedom after it'. This needs to be balanced with an understanding that Palm Island had been gutted of a significant number of community leaders. Certainly there were some advances. Cargo workers received a wage rise and rations were delivered to the homes of those not well enough to carry them. Better homes were provided, a new store and butcher shop were opened, and in 1958 a reserve was established on 60 acres (24 hectares) at Aitkenvale for Palm Islanders who required residence on the mainland.

For the remainder of the decade, Murris in North Queensland were subjected to a second wave of dispossession and removals with the mining invasions into reserve lands. The British–American aluminium cartel, Comalco did well from the negotiations it held with the state government and Presbyterian missionaries managing reserved lands. In 1957, the discovery of large deposits of bauxite on Weipa mission at Cape York resulted in a subsequent reduction of Aboriginal reserve lands by 723,200 acres (292,667 hectares). The Department of Native Affairs report for 1958 noted the reduction of reserved land at Mapoon by 787,200 acres (318,568 hectares) and at Aurukun, where 422,400 acres (170,940 hectares) were lost. By 1963 Mapoon residents would face eviction from their homes which were burnt to the ground, and brutal deportation to Bamaga.

In addition, the punitive banishment of reserve residents, so recently witnessed on Palm, was soon repeated at Yarrabah, when again the government sought rigid internal control of the institution, despite the fact that in this case the settlement was a mission. In 1958, in the course of a strike at Yarrabah, Superintendent Bartlam was summoned from Palm Island to provide his expertise in crushing the resistance to the authoritarian and brutal control of mission manager, Captain J Wilcox.

Wilcox was a member of the Church Army, a lay evangelist movement within the Church of England, which had taken control of Yarrabah four years earlier. Known as a 'very tough man', he was prone to assaults upon the culture of reserve residents. At the time of the uprising, he had forbidden hunting and fishing on the Cairns side of the bay on weekends and exiled individual residents who challenged his reign. Like Bartlam, he eventually faced a major refusal of this authority when Murri residents took strike action. With the assistance of the Waterside Workers' Union, Bessie Point was again opened to Murris and representations were made to Bishop Shevill in Townsville, calling for the removal of Wilcox.

While these events at Yarrabah are poorly documented, there is evidence that Palm Islanders had been communicating with residents from the mission for some time, both through meetings for annual shows and contact in mainland employment. Moreover, the original plan had been for a joint strike on both settlements to occur simultaneously, but the difficulties in coordination resulting from the restrictive 'protection' Act had made their goal unrealisable.

On 18 January 1958, the *Courier Mail,* under the headline: ABORIGINALS EXPELLED FOR MISSION BRAWLS, reported that Yarrabah residents had been removed from their homes 'for attacking mission staff'. Like their predecessors on Palm, the Yarrabah strikers were maligned as 'troublemakers' who 'should not have been at the mission because they were quite capable of earning their own living'.[15]

Following his ruthless defeat of the strike in 1957, Bartlam served for another eight years as Palm Island's Superintendent, before receiving a position as a regional district officer with the Department of Labour and National Service. Palm was in this period still being used as a dumping ground for exiles from the mainland, with 514 arrivals to the reserve in 1959. In the following decade, Bartlam expressed his philosophy on race relations when he was asked for a submission to the 1961 Commonwealth Select Committee on Voting Rights of Aborigines. On the fourth anniversary of the defeat of the strike, Bartlam advised the committee that 'settlements' housed Aboriginal people 'who are not yet educated enough to reach a standard of thinking for themselves'.[16]

As this chapter of Palm Island history makes clear, Bartlam was amongst many Queensland officials who were determined to exercise the kind of control designed to ensure that they never did. Indeed, the apparent absence of Aboriginal mobilisation on reserves between the Taroom strike of 1916 and Palm Island in 1957 — a 40-year interval — is telling evidence of the iron-clad control exercised by the reserve system, and its success in servicing the interests of Europeans.

Given events in Queensland at the close of the 1950s, the change in the name of the Department of Native Affairs to that of the Aboriginal Advancement was, in 1958, something of a paradox. The real progress for Aboriginal people was in fact taking place outside the realm of governmental bureaucracy, with the formation of the first national organisation of representatives from Indigenous communities, which came to be known as the Federal Council of Aborigines and Torres Strait Islanders (FCAATSI). The campaigns by this organisation for citizens' rights and for self-determination on reserves would lead, eventually, to a gradual dismantling of white control. By 1984, Palm Islanders would finally receive papers from the government officially acknowledging that management of their island would be placed in the hands of their own elected council, and the settlement bell which had dominated their lives would be dumped into the sea. The death of Roy Bartlam later in that decade seems to have caused little remorse amongst Palm Island residents.

The Palm Island strike of 1957 received scant historical attention outside the reserve until 1974, when Alessandro Cavadini and Carolyn Strachan began their research for the film *Protected*. A subsequent media outcry berated their efforts, referring to the events in question as an 'ugly incident of history' and a 'riot' that was better left forgotten. Links were drawn by the *Townsville Daily Bulletin* between the strike of 1957 and 'Black Power', while a representative of the department was cited as condemning the film-makers for 'racking around in the much-heap of the past'. Disapproval of the film and a refusal to participate on the part of two ex-Palm Island residents, previously involved in the strike of 1957, was heavily exploited.[17] Despite constant threat of expulsion from Palm Island by the white manager and the Department of Aboriginal and Island Affairs, either the strikers themselves or a close relative re-enacted all parts of the film. While the press had portrayed the strikers' indecision regarding the film as definite, 'their revolutionary spirit prevailed'.[18]

Chapter 9

Whistleblowers' Time:
'A Certain Paradise for Certain People'

> In recent years...Queensland has been subjected to considerable criticism...This is a very healthy and desirable situation because it means that Queensland is really doing something...It is not, however, government policy nor thinking that Palm Island or any other reserve is a penal centre.
> Pat Killoran, Director, Department of Aboriginal Affairs, 1968[1]

> We say quite bluntly that Palm Island is a penal settlement despite the fact that the Queensland government says it is not.
> Evelyn Scott, Address to FCAATSI, 1970[2]

In June 1961, Leslie Foster of Palm Island was asked by Mr Nelson of the Commonwealth government's Select Committee into Voting Rights, 'What would you say would be the most important thing that your people require?' Foster replied, 'What they want is their rights, which have been taken from them a long time ago.' Questioned further he added, 'We want our rights and I do not think it will be long before we get them.'[3] Foster's words were indicative of the commitment of the Palm Island people to self-determination, expressed in the strike of 1957, and persisting, despite the brutal conclusion of the strike, in the years that followed.

Throughout the first half of the 1960s, Palm Island continued to operate as a penal settlement under the excessively brutal dictatorship of Roy Bartlam, but with the Superintendent now repeatedly faced with public exposure of his reign. Murri residents increasingly used the facilities of the mainland to draw attention to their plight. Officials of the select committee were told by Joseph Garbutt that he had been sent to the island as punishment for drinking alcohol, that his sentence appeared to be indefinite, and that living on Palm was 'like being in prison'.[4]

Two months after these sittings the Townsville Trades and Labour Council (TLC) attended the Coroner's Court inquest into the death in custody of Henry Pitt on Palm Island, following representations to the TLC by island residents, Jimmy Daisy and George Johnson. Hearings in August and September provided evidence from Pitt's colleagues alleging that he had been assaulted by police. It was the opinion of Townsville Medical Officer, Leslie Halberstater, that Pitt's life could have been saved if the condition of his health had been ascertained and treated four or five days prior to his death, while in the custody of Palm's police.

Henry Pitt was a 29-year-old sanitation worker, known to residents as a person who 'was always voicing his opinions' and who defended himself in the face of authorities who were 'dressing him down in any way'. Previously locked up for not having a haircut, Pitt was sentenced to three weeks jail on 8 July, 1961, for 'refusing to keep himself clean'. Resident chaplain, Robert Jones, advised the inquest that Pitt worked on sanitary and garbage wagons at the time of his arrest — 'not,' he added, 'a very clean job in my opinion.' Jimmy Buchanan stated that he was serving four weeks jail at the time of Pitt's arrest, for 'being out of bounds', while Ron Shadford told the court that at 32 years of age he had been imprisoned 'at least 30 times', his latest arrest being for evasion of work.

The inquest was advised that prisoners were confined in a small concrete building with three cells. They were put to work on road construction and in clearing scrub, while only officials and missionaries were allowed to visit them in jail. Palm Island's prison was subject to little scrutiny. The Superintendent visited once every two or three weeks, the hygiene officer every three to four weeks and a magistrate visited only once every three months.

Witnesses testified that Henry Pitt had complained to the police sergeant of being ill on 12 July and was allowed to stay in his cell. On several occasions in the days that followed Pitt was provided with aspirin tablets by Constable Gunnawarra when he complained of headaches. On Monday, 23 July, Pitt began vomiting blood, but the Constable was unable to take him to hospital until he had the approval of Superintendent Bartlam. When Pitt was taken to hospital later that day, Dr Flynn prescribed two tablets of Largactil, a medication usually administered for management of psychotic disorders, to be taken four times a day, and for reasons not explained, performed a blood test for venereal disease. [5]

Dr Flynn was at this stage dealing with a patient who was suffering from a fracture to the skull which had caused cerebral compression, and the injury was between two and four weeks old. Despite the fact that Pitt had been carried to hospital on a stretcher, when asked if he ever thought or suspected 'Henry Pitt may have been pretending to be sick,' the doctor replied, 'I thought he may have.' Pitt was returned to his cell and in the days that followed he continued to vomit blood, 'couldn't stomach food', was unable to rise from his bed and was occasionally given aspirin.

The late Ivy Sam, who lived next door to the jail at this time, recalled:

> I remember Henry Pitt...I used to hear him calling out at night... from the cell...cryin' out and you could tell it was a cry that he was in pain...I'd walk out to the fence and ask him how he felt... he used to say, 'No good,' and he couldn't balance. He had police, each side of him in the end, leading him down there (to hospital) and back...You could tell there must have been some damage done to his head.[6]

On Friday 28 July, Henry Pitt was taken out into the compound of the jail where he lay on a blanket. All of the police had left the jail at 9am that morning to collect their wages. They were still absent at 11am when Henry Pitt passed away. Watch house keeper, Jack Gunnawarra, was walking past the picture theatre when Beatrice Dodd ran up to say that 'something has happened to Henry'. When Gunnawarra arrived back at the jail, the prisoner Johnny Jumbo informed him that during his absence Pitt had died.

At the subsequent inquest, Murri residents George Johnson, Ron Shadford, Keith Bligh and Robert Wilson all stated that Pitt had been assaulted by police on the day of his arrest. When asked why he had not reported this information, Shadford stated, 'I knew I would be sent for later on.' Questioned by J Aboud of the Department of Native Affairs, Bartlam argued that he was unaware of evidence from Sergeant Stanley that another police officer had pushed Pitt into a set of lockers on the day of his arrest, and that he was knocked off balance and had hit his head. He added that 'knowing' the police officers on Palm, 'I do not think they intended it as a punitive action.' Aboud responded, 'Would it surprise you that some lawyers regard it as unlawful assault?' to which Bartlam responded, 'It would not surprise me at all.'

It was after Pitt's death that one of the police allegedly reported to Bartlam that Henry Pitt had fallen on a log while at work on 17 July. Constable Gunnawarra stated that Pitt had mentioned nothing of an accident, while fellow prisoners, Fred Fulford and Paddy Sarabo stated that they had not seen nor heard from anyone on the gang that an accident had occurred. Paddy Sarabo commented that workers on the logging gang 'were all lined up so we could see one another', and that Pitt's job as tea boiler meant that 'he didn't pick up any branches or logs and put them on the stack... just little scraps to start the fire.' Fulford stated that if an accident occurred, workers would have informed policeman Diamond Bell, in charge of the gang. Moreover, Bell testified that he had not been told of any accident involving Pitt, despite the fact that as the person 'in charge' he would 'generally' be advised.

Despite this evidence, the testimonies of Superintendent Bartlam and one police officer dominated the findings of the coroner's inquest which concluded that Pitt's death: 'was the result of an injury received when he accidentally struck himself on the back of the head with a log, when he tripped and fell while attempting to throw the log onto a heap of logs for burning...There is no evidence of any criminal act or omission on the part of any person to which the death of the deceased can be attributed.'

Jimmy Daisy, the resident who had made an excuse to Bartlam in order to get to Townsville and raise the issue of Pitt's death with the TLC, was subsequently removed from Palm Island and separated from his family, who did not see him again until eight months later when they met with him on the mainland. His daughter Leonie recalled the period as a traumatic time for the Daisy family, who were unaware of why he was being punished or where he had been sent.[7] In the aftermath of the inquest, Percy Tucker, the Labor member for Townsville North, questioned the Minister for Health and Home Affairs during Parliament's October sittings: 'As it is normal human practice to make critically ill patients as comfortable as possible in hospital, has he inquired as to why Pitt was allowed to spend the closing hours of his life on a bag on his cell floor?'[8]

The outcome of the inquest did little to develop faith amongst the community in the island's police force or the state's legal system. The belief that Pitt had died as a result of assault by police and negligence while in custody remained widespread, compounding tensions on the reserve.

Public health on the island remained appalling, most homes had only one cold water tap, and outbreaks of chronic dysentery occurred. In 1963, twelve children died from amoebic dysentery as a result of cross-infection at the hospital. The impact upon families can only be imagined. Dr Allen Saltau was resident on Palm for the standard six week practice as a general practitioner at the hospital in 1967. He noted that some residents were housed on the bay, in a marshy area, below tide level, so that when the water rose the sewage system erupted, causing illness and cross infections. He described a butchery that was a 'disgusting disgrace, being filthy and fly blown', and lacking a working refrigeration system; housing that consisted of 'two roomed, dirt floor hovels, usually fibro', while the only curbed and guttered streets were those surrounding the spacious homes of white staff.[9]

Saltau's partner, Jan Mills, nineteen-years-old and pregnant when she arrived on Palm Island, recalls that the meat available to Murris 'wasn't even a recognisable meat colour'. White staff and their families were offered 'big thick T-bone steaks for about forty cents...they were practically giving it away to white people'. Jan developed a friendship with the late Iris Clay. Palm Island women provided her with maternity dresses and visited her in Townsville when she gave birth. The white community on Palm Island ostracised her. Jan summarised her experience:

> ...the sea, the palms, it was just paradise. But it was a certain paradise for certain people... It used to make me very sad...I can remember walking home, it was my nineteenth birthday, and I just cried and cried and cried...I couldn't stand it, it was so beautiful, but it was just such a lie, it was so unhappy...I remember being horrified that people could be so mistreated.[10]

Dr Saltau's observations and his map of the island's segregation system were published in the national university student magazine, *Aboriginal Quarterly*, which triggered a government orchestrated witch-hunt in search of the author.

The emergence of the publication was indicative of the burgeoning mainland movement of Indigenous people and their supporters, campaigning around human rights. This movement was enhanced by struggles for decolonisation internationally and links were drawn with people in the Third World. Contact with visiting African–American troops during the Vietnam War and Black Power philosophies provided further inspiration. The Federal Council for Aboriginal Advancement and the all-Aboriginal National Tribal Council evolved in this context and both bodies took a strong interest in exposing conditions on Palm Island.

Bartlam's reliance upon stealthy deportations seemed to have backfired by the end of the decade, as word of conditions on the island was made public by exiled residents.[11] In the late 1960s, the Department of Aboriginal and Island Affairs still had control over the island and access to the files of all Palm Islanders. Changes to the Queensland Act in 1965 proved to be largely cosmetic and with the ascendancy of Johannes Bjelke-Petersen as the Country–Liberal Party Premier, following the sudden death of Jack Pizzey, the political climate for Indigenous activists became decidedly dangerous. Even attending meetings risked incurring sustained police harassment.

Over the course of the 1960s, some concessions were won in the shape of legal reform. The *Commonwealth Electoral Act* 1962 gave Aboriginal people the right to vote in federal elections. (Before this Aboriginal people could only vote where they were allowed to vote under state legislation.) It was not until 1965 that Queensland finally amended its legislation to permit Aboriginal people to vote. At this stage while the country's sheep and cattle were counted on the census, Aboriginal people were not. In 1967, a federal referendum proposed amendments to Sections 51 and 127 of the Constitution which prevented the Commonwealth from making 'special laws' regarding Aboriginal people and failed to acknowledge the existence of Aboriginal people in the census.

The discrepancy between what the referendum has been presented as achieving and the limited gains that it meant in practice has been thoroughly examined by Bain Attwood and Andrew Markus.[12] While in the strict legal sense Aboriginal people were automatically citizens from 1948 (under the Nationality and Citizenship Act) they remained, in practice, 'citizens without rights in their own country'.[13] Those campaigning for the 'Yes' vote hoped that it would lead to the Commonwealth taking over control of the administration of Aboriginal affairs and assist moves towards equality by removing discrimination. Moreover, the successful campaign for the 'Yes' vote brought together many activists from all states and boosted confidence and expectations.

The demand for equal wages also became a central call of all Aboriginal organisations, and drew support from the Australian Council of Trade Unions' Congress. Across the country Aboriginal stockmen were being paid a few dollars a week and sacks of flour, sugar and tea while living conditions were appalling. In the Northern Territory, the Gurindji campaign for equal wages, which started as a walk off at Wave Hill pastoral station, evolved into a land claim as the Traditional Owners continued to squat on land at Wattie Creek 30 kilometres from Wave Hill. Their nine-year strike action drew international interest. But while equal wages were awarded in the pastoral industry over the course of the late 1960s, with benefits felt in some areas, the aftermath of this change, in the context of an economic downturn, involved the dismissal of longstanding Aboriginal stockmen, no longer attracting employment as cheap labour. Faith Bandler commented that the issue of unequal wages,

> evolved into the present problem of unequal opportunity. However, at the time, these changes brought tremendous relief from crippling poverty and virtual slavery in rural areas...and helped to instil in the black community greater optimism about the future...Confidence grew among the young.[14]

In November 1968, a cash economy was introduced to Palm Island. No funds were made available to assist the transition, which was accompanied by the 'dumping' of Palm Islanders on the mainland. In

1969, David Gundy advised *Aboriginal Quarterly* that he was caught gambling, taken straight to the wharf and not allowed to return to the island.

> If you go down to the Strand (in Townsville) you'll see a lot of coloured men — ask them and they'll tell you they are from Palm. It's the same in the watch house ...They are just dumped ashore...They steal for food and drink and get into trouble, they don't know what else to do.

Some Palm Islanders were convinced that the emergence of an Aboriginal council on Palm by the late 1960s was enough infringement upon 'the Red Emperor's power' to drive him to the mainland for an alternative career.[15] While wages on the island were increased — following strenuous representations from unions and FCAATSI — the rise was not to the level of awards and led to the sacking of half of the island's workforce. In 1974, the Palm Island Council reported that only one of the 1,200 workers on the island received an award wage.[16]

Some Palm Islanders became active in forming the Foundation for Aboriginal and Islander Research and Action (FAIRA) in this period, with Beryl Castors and the late Monty Prior playing important roles as contributors to this fusion of churches, trade unions and Indigenous people from across the state. Qwanji (the late Pastor Don Brady), Mick Thaiday, Steve and Pam Mam, Fred and Iris Clay, Rachael Cummins, Erykah Kyle, Tom Geia and many others worked hard to establish some semblance of justice for their community on the island. The 'Concerned Palm Islanders' group tried to inform people of their rights and to explore models of self-government with the community.

While the federal Whitlam Labor government raised expectations of support for health, education and services, much of the funding earmarked for Aboriginal communities in Queensland was rejected by the Bjelke-Petersen government. State Leader of the Opposition, Percy Tucker, noted that $2.4 million federally allocated to Indigenous health in the period 1972–74 had been refused.

In 1975, the Whitlam government introduced legislation attempting to redress some of the injustices in Queensland, with the *Aboriginal and Torres Strait Islanders' (Queensland Discriminatory Laws) Act*. This legislation was designed to protect the rights of residents and to allow appeals against reserve court decisions directly to a judge, but the Queensland government simply chose to ignore the federal Act. At this point the Queensland Acts continued to contravene the Universal Declaration of Human Rights, and numerous international covenants on civil and political rights, all of which had been ratified by Australia.

The separate school for white children was maintained on Palm Island until the late 1960s and Murris were again denied access to Mango Avenue. Dormitory children considered to be misbehaving were imprisoned in a dungeon-like room with little ventilation for two-week periods. Residents continued to be stealthily removed for complaining about wages and conditions. A delegation from the federal Labor Party's Aboriginal Affairs Committee in 1971, requested by both FCAATSI and Palm Islanders themselves, reported to the *Australian* that the reserve as a whole was 'the ultimate in white control over Aboriginals'. The federal member for Hughes, RL Johnson, took headline attention, with MP SAYS ISLE RESERVE IS LIKE ALCATRAZ. In 1974, Amnesty International described Palm Island as 'little more than a concentration camp'.[17]

The Premier responded with a campaign of demonisation, equating Aboriginal activism with 'black terrorism' and land rights with the creation of 'an Aboriginal state'. From the late 1960s, Palm Island was targeted as a potential site for a profitable tourist industry and in 1971 the *Australian* publicised state Cabinet approval for the calling of tenders for the whole Palm Island group. Bjelke-Petersen later acknowledged that Palm's tourist potential had been 'advertised on a worldwide basis'. At this time the long-standing activist Fred Clay, had been elected Chair of the Palm Island Council. Edith Lenoy, Mary Twaddle and Bill Congoo became Councillors, and with the election of this team came a new drive to expose conditions on the island, with support engaged from members of Queensland's Act Confrontation Committee.

While the Queensland Act still maintained the authority of the manager over councils in determining who could visit Palm Island, Clay's council made its own decisions and involved Murris from outside the reserve to provide assistance. Qwanji, Bobbi Sykes, Denis Walker and Bill Rosser visited Palm Island in this period. Clay's council also contacted the trade unions and the Labor Party, seeking assistance to achieve wage justice on Palm.

Government moves to force the issue of providing land for tourism on Palm came amidst the concerted protests against the Acts in Brisbane in 1974. Denis Walker and members of the Brisbane Legal Service visited Palm at the request of Clay's council, and prepared a comprehensive report on the island's conditions which was submitted to the federal government. The document argued that the Palm community was capable of running the reserve without interference.

In June, it was announced that the Queensland government intended to include Palm Island within the boundary of the Townsville Shire Council. The Department of Aboriginal and Island Affairs set aside blocks of land in Townsville on which it planned to relocate Palm Island residents. On

21 June, at a meeting between the Townsville Shire Council and Palm Island's Aboriginal Council, Palm Islanders made it clear that they were opposed to the move. The council mobilised supporters throughout July, and meetings and seminars which were attended by Brisbane representatives of the Act Confrontation Committee.[18]

In the week leading up to a planned protest against 'the Act' on 13 July, the *Courier Mail* announced a '24 Hour Guard On [the] Premier' had taken effect from 4 July, and alleged that Bjelke-Petersen's life had been threatened by 'a radical aboriginal element' seeking a federal takeover of Aboriginal affairs in Queensland.[19] Two weeks after the arrests of Denis Walker, John Garcia and Lionel Lacey of the Aboriginal Coordinating Council (ACC), the state government dissolved the council on Palm.

State Aboriginal Affairs Minister, Neville Hewitt, claimed the sacking of Clay's council on 28 August and appointment of an administrator was in response to a petition from a 'two-thirds' majority' of Palm residents. The authenticity of these signatures was later questioned by federal Senators, Jim Keefe and Neville Bonner. Labor Party member for Bulimba, John Houston, subsequently advised Queensland Parliament that Senator Bonner had claimed that 'at least 100 names out of 300 names on the petition had not been personally signed.' He then requested that the Minister table the petition, to which Hewitt replied, 'A firm "No".'[20]

Councillors Fred Clay, Edith Lenoy, Mary Twaddle and Bill Congoo sought an injunction in the Cairns Supreme Court against a new election, but the move was defeated. Hewitt refused to discuss the issue with federal Minister, James Cavanagh. With characteristic 'double-speak', Premier Bjelke-Petersen argued that he wanted 'all outsiders to leave the aboriginal people of Palm Island alone'. Senator Keefe stated that the dismissal of Clay's council had 'led to a breakdown in community relations' and the imprisonment of Palm Islanders 'for the first time in months' in the island jail. Fifteen arrests were made over the weekend following the council's dismissal.[21]

A new election of the Palm Council was held amidst rumours that 'extremists' were attempting to run firearms to the island. On 14 September a new council took office, with John Watson, foreman of the powerhouse, as chairman. Palm's manager, John Dillon, described the outcome as 'a victory for non-radical elements on the island'. The transfer of Palm Island into the authority of the Townsville Shire Council took place 'in embarrassingly quick time' three days later. While the state government had consistently denied any links between moves to bring Palm Island under the local shire and plans for a tourist industry in the

Palm Island group, a portion of Orpheus Island was subsequently offered for auction as perpetual leasehold for tourist development.[22]

The advice of Fred and Iris Clay continued to be sought by the new council regarding affairs on the island, and their son Ricky became active in speaking to young men about the need to challenge the Act. While in September 1974, Bjelke-Petersen had told Parliament that accusations that Palm Islanders were being forcibly removed from the reserve were 'deliberate lies', several months later Ricky Clay, Iris Clay's nephew Abe Johnson, Fred Clay's nephew Zacky Sam, Paddy Lightning, a boarder with the Clay family, and Patrick Bonner were all deported from the island by state police.[23] Iris Clay and Abe Johnson have recalled the events in which more than 40 armed police — two plane loads of them arriving from Townsville — had surrounded the Clay residence. Indicative of official paranoia concerning dissidents on Palm Island, some of the police had hidden in the mango trees nearby. The men were handcuffed at the airport and flown to Townsville where police 'just told them to go'. No charges were ever officially laid.

The pattern of dismissing reserve councils and using police intimidation to enforce subservience to government plans, as illustrated on Palm Island in 1974, was repeated in events at Aurukun and Mornington Island in 1978. At the federal level, Justice Woodward had submitted his report, providing guidelines for the introduction of land rights. In August 1975, the Whitlam government presented Vincent Lingiari of the Gurindji with a lease of 1,250 square miles (3,237 square kilometres) of land at Wattie Creek – a successful outcome for what would become a more widespread of outstation movement, wherein Murris squatted on their traditional lands in a direct confrontational tactic, to win the return of some lands to their Traditional Owners and to increase the capacity of people to maintain their cultures. By the early 1970s, the outstation movement had spread to other states.

In 'Australia's Deep North' race politics continued to be conducted 'the Queensland way'. Having rushed through Parliament the *Aurukun Associates Agreement Act* 1975, to allow further bauxite mining on Cape York Peninsula, contrary to the wishes of the Aurukun community, in March 1978 the Queensland government announced that it would take over control of Aurukun and Mornington Island from the Presbyterian Church. Federal government legislation, hastily constructed in 1978 to prevent the Bjelke-Petersen government's takeover, was rendered ineffectual when the Queensland Parliament rescinded the reserve status of Aurukun and Mornington, and declared these areas local council shires. The Bjelke-Petersen government then sacked the councils at both Aurukun and Mornington and appointed an administrator.

The following month, the multi-portfolioed Minister, Russ Hinze vowed that he would 'mop up' land rights campaigners in the two communities, a pledge seemingly extended to all reserves. Vocal in his support for the people of Aurukun and Mornington, Steve (Stumbo) Walsh, Palm Island's Welfare Officer, and his entire family (including eight children) were deported in 1979. The federal Community Relations Commission, claimed the Bjelke-Petersen government had 'a veritable touch of 1984' (referring to George Orwell's novel) in its treatment of reserve residents.

The appalling conditions and widespread poverty on Palm Island continued unabated and by 1980 there was one wage earner to every 99 people, with an average of twelve people living in each house. 'Self-management' strategies created fiefdoms of power and intensified internal conflict as people vied for the small number of jobs on the island. But perhaps the most destructive and enduring legacy of the 1970s, significantly compounding these problems, was the imposition of an alcohol canteen in 1972, without community consent.

The *Queensland Aborigines Act* 1971 liberalised access to alcohol, opening the scope for government to develop contracts with the alcohol industry. While a meeting was held in 1972, with state government intervention, no vote was ever taken on the issue of whether to establish a beer canteen. I have encountered a good deal of anger over these events from elders on Palm, who state that they foresaw poverty and violence as the likely consequences, for which they, their children and grandchildren would pay a hefty price. Some of those present claimed that a motion to introduce alcohol would have been defeated. Instead the government simply announced to the assembly that it had decided to open a beer canteen on the island in the near future.[24]

The first canteen was established in the town hall, with rations of two cans of beer per person, to be consumed on the premises. Fred Clay's council administered the vexed issue of alcohol supply in the context of an extensive history of sly grog trading and other damaging consequences of prohibition. In March 1970, Senator Keefe had advised federal Parliament that 'cheap bottles of "plonk" were being sold for $10 each, methylated spirits for $5 a bottle...Significantly the rum running... was done by white people running boats to the island and making exorbitant profits.'

Moreover, 'home brews' manufactured in the pre-canteen era, often had lethal results. In 1973, three residents died as a result of methanol poisoning, the liquid having been consumed in the belief that it was rum.[25] In addition, under the 1971 Act, profits from sales of beer became the property of councils to spend for the benefit of residents. The devastating and ultimately disempowering influence of alcohol sales on the lives of many hundreds of residents was not foreseen by all, though it would only be a few years before widespread damage was obvious. Within the context of reserve life, drinking and violence would become the both a symptom and a cause of social dysfunction and misery.

In 1977, a federal government inquiry into Aboriginal drinking patterns reported that 'over 90 per cent of men and 80 per cent of women' on Palm Island drank 'heavily'.[26] It is no accident that the effects of alcohol are most detrimental where people had the least chance of escape from conditions of chronic stress and poverty. The Palm community experienced between 70 and 80 per cent unemployment in the late 1970s. There is a 'not coincidental' connection 'between being on welfare, at the bottom of the social order, and being drunk most of the time'.[27]

By the late 1970s, a rise in violence, chronic ill-health and the need for alcohol rehabilitation facilities were major concerns of the Palm community. The canteen had become the centre of social life and by the 1980s, 650 kegs of beer were being sold each week on the island. At the same time, after only two and a half years of operation, profits from the canteen were enough to allow the opening of a $160,000 hotel, to restore old buildings and to provide new shops.[28] Sales of alcohol have since been used to fund roads, parks and gardens, wages for staff, fruit supplies to schools and freight, as well as supplementing wages of DAIA staff. An absence of alternative forms of economy, led to the entrapment of the community in the process of the destruction of Murri culture and lifestyles.

Former Deputy Chair, Rachael Cummins, has commented: 'We are the only local authority in the world which has got to keep our constituents drunk to operate.'[29] Past Mayor of Palm, Erykah Kyle noted:

> It is a sad fact of life that the canteen is the main source of income for the Community Council, but it is also the main source of problems — crime, bashings, family break-ups, imprisonments, injuries and death. It is nothing unusual in our community to see emergency flights (to Townsville Hospital) at all hours.[30]

Palm's annual death rate from accidents and violence in the years 1976–78 figured at 37.8 per 10,000, while the general Queensland rate was 6.9 per 100,000. The Palm community experienced an 'enormous and staggering' rate of homicides — 94.3 per 100,000 in the period 1976 to 1984, compared to a general Queensland rate of 6.9 per cent.[31] Surveys by David S Trigger, C Anderson, RA Lincoln and CE Matis in the late 1970s revealed that of fourteen reserves studied, those with the highest rates of death from accidents and violence were receiver reserves which operated beer canteens.[32] By 1979, the Chair of the Palm Island Council,

Jacob Baira, was defining the two core issues confronting the community as unemployment and alcoholism.

Indigenous cultural practices, protocols of demand sharing and an emphasis upon personal autonomy exacerbated problems, as did the history of prohibition and the gulping of 'forbidden fruit' in the long grass. In addition, rather than the daily 'obsessed and driven alcoholic of the Western world', alcohol consumption in Indigenous communities predominantly follows binge patterns (eight or more drinks in a weekly or fortnightly session) — short lived periods or 'bouts' that can be enormously chaotic and often with fatal consequences. Alcohol abuse has served to erode and undermine the authority and function of the family as an agent of social order and control. For people whose lives had been subjected to claustrophobic levels of external control, becoming drunk provided the rare experience of being, quite literally, out of control.

It should be noted that alcohol consumption was increasing amongst the mainstream community in Australia throughout the 1960s and 1970s. By 1981, Australia's 10.0 litres of consumption per head was the highest of the English speaking countries.[33] But outcomes were most severe in small communities suffering poverty, isolation and despair. Moreover, as David Knight notes of Mornington Island and Richard Trudgeon of Arnhem Land, the introduction of alcohol alongside the imposition of Western forms of local government stripped people of control over their lives. The depersonalised power and domination of Western democracies and their bureaucratic institutional processes are an anathema to Aboriginal people and drinking is pursued from a site of despair.[34]

Anger and violence unfurl in these setting. Alcohol was involved in almost all forms of crime on Palm in the late 1970s, and over 70 per cent of assaults were 'committed on females and most of those involved boyfriends and husbands who were said to be drunk at the time'. While five rapes were reported in the three and a half year period from January 1978 to August 1981, four of which were gang rapes, police advised that most incidents went unreported and that rape 'is an almost daily occurrence on Palm Island'. All cases of murder and attempted murder were 'committed by Aborigines against Aborigines'. Barber, Punt and Albers comment: 'The social cost of alcohol, introduced by whites and used to exploit blacks, is borne almost entirely by the black community itself.'[35]

Researching this issue in the early 1990s, I found insights and parallels to Palm Island in Anastasia Shkilnyk's examination of the Ojibwa community of the Grassy Narrows reservation in Canada in the 1960s and 1970s, *A Poison Stronger Than Love*. It says something that I had to look to Canadian sociology to find a comprehensive treatment of the impact of alcohol on an Indigenous reserve, at a time when its devastating repercussions had been felt for decades in such communities across Australia. One of the most pressing issues to Shkilanyk's mind, and one that resonated so much with Palm history — was the traumatisation of the people of Grassy Narrows, particularly following the dumping of methyl mercury into the water supply.

For Palm Islanders had experienced decades of trauma, not least of all the loss of child lives, which were, across all Queensland reserves, occurring at a rate at least six times higher than in non-Indigenous communities. Indeed, as alcohol was imposed for commercial purposes, another wave of dysentery took its toll as a result of a poisoned water supply. Scientific studies would eventually determine that the 1979 outbreak of gastroenteritis — blamed by government ministers on children 'eating green mangoes' — was the result of 'a tropical blooming of blue green algae' that was subsequently observed as 'regularly appearing in the late dry season' of October to December. Of the 150 Palm Islanders hospitalised, 140 were children and several died.[36]

Judith Hermann's study of trauma linked survivors of domestic violence, refugees and war veterans to the plight of communities living under tyrannical control. She noted the effects of self-medication in assisting dissociation from the feelings of past and present trauma, while also blocking the integration of experience required for healing, setting up conditions for inter-generational abuse and violence. Judy Atkinson also explored the process from an Aboriginal perspective in her work, *Trauma Trails* (2003).[37] Survivor guilt, a victim mentality, anxiety disorders and depression are amongst the range of psychological disturbances that become masked by intoxication.

Contemporary journalists regularly visit Palm Island to focus voyeuristically upon alcohol-related violence. Random connections are made with residents in the streets, no accountability is established with anyone who lives there, and return flights to cities are followed by lurid writings and photographic 'exposes' for white audiences, in which violence is the new exotica — extreme, incomprehensible and bearing no resemblance to that in our own communities. Attention to the island's history is most often non-existent, superficial or distorted. As in the colonial 'anthropological' circuses and vaudeville of old, viewers no doubt gasp in shock and horror, taking comfort that such communities remain remote from their own — both physically and psychologically. Yet part of recovery for traumatised peoples, writes Hermann, is for the sufferer to 'rediscover history' — 'The conflict between the will to deny horrible events and the will to proclaim them aloud is the central dialectic of psychological trauma. When the truth is fully recognised, survivors can begin their recovery.'[38]

Chapter 10

Campaign Time:
'Heady Days'

The 1980s and 1990s were a time of mobilisation across Aboriginal Australia. The push for land rights was given urgency through the passing of the *Land Rights Act* 1976 in the Northern Territory and by successful campaigns for land in some areas. In Queensland in 1982, the impending Commonwealth Games, to be hosted in Brisbane, added impetus to the land rights campaign.

For those residing in Queensland, the continuing reign of a fanatically anti-Aboriginal government under Premier Bjelke-Petersen, made for a volatile climate in the lead up to the Games. On the eve of the Games' opening, the Premier told the *Sydney Morning Herald* that the Queensland government was nonplussed by international media attention to the state's record on race relations. Aboriginal people in Queensland he said, 'live on clover' — they are 'as rich as the sheiks of the Middle East'.[1] His comments were uttered at a time when death rates on reserves were more than three times the rates for the state's non-Indigenous people.

Issues of poverty and dispossession, poor health and sanitation, lack of access to education and employment, high rates of imprisonment and police brutality would continue to shadow the tenor of people's lives on Queensland's Indigenous communities throughout the 1980s. Hundreds of protestors converged on Brisbane from around Australia in the lead up to the Games and a camp was established in Musgrave Park for the duration. Frank Brennan has described the early 1980s as 'heady days' and notes,

> Back then young leaders from Palm Island like Tom Geia and Rachael Cummins led the charge, appearing on national television prior to the Brisbane Commonwealth Games and challenging the misrepresentations made by government and their media chorus. Remember, keep it local. Keep to the facts.

Be principled. Don't overstate your case. Be committed to dialogue with your neighbours even when the media is selling a government message.[2]

Large gatherings took to the streets throughout September and October of 1982. Queensland's *Commonwealth Games Act* 1981 added nineteen offences for curtailing protests and the ban on street marches was resuscitated. Hundreds of arrests were made. In an effort to stem the groundswell of indignation and to divert the spotlight of the world's media, the state government passed the *Land Act (Aboriginal and Islander Land Grants) Amendment Act*. The Act promised a system for granting Deeds of Grant in Trust (DOGITS) to Indigenous communities, rather than open title, to Aboriginal councils. Deeds were revocable and approval was required before councils could lease or rent land to residents. The government maintained control over services and facilities. The Queensland Aboriginal Advisory Council voted to reject the DOGIT proposal and was never reconvened.[3]

The *Community Services (Aborigines) Act* 1984 transferred administration of communities from the government to locally elected Aboriginal councils. The first DOGITS were issued in 1985 under the new *Aborigines and Torres Strait Islander (Land Holding) Act*. For Palm Island the result was the receipt by council of title deeds for a form of perpetual leasehold over the former reserves lands of Palm and the ten surrounding islands of the Palm Island Group.

Yet the deeds of grant system reserved Crown ownership over mineral, petroleum and forestry rights. Greater powers for administration by elected councils were offset by the almost instantaneous removal from the island of services and infrastructure. Older residents of Palm recall the barges arriving to convey the dismantled houses, shops, dock, timber mill and community farm to the mainland. George Friday Senior recalled, 'They took everything, even the cattle.'[4] As the 'reserve' made the transition to 'community', jobs disappeared. Skilled tradesmen were left without work and there developed the phenomenon of the 'fly in — fly out brigade' — white contractors and public servants performing in positions that Palm Islanders were capable of doing.

Palm Islanders continued to live with inadequate housing, water and sewage systems and regular outbreaks of infectious disease. The island's water and waste system was suitable to a population of 1,500 in a community which, at peak periods, was more than double that size. Tellingly, a state government advertisement for a position at Palm Island's hospital called for 'Third World' experience as a preferred qualification.[5]

By 1983, the efforts of the 'Concerned Palm Islanders' had resulted in the election of four new Councillors who were part of the concerted campaign for secure land tenure and self-determination. Tom Geia, Rachael Cummins, Erykah Kyle and many others were part of a state-wide struggle throughout the 1980s, which saw the passing of ten Acts of Parliament between 1982 and 1988.[6] This included the 1982 Lands Act Amendment Act that facilitated Deeds of Grant in Trust, the *Aborigines and Torres Strait Islanders (Land Holding) Act* 1985, the *Community Services (Aborigines) Act* 1984 (which involved a separate act for the Torres Strait Islands), as well as heritage legislation (to protect sacred and significant places, areas and objects) and a cultural renewal Act around land management.

In 1985, seven Palm Islanders brought action against the Queensland government before the Human Rights Commission, charging it with discrimination towards Aboriginal reserve employees. The case raised the illegality of the government paying below award wages between 1975 and 1985, in the context of the federal *Racial Discrimination Act* 1975 and in terms of its own state industrial laws. Palm Islanders, the late Jack and Jean Sibley, Buller Coutts, Maurice Palmer, and Kitchener Bligh, as well as Mavis Foster and Fred Lenoy, demanded their rights to receive the same wage levels as their non-Indigenous counterparts, employed by the Queensland government. All had worked since childhood 'for a pittance'.

Historian Rosalind Kidd, members of FAIRA and lawyer Bob Haebich were active and vocal in supporting the Palm campaign. While the case was lodged with the Human Rights Comission (HRC) in 1986, the commission did not begin hearing evidence until an inquiry was conducted on the island ten years later. During that decade Queensland's political climate proved tumultuous. Journalistic exposés of endemic corruption amongst ministers of Bjelke-Petersen's government led to the Fitzgerald Inquiry and the Premier's resignation.

The year 1989 marked the first Labor government in 32 years. The Goss government embarked on an extensive agenda of reform, but its *Aboriginal Land Act* 1991 incurred the contempt of large sections of the Aboriginal populace. The truncated consultation process — a mere three weeks — allowed little space for garnering Aboriginal aspirations for land and the Act failed to provide a mechanism for claims for most Aboriginal Queenslanders.

In 1996, a recently united Coalition of Liberal and National Parties narrowly took office when it won the support of a Gladstone Independent. Goss withdrew from active political life and Peter Beattie became Leader of the Opposition. The Rob Borbidge government pursued an agenda of unbridled development, resurrected a 'cosy relationship' with the police service and the Criminal Justice Commission had its powers curbed. When the Human Rights' Commission judgment found that the Queensland government had deliberately, knowingly and intentionally discriminated against Palm Islanders and recommended a public apology and payment of $7,000 to each person as compensation, lawyers for the Borbidge government attempted to derail the process. They sought suppression of historical evidence and threatened legal action against Palm Islanders.

When the state government refused to pay the compensation, Palm Islanders commenced federal court action. Borbidge's government capitulated. While amounts actually underpaid to each of the seven Palm Islanders varied widely — with none being calculated at less than $8,000 and in one case at more than $20,000, and with these figures being accepted by Commissioner William Carter — the HRC determined that the same amount (of $7,000 for 'hurt and humiliation') be received by all.

Commissioner Carter noted that while each individual complainant had different 'skills and talents', 'one can recognise a certain commonality. They were treated alike; they lived as part of the same community', they had suffered a similar 'personal anguish'. On that basis he concluded that the complainants should each receive the same amount of compensation. When compared to the individuality accorded to non-Indigenous claimants before the HRC, it is difficult not to conclude that even their compensation was awarded in a discriminatory fashion, being determined by their Aboriginality and location.[7] The Palm Island campaign would inspire further claims for compensation by residents of Queensland's reserves.

These claims would be managed by the Beattie Labor government, which took office in 1998. In response to the decision in the *Palm Island Wages Case*, Beattie's government introduced the Underpayment of Award Wages Process on 31 May 1999. This process made a single payment of $7,000 available to people who had been employed by the government on Aboriginal reserves between the commencement of the federal *Racial Discrimination Act* 1975 and the delivery of award wages to all workers in 1986. The public was not told that the government's own research showed that the average liability was around $20,250.[8]

Following the initial Palm Island case and its results, activists focused upon the return of stolen wages for all those who had been subjected to the Trust Fund system. By the year 2000, the Queensland Aboriginal and Islander Legal Service Secretariat had collected testimonies from

2,000 people in relation to missing, unpaid and under-paid wages, misused trust funds, unpaid child endowment, workers' compensation and deceased estates. In 2002, the Beattie government offered $4,000 to some people and $2,000 to others. Those born on or before 31 December 1951 and subjected to government control over their wages and savings were eligible for $4,000; those born after that date and up to 1956, to the latter amount. Referred to by the government as 'reparations', these limited and arbitrary amounts were greeted with much anger as an insult.

Large numbers of potential claimants voted to reject the offer of 2002. Alf Lacey of Palm Island, then Councillor on the island and deputy chairman of the Aboriginal Coordinating Council, argued that the government needed to lift the offer to include all withheld wages and savings, as well as child endowment that had been placed in state coffers. The last of these issues was an historical wound for Palm Islanders, since thousands of dollars worth of payments had been denied Palm Island mothers and used instead to finance a hostel at Aitkenvale until the 1970s.

Widespread poverty, stressful living conditions, cultural dislocation, incessant bureaucratic control and a lack of funding and infrastructure gave rise to despair and a sense of anomie, compounded by increasing access to alcohol on most communities. When Aboriginal councils became responsible for delivering local government services from the mid 1980s, alcohol sales became crucial to keeping services functioning. By the mid 1990s, Palm Island's Coolgaree Bay Hotel had a turnover of almost $3 million, while revenue from other enterprises amounted to only $35,000.[9] The social outcomes included shocking levels of family violence and children raising children in many homes.

Noel Pearson documented the process whereby access and opportunities to drink, combined with exclusion from the 'real economy', increased interactions with police and rising rates of incarceration throughout the 1970s and 1980s. The result was the cyclical movement of Aboriginal people through revolving doors into 'the sausage machines of the criminal justice system'.[10] It was this gross over-representation of the numbers of Aboriginal people in police custody that the Royal Commission into Aboriginal Deaths in Custody (RCIADIC) would define as the determining factor in the disproportionate numbers of these deaths.

From the early 1980s, Aboriginal Legal Services and the Committee to Defend Black Rights had demanded a government inquiry into Aboriginal deaths in custody. The commission examined 99 such deaths between January 1980 and April 1991. It found that almost half of those who died had been Stolen Children. Other studies have noted the higher rates of substance abuse, mental health issues and histories of multiple institutionalisations amongst Indigenous people who had been taken into state care.

Vincent Roy Ryan, one of the cases examined by the commission, had been exiled from Woorabinda to Palm Island as an adolescent. Ryan spent a significant proportion of his life in welfare institutions and in jail. Efforts on the part of his parents to visit him in the various institutions were thwarted by bureaucratic procedures. He died at 39 years of age in Townsville prison. Dr Josef Reser has commented that Vincent Ryan's life was 'not untypical of the experience of many middle-aged Aboriginal men in and out of custody' in Australia and was indicative of 'the dismal cycle of arrest and incarceration which characterises so much of so many people's lives'.[11]

The commission delivered more than 300 recommendations – some addressing the over policing of Indigenous people and others establishing protocols for arrest and imprisonment processes. By the late 1980s, the commission had generated extensive publicity and had cost more than $40 million. Yet the avoidable deaths continued. In North Queensland, in 1989 two young Aboriginal men, aged 21 and 26, died while in custody in the space of one month in the Townsville watch house. Two coronial inquiries were held at the Townsville Coroner's Court, one on the 25 January 1990 conducted by Coroner BD Barrett and the other on 11 December, conducted by Coroner DG Evans.

Barrett noted that the 26-year-old male had previously been arrested 34 times for offences related to drunkenness. On the occasion of his arrest on 13 July, he had been placed at 3am in an enclosed cell, with occupant vision impossible. One hour and forty minutes later he was found hanging in the cell. Resuscitation attempts proved futile. The Coroner recommended that video equipment be installed in all enclosed cells where occupant vision is impossible, and 'also pointed out that he had made the same recommendation in February 1989'.

Coroner Evans investigated the death of a 21-year-old male who died after he was arrested for 'public drunkenness' in Hanran Park, Townsville, where he was found unconscious on 5 August. That such an arrest occurred represented a failure to implement the recommendations of the royal commission's interim report – that unconscious persons should receive immediate medical care, that public drunkenness be decriminalised and that police find alternatives to police cells in such circumstances.

Instead, having been arrested at 11.30am, the deceased had been dragged to the cell and his condition had not been checked by police until 3.45pm. The Coroner recommended that medical assistance be immediately sought for persons arrested who are habitual drinkers, that police receive training in 'identifying the differences between those who are asleep, unconscious or needing help and when medical attention should be sought' and that 'persons in charge of watch houses make their own observations regarding the health of prisoners'. Police argued in the case of the 21-year-old, that they were unaware of the existence of the royal commission's interim report in relation to arrest and detention of Aboriginal people.[12]

Coinciding with the royal commission, the Human Rights and Equal Opportunity Commission (HREOC) commenced the National Inquiry into Racist Violence. Its report of 1991 noted that 'racist violence against Aborigines and Torres Strait Islanders is endemic, nation-wide and very severe' and that there was a 'crisis in Aboriginal–police relations'. The report further noted a failure to respond to racist violence on the part of authorities of 'public institutions'. In particular:

> Aboriginal-police relations have reached a serious level due to the involvement of police in acts of racist violence, intimidation and harassment. We regret that we have come to this conclusion but the evidence is overwhelming. It is apparent that the climate of racism is so pervasive in our police forces that there is a need for fundamental changes in policing practices.[13]

Henry Reynolds recorded that in 1992 in Townsville club bouncers, other staff of a popular nightclub and several air force personnel who were also patrons at the club, pursued two Aboriginal brothers who were seen attempting to break into a car. One brother was captured and bashed, the other evaded pursuers after a struggle in the water. A witness later reported that from the bridge a police officer had cast a torch light upon the fleeing victim, assisting the bouncers to find him. The victim bit his assailant's hand while fighting for his life, as the bouncer held his head under the water. His drowned body was found in the creek the following day. A taxi driver who witnessed the events described the pursuers as behaving 'like the KKK'. Police who attended the scene, he said, 'stood by and did nothing' to stop the assaults. The coroner declared death by misadventure and determined that no charges would be laid.[14]

In September of that year, Australian soldiers in Townsville's Lavarack barrack posed in hoods as members of the Klu Klux Klan, and stood behind several dark skinned recruits towards whom they made threatening gestures, while having photographs taken. An inquiry was held but no disciplinary action taken. Some of the officers involved were later promoted, while the local Liberal member of federal Parliament, Peter Lindsay referred to the event as 'just a fun thing…out in the community,' he stated, 'no one would turn a hair.'[15]

In an effort to address the issues raised by Royal Commission into Aboriginal Deaths in Custody and the National Inquiry into Racist Violence, Paul Keating's federal Labor government established the Council for Aboriginal Reconciliation and the Queensland government moved to facilitate the input of Community Justice Groups (CJG) regarding the operations of the criminal justice system on Indigenous communities. Palm Islanders established their CJG in 1993. The group sat on the bench with visiting magistrates, settled family disputes, addressed anti-social behaviours, prepared sentencing reports for courts and supervised community correctional orders. This proved an effective measure in reducing juvenile crime rates and charges.

The Keating government sought to follow through on the Whitlam government agenda, resurrecting compassion, an historical awareness of human rights abuses and the legal recognition of land rights. Prime Minister Keating's Redfern speech in 1992 was a seminal moment in Australian race relations, acknowledging the history of frontier warfare, the taking of Aboriginal children from their families and the destruction of Aboriginal culture, and urging non-Indigenous Australians to adopt a sense of responsibility for addressing the impacts of these issues.

The federal government introduced the native title bill, following the successful High Court claim for native title rights on Meriam Island in the Torres Strait, inspiring optimism regarding the prospects for widespread and substantial change. At an international level, advances were being made in the passing of covenants and laws to protect the continuation of Indigenous lives and cultures. Aboriginal Australians were also making gains in campaigns for the return of human remains from overseas museums and institutes.

On Palm Island the return of the body of Kukamunburra (Tambo) from the basement of a funeral home in Cleveland, Ohio in America was secured by his great-great nephew, Walter Palm Island Jnr, in 1994. Accompanied by two other Palm Islanders, Walter travelled to the United States to bring him home. Chapter Three recorded the removal in 1883 of six Palm Islanders, as well as three from Hinchinbrook Island, who were lured to America and Europe to perform as part of Barnum, Bailey and Hutchinson's 'Greatest Show on Earth'.

Kukamunburra had died of pneumonia at aged 21 and within twelve months of his removal. His companions had grieved deeply over his death. The troupe's 'keeper', RA Cunningham, refused to allow them to perform traditional rites for the body. Instead Kukamunburra was mummified and displayed in a dime museum. Officials at the Australian Embassy in Washington were contacted when the body was discovered and were directed to Walter Palm Island Jnr, a 35-year-old resident of Palm Island.

Walter's surname was in recognition of his people's claim to traditional ownership of Palm. It was Walter Palm Island Jnr's grandfather, Dick Palm Island, who had called all the groups together at a time when many of the forty-six language groups were in conflict with each other. He had suggested that they call themselves Bwgcolman, meaning Palm Island. As a child, Walter Palm Island was told by his grandfather of a great uncle who went overseas, never to return, and of an old woman's spirit which kept a nightly vigil for the return of lost souls, under the mango trees on the site of a traditional camping ground. The story of Kukamamburra's abduction and return are recorded on a headstone at the site on Palm Island where he was finally laid to rest in a poignant ceremony one hundred years after his death.[16] The completion of these burial rites was a part of the cultural revitalisation and spiritual healing that was unfolding across the country.

Yet feelings of optimism inspired by changes in the first half of the 1990s were dashed when Liberal leader John Howard won the 1996 federal election. Upon taking office Prime Minister Howard declared his intentions to encourage Australians to 'feel comfortable about the past' and to promote a singular pride 'in our achievements.' Minister for Aboriginal Affairs, John Heron, rejected the findings of HREOC's *Bringing Them Home Report* commissioned by the Keating government, dismissed the term 'Stolen Generations' and argued that the removal policy had been 'essentially benign in intent'.[17]

The federal government's 'ten point plan' dismantled much of the advances made by the Keating government's *Native Title Act* 1993 (Cwth). Moreover, despite RCIADIC's recommendation that arrests should be seen as 'a last resort', incarceration rates of Indigenous people and deaths in custody increased between the early 1990s and 2001. In the late 1990s, John Howard removed the requirement for states to report their progress in implementing the recommendations of RCIADIC.[18]

Mental health researchers Josef Reser and Ernest Hunter struggled to draw public attention to the escalating rates of suicide that were occurring both in and out of custody, documenting that North Queensland suicide rates in Aboriginal communities had reached 'epidemic' proportions by the mid 1990s. On Palm Island Vincent Thimble, an ambulance officer, attended 40 suicides over the years 1988 to 1999. A men's group was established on Palm Island in 1997 in response to sixteen suicides on the island over a past eighteen month period. There had been many more attempted suicides — four to five times more. Some presented to hospital for resuscitation and medical aid; others did not.[19]

On Cape York, Merv Gibson and Noel Pearson offered extensive insights into the impact of substance abuse on communities, from a perspective that emphasised the nexus between alcohol and social breakdown in communities in the context of Aboriginal culture and the role of violence in silencing the abused and paralysing the political will of communities. Commissioned by the state Beattie government, Tony Fitzgerald's *Cape York Justice Study* in 2003 followed Pearson's strategic inclination towards restrictions on alcohol access in communities, and argued for community alcohol action plans as a first priority for addressing social disorder.

Palm Island was one of the first communities to implement alcohol restrictions. Developed by the council chaired by Delena Foster, the management plan banned the sale of spirits and wine in April 2002. This move coincided with the state government's release of the *Meeting Challenges, Making Choices* policy, which would lead to nineteen communities adopting a range of restrictions upon access.

Within a few years, some communities reported evidence of a reduction in alcohol-related crime, violence and hospital admissions on Cape York, with quieter environments, improved school attendance and greater food sales in many of the affected communities. Yet anecdotal evidence from professionals, health workers and communities indicated that results also included an increase in 'sly grogging', the use of methylated spirits, glue sniffing and consumption of other drugs and a shifting of the problems of alcohol-related violence to areas outside of council boundaries, thus further away from services and support for victims of violence. Movements have also occurred towards nearby towns, where alcohol is more readily available.

Moreover, the most dramatic documented reduction in social problems occurred at Aurukun where the community had initiated an Alcohol Law Council as early as 1995 — eight years before Fitzgerald's report. This suggests that community-based initiatives have proven more effective than the arbitrary imposition of government decrees. The government's own evaluation report noted that the effectiveness of the restrictions had been limited by a failure to map the changes to the needs of each community, inadequate attention to communication with communities and a delay in addressing the issue of demand, with a singular focus upon supply.[20]

Contrary to the recommendations of RCIADIC, for many of those suffering alcoholism, the main impact of recent changes has been the imposition of arrests and fines which, in a context of poverty, are left unpaid, resulting in criminalisation and jail sentences. By January 2005, the *Townsville Daily Bulletin* reported that Aboriginal people in remote communities had been fined a total of $250,000 and at least five people had been jailed over breaches of restrictions.[21]

A spate of previous reports — including the Royal Commission into Aboriginal Deaths in Custody, the National Aboriginal Health Strategy and the Fitzgerald Report — highlighted the need to address the demand for alcohol, through the development of culturally appropriate screening, assessment and intervention tools. Despite the recent successful validation of tools for this type of intervention in Queensland,[22] systematic and substantial movement in this area is yet to be achieved.

The Aboriginal and Torres Strait Islander Women's Task Force Report of 1999 and *'The Safe House Project' Report — Sustainable Responses to Family Violence in Remote Aboriginal and Torres Strait Islander Communities in North Queensland 2004* have both developed comprehensive, detailed and holistic recommendations regarding culturally appropriate solutions to problems of substance abuse, family violence and community breakdown, built upon substantial research and consultation with Indigenous communities. Like the 339 recommendations of the Royal Commission into Aboriginal Deaths in Custody, most of their projected solutions are yet to be implemented.

Indeed, over 40 reports addressing social dysfunction in Indigenous communities are currently gathering dust. The need for funding of capital works, infrastructure and sustainable programs has yet to be realised. Without the access and opportunities that this base line facilitates, talk of recovery and self-determination will likely remain just that. Those who work 'at the coal face' in this area, know that efforts to address the misuse of alcohol and drugs require concerted attention to countering the impacts of racism, since feelings of low self-worth, victimisation and hopelessness are so much a part of current dilemmas in treating addiction in Indigenous communities.

The use of legal 'solutions' to social and health problems is clearly not new to Palm Islanders. Much of this history — from the origins of the Palm reserve to the present — has been about the criminalisation of Aboriginal people for trivial offences, the role of police in the colonisation of Aboriginal lands, the over policing of Indigenous communities and the use of prisons as a means of social control.

Recent events on Palm Island suggest that the 'benevolent dictatorship' model of governance continues to shape interventions on Palm Island today, giving credence to the words of Spanish philosopher George Santayana: 'Those who cannot remember the past are condemned to repeat it.'

Chapter 11

The Inquest and its Aftermath:
'Our Day in Court'

The Coronial Inquiry that began at the end of March 2005 would eventually consume seventeen days of hearings spread over eighteen months. Brisbane pathologist Dr Guy Lampe, who examined Mulrunji's body after he died, told the inquest that the injuries could not, in his opinion, have been sustained in a fall alone. He noted that the liver was 'virtually cleaved in two' — the kind of injury usually associated with 'very severe force', such as in a 'high speed motor vehicle trauma'. Evidence from re-enactments performed on 19 November 2004 by both Hurley and Bengaroo, noted that Hurley had fallen to the left of Mulrunji, and onto his knees on the linoleum floor.

Hurley had maintained clearly, in his recall of events to Sergeant Leafe, within hours of the events, that he had fallen 'to the left of him, and he was to the right of me'. This account had also been given to police investigators on three occasions and in an interview with the CMC's investigating officer. After the release of a medical report, outlining the nature of Mulrunji's injuries, Hurley changed his recall when he appeared before the Coroner's Court, arguing that he had in fact fallen 'onto Mulrunji'. Hurley had never been asked by investigating police if he had at any time hit Mulrunji.

On 27 September 2006, Deputy Coroner Christine Clements delivered her findings to the Coroner's Court in Townsville. She questioned that there was even any basis for Mulrunji's arrest and accepted expert medical evidence that 'a fall together, side-by-side, of the two men onto a flat surface was unlikely to have caused the injury that occurred'. She further stated 'the application of a knee or an elbow…was accepted as a possible means by which the injury could have occurred'. Clements found Hurley's denial of an assault upon Mulrunji to be 'untruthful' and his explanation that he had fallen on top of him an expedient move, only adopted 'when he realised the nature of Mulrunji's injuries'. Clements would later note that 'it would seem commonplace that anyone would be able to say whether they had got up from a fall, either removing themselves from on top of another person, or up from a hard, flat, lino [sic] covered surface'.

The Coroner found Hurley responsible for the fatal injuries and accepted Roy Bramwell's account of witnessing punches thrown by Hurley at Mulrunji. She stated:

> Senior Sergeant Hurley's response was to deny the accusation of punching and to explain it as an attempt to lift Mulrunji by the shirt. The shirt kept ripping, thus causing him to perform a repetitive action which he says was misinterpreted by Bramwell...the description is reminiscent of what is frequently seen in football matches when hot headed players seemingly grab at shirt front, but take the opportunity to punch the opposition in doing so.

She found that Hurley's 'so called arousal technique' of nudging Mulrunji with his foot 'could not be sanctioned' and was 'demeaning' and 'inappropriate'. Hurley's discharge of his duty of care as regards Mulrunji and Patrick Bramwell was 'callous and deficient'. It was 'inappropriate' for officers who knew Hurley personally to conduct the investigation, 'inappropriate' for them to be collected from Palm Island's airport by him and 'completely unacceptable' for investigators to dine with Hurley at his home as the investigation was being conducted.

Clements also levelled criticism at previous complaints on Palm Island regarding Hurley's conduct. After two failed attempts by the police service to have the Supreme Court suppress the material, lawyers for the family had been able to submit evidence from a number of prior complaints against Hurley. While confined to those incurred on Palm Island, some have suggested that other complaints referred to Hurley's conduct in Doomadgee and Burketown and that he had been 'driven out' of the northwest prior to his arrival on Palm.[1] Submitted as propensity evidence, Clements 'gave regard to' the cases of Barbara Pilot (a niece to Mulrunji), Noel Cannon and Douglas Clay, but made no findings in these matters. Shock headlines followed.

The press reported that on 19 May 2004 Barbara Pilot's foot had been so badly injured, after Sergeant Hurley ran over it with a police car, that the bone protruded from her foot. Hurley later stated that Pilot had stepped away from the vehicle 'after a couple of requests' and had then fallen down. Asked 'Did you get out of the vehicle?' he stated that instead he had 'looked her up and down...I didn't see any injuries whatsoever.' Hurley had then driven off. Barbara Pilot said that after questioning Hurley as to why he had come to the house, he 'was going forward and he slammed the brakes and he spinned the back wheel onto my foot'. Pilot stated that she showed Hurley how the bone was protruding from her foot.[2]

She was accompanied by two others to the hospital in considerable pain and transferred to Townsville for medical treatment. Sergeant Hurley and Constable Fuller drove back to the station where they placed Arthur Murray in the cells. Severely intoxicated, Murray was left alone while Hurley and Fuller (the only police on duty) went to the hospital, where Hurley attempted to convince Dr Clinton Leahy that Pilot's injury could be 'the result of alternative scenarios', rather than 'his running her over'. Leahy stated that Hurley 'made an effort to push him to agree'. With Murray still in the cells alone, Hurley and Fuller then drank tea with the nurses.

Hurley would later tell the Coroner's Court that the doctor 'informed him that the injury was more consistent with kicking the ground than a tyre or car going over the foot'. Hurley also gave this account of the doctor's words to the police service communications coordinator. Dr Leahy would dispute that claim. At the request of Inspector Hickey, Hurley had returned to the scene and attempted to interview witnesses. The matter was the subject of an investigation by Detective Sergeant Darren Robinson, Hurley's close friend, who determined that the complaint was 'fictitious'. Robinson later admitted to lying in his report on the case when he described two witnesses — whose names were in the logbook — as being 'unidentifiable'.[3]

Noel Cannon's complaint concerning events in July 2004 related to his arrest for breaching a restraining order by visiting his ex-girlfriend. The *Courier Mail* reported:

> A Palm Island man urinated in his pants after having his throat squeezed by a police officer at the centre of a death in custody controversy…He said when he asked Sergeant Hurley for a mattress at the watch house he was told to wait twenty minutes while the sergeant did the paperwork. When he repeated the request several times Sgt Hurley became angry and attacked. 'And he gave me a knees up in the guts, winded me.'[4]

Sergeant Hurley was adamant that he did not assault Cannon.

Douglas Clay, a 24-year-old suffering from speed-induced psychosis, complained that Hurley had assaulted him with a 'flurry of punches'. Clay acknowledged that he had entered the police station and was verbally abusive. Police stated that Clay made a movement towards Hurley; Clay disputed this. Hurley who was seated at the time, rose and hit Clay with what he claimed was a slap: 'I slapped him. I pushed out — hard in his face and I slapped his face hard and pushed it towards the wall.' Police varied in their descriptions of events, using the terms 'hit', 'push' and 'slap', and providing different accounts as to whether it was an open-handed movement or a closed punch. This complaint to the CMC was also dismissed.

Clements explored the second autopsy and its findings of deep bruising adjacent to the right mandible and a scalp contusion (bruise) on the right front temporal lobe. The right upper eyelid was swollen and Dr Lynch noted that these injuries had to have occurred from the front or on the right side of the body. Clements concluded, 'It would be difficult in such a scenario to then explain the injury to the right eye as being incurred in the course of such a fall.'

Coroner Clements found that Hurley had assaulted Mulrunji, causing internal damage and death. The finding triggered outrage amongst the police service. Hurley was not stood down as a result, but retained a non-operational position on the Gold Coast, where he was reportedly 'holed up' in 'one of the four apartments worth $1 million he is listed as owning on the tourist strip'.[5] Coroner Clements' referral of matters to the Department of Public Prosecutions (DPP) incited QPUE President Gary Wilkinson to publicly dismiss the findings as 'a witch hunt', for which he was later forced to apologise under threat of a charge of 'contempt of court'.

Over the course of 2006, Coronial inquiries, the flooding of the island with journalists, the psychological violence and intimidation experienced in watch houses and jails across the state, took an enormous toll upon Palm Islanders. Calls for counsellors to assist people testifying went unheeded, as was Sydney lawyer, Stuart Levitt's call for federal agents to protect Aboriginal witnesses. The impact fireballed when, in July, Mulrunji's son Eric, aged only eighteen, killed himself and on 4 October Mulrunji's niece Desley Johnni, aged 35, hanged herself at her Doomadgee home. Eric's death was noted at the conclusion of an episode of the ABC television broadcast *Message Stick*. Called 'A Line in the Sand' the documentary covered the events of 2004 and included a poignant interview with a grief stricken Eric, in which he spoke of what a good father Mulrunji had been.[6]

Jail sentences also took their toll. On 9 October the Attorney-General, Kerry Shine, urged the Queensland Court of Appeal to extend the sentences received by Jayson Poynter, aged 26, Alissa Norman, aged 31, Wayne Russel Parker Snr, aged 37 and Russel Parker Jnr, aged 22. All had pleaded guilty to 'rioting', with Poynter and Norman given twelve months' intensive correction orders to be served in the community, and Wayne Russel Parker Snr sentenced to eighteen months jail, to be suspended after six. Chief Justice Paul de Jersey determined that the original sentence did not send a strong enough message needed 'to deter similar behaviour'. Poynter and Norman were sentenced to jail and Russel Parker Jnr's sentence was extended. The children of Norman, a single mother, were made wards of the state.

Evidence from the Coroner's Inquest was referred to the Director of Public Prosecutions. Leanne Clare had a trifecta of controversies behind her – the Volkers case, the Pauline Hanson and David Etteridge cases and the Fingleton case. In 1982, swimming coach Scott Volkers was not prosecuted for rape allegations after Clare advised Nicholas Cowdery, QC, not to proceed. In response to the controversy, Premier Beattie referred the case to the CMC, which found 'serious shortcomings' in the Queensland Public Prosecutor's decision. When fresh allegations of indecently dealing with a teenage girl were raised in the following year, the QPP again decided not to proceed. In 2003, Etteridge and Hanson, political party One Nation's founders were released from prison by the Court of Appeal, their convictions for fraud and electoral charges quashed. Then in 2005, Chief Magistrate Di Fingleton, imprisoned in relation to intimidation of a witness, was found by the High Court to have been immune from prosecution.

Clare's decision, in December 2006 – that Hurley had no case to answer – triggered a furore in legal circles and outrage amongst the Palm community and its supporters. Clare went further, redefining the death as 'a terrible accident'. Her claim to have sought and received further evidence, which she was not prepared to disclose, was unprecedented.

Noel Pearson accused the Leanne Clare of incompetence, civil liberties lawyer Terry O'Gorman called for an interstate review and protestors took to the streets in Brisbane. Premier Beattie visited the island, aiming to calm the situation, and was greeted by an angry demonstration of 400 Palm Islanders demanding justice. Aboriginal leaders from across the east coast attended and called for a review. By 23 December, the government had backed down, appointing former District Court Chief Judge Pat Shanahan to the task. As if to ensure the incessant continuation of fiascos in every milestone of official responses, the government had chosen a member of the panel that had selected Leanne Clare.

Harassment of Aboriginal members of the Palm community continued, both on the island and in Townsville. Roy Bramwell, serving time in Townsville Prison (also known by its previous name, Stuart Prison) for the domestic violence charge that had brought him into custody on the day of Mulrunji's death — and who told investigators that he had witnessed Hurley assault him — was allegedly subject to regular death threats from prison guards.[7] On 13 January his nephew

Patrick was taken into custody by Palm Island's police, over an incident involving his 'frightening people with a live snake'. Police later dropped him at the Chook Farm area where some of his relatives lived. Later on the night of 13 January, Bramwell walked to his grandmother's house in Dee Street, where he hanged himself from a tree. The location was the site where both he and Mulrunji had been arrested.

It will probably never be known what the police said to him that night, though it was reported that police in Townsville had already told him not to discuss the incidents of 19 November or he would be 'dealt with'. It is feasible that in the lead up to a potential trial of Hurley, the whole experience had simply become too much. That potential Aboriginal witnesses in such an important case could be left to their own devices in this deeply traumatised community says a great deal about the plight of people on Palm Island. The community was devastated by Bramwell's death.

On 4 January 2007, former New South Wales Chief Justice Sir Lawrence Street commenced his duties in reviewing Clare's decision. The day after Bramwell's death, Street arrived on the island as the community mourned. Several weeks later, at an Invasion Day rally on 26 January, outside Parliament House in Brisbane, lawyer Andrew Boe announced that he had received a phone call from the Attorney-General's Department advising that Street's report had recommended that charges of manslaughter and assault be laid against Sergeant Chris Hurley. A spirited march of Palm Island supporters made its way to the police headquarters in Roma Street where speeches were made. On Palm Island the family of Mulrunji remained calm and focused on the need 'to have our day in court'.

Hurley was for the first time officially suspended, but with pay, nearly two years after the death. The QPU held protest rallies in every major town in Queensland. These were attended by hundreds of police — record numbers for the QPSU, including 500 at a meeting in Townsville, 650 on the Gold Coast and 2,000 at the Broncos' Club in Brisbane.

Police Minister Judy Spence was criticised for attending these meetings against the need for government impartiality. Across the state, police donned blue wristbands in support of Hurley. Their flaunting of these symbols at the opening of a new Indigenous court in Brisbane triggered the lodging of an official complaint. The production of yellow wristbands in memory of Mulrunji soon followed.

On 5 February, Hurley faced the Supreme Court in Townsville where he was formally charged. The following day's planned protest by police was cancelled after the Premier agreed to install closed circuit cameras in watch houses in Aboriginal communities. The police service was suddenly passionate about following one of the recommendations of RCIADIC. It was no doubt cold comfort to Palm Islanders when Police Minister Spence announced that another 29 police officers would be sent to Indigenous communities.

After two years of stress over legal charges, on 22 March 2007 William Blackman, John Clumpoint, Dwayne Blanket and Lance Poynter were found not guilty of rioting with destruction by a Brisbane Supreme Court jury. On 8 May 2007, Terence Kidner was sentenced to sixteen months jail in the Townsville District Court after pleading guilty to rioting on Palm Island. His barrister, Bruce Mumford, told the court that Kidner 'had the mental capacity of a seven-year-old'. Nine others were at the time serving sentences ranging from six months to two years of jail, with a juvenile ordered to do 150 hours of community service.

In the winter of 2007, a survey of Townsville residents, commissioned by Stewart Levitt, and involving interviews with four hundred residents, revealed that 'over half of Townsville residents (interviewed) claimed that they could not disregard negative beliefs held about Aborigines, even if instructed to do so by a judge in a courtroom setting.' Moreover, only one in twenty had a positive attitude towards Palm Islanders.[8] While this research proved useful in moving the trial of an alleged 'rioter' from Townsville to Brisbane, Hurley's trial, scheduled to take place on 12 June, in Townsville, would proceed in that town despite the apparent risk of the recruitment of racially-biased jurors.

Harassment of politically active members of the Aboriginal community in Townsville, in the weeks leading up to Hurley's trial, failed to make headlines. Some were offered rides in police vehicles to 'very important meetings'; others were faced with police visits to their workplaces. Many were reminded of the days of Bjelke-Petersen's 'Deep North'.

Large numbers of Palm Islanders fronted the courtroom to watch Hurley's trial on 12 June. Two key witnesses — Police Liaison Officer Lloyd Bengaroo and Roy Bramwell, whose evidence had been crucial to Clement's findings — were dismissed as unreliable in the first twenty minutes of the opening. The prosecution, conducted by Peter Davis QC, centred on the claim that Hurley must have kneed Mulrunji during or after the fall. This opened the path for police to 'concede' that Hurley's knee must have accidentally struck Mulrunji.

The defence opened its case by calling Hurley as their first witness. Hurley stated that he accepted that he must have caused the death by landing 'on top of' Mulrunji', but denied any deliberate intention to cause harm. When Davis argued that he had described the fall differently in initial interviews because he believed Mulrunji had died of a heart attack and so there would be no case to answer, Hurley replied 'No'. He clenched his fists and his face twitched while viewing earlier video footage of himself telling the camera that he had fallen alongside Mulrunji.

At the conclusion of the seven day trial, Robert Mulholland, summing up for the defence, spoke for six hours, arguing that Hurley dealt regularly with 'drunken disorderly residents...who made a nuisance of themselves'. Playing to local sympathies, Mulholland asked, 'Members of the jury, isn't he precisely, precisely the sort of officer you'd like to have as your local copper?...When Senior Sergeant Hurley went out that morning ...he was performing a service for all of us...When Senior Sergeant Hurley went out that morning to respond to the request,' he said, 'he did it on our behalf.'[9]

On 20 June 2007, with less than two hours of discussion, the jury had acquitted Hurley, unanimously, on both charges. Outside the courthouse, Mulrunji's family wept and Andrew Boe spoke of the 'long journey' that had seen people take Indigenous justice further than ever before. On Palm Island there was an eerie silence. Premier Beattie told the community it was time to 'move on'. When I telephoned the island after the decision, I was told, 'The difference between them and us mob, is that when we put our hands on the Bible, we really mean it.' Calls for a royal commission were rejected by the Police Minister. Hurley was immediately reinstated on active duties on the Gold Coast.

The only people to have served any time in jail as a result of the events of November 2004 have been Palm Islanders, with thirty charged over the riot and more than half of them having served sentences ranging from a few weeks to two years. Some saw Hurley's acquittal as 'a license to kill', a suggestion born out by subsequent events when Palm Islander, Les Beckett, was bashed in Townsville, his assailants used a wooden truncheon and accused him of being responsible for 'causing the trouble with Sergeant Hurley'. The three unidentified non-Indigenous men left Beckett with brain damage and broken bones, which landed him in Townsville's intensive care unit.

No disciplinary action has been received by any of the police involved in the events of November 2004. Four years later, the CMC expressed its frustration with QPS delays in releasing its report concerning the initial investigation into the death. The CMC's review of the SERT noted that their actions 'may have been unlawful, since the state of emergency declared under the Public Safety Preservation Act did not authorise police to enter and search residents' homes', but the inability to identify any of the officers involved meant that no action would be taken.[10]

An examination of history shows that police have played a central role in the control of Aboriginal people, and that in the early colonial period it was their primary task. Many of those recruited to Indigenous communities are chosen for their abilities to apply force, and often land in these settings with no introduction to cultural awareness. Officer Kristopher Steadman, on Palm at the time of the death, had arrived the day before with no education in relation to interaction with Indigenous people.[11]

Moreover, we are all of us influenced by the nature of our work, at times assuming habits directly connected to habitual behaviours in our jobs. Hurley's history was in the police force, where exposure to violence and corruption is a regular part of the work routine. It is these issues — of culture, history, sociology, politics, power and over-empowerment — that provide a more valuable framework for understanding Chris Hurley's place in Palm Island history, than the issues of 'good and evil', presented in Chloe Hooper's recent publication on this topic, *The Tall Man* (2008).

Hooper was explicit about her goal of presenting the side of the 'misunderstood' cop and wrote about the death in custody 'in the mode of a good thriller'. Hurley is described as 'an enigma', while much is made of his efforts to play football with Aboriginal kids and that fact that he had Aboriginal friends in Doomadgee. Yet one could argue that this kind of community engagement is — and should be — simply part of the job description of police, teachers and others who work in these communities.

In Hooper's account, instead of just doing his job, Hurley is a white 'pioneer', 'charismatic' and 'classically handsome', venturing into 'the badlands'. While sympathy is shown for the Doomadgee family, the community consists of violent alcoholics, sober Christian women whose faith Hooper cannot understand and community leaders who, in the figure of past Mayor Erykah Kyle talk an archaic language or in that of Lex Wotton, are 'almost megalomaniacal'.[12] Little wonder, then, that reader/reviewers of *The Tall Man* have concluded that Palm Island is 'a Hogarthian painting of booze and violence, from wife beating to riots', a place where 'Most of the women have lost their front teeth, knocked out in drunken domestics.'[13] For in Hooper's account Palm Island is 'a black hole into which people have fallen' and the future is hopeless.

In later writing, Hooper drew upon my research into Superintendent Robert Curry to draw parallels with Hurley.[14] Like the first Superintendent — who had served in the First World War — Hurley is said to have arrived on Palm from the northwest, 'returning from a war that he couldn't get out of his system' — 'a war against savagery'. Yet Hurley is neither a war veteran nor a product of the inter-war years, but a member of Generation X — known for its pragmatism, its savvy, its focus upon money and, in harsher definitions, a tendency to amorality. Hurley is more akin to later Superintendent Roy Bartlam, trained in the police force, built like 'a mountain of a man' and used to having 'the law in his own mouth'.[15] What all three men share in common are explosive repercussions to their roles.

Hurley had acted as quasi-Superintendent in a period in which federally the Howard government fostered a culture of blaming Aboriginal people for the pain and dysfunction in their communities. Prime Minister John Howard had overseen the scaling back of efforts to implement the recommendations of RCIADIC. At a state level, Hurley operated within a political climate where Premier Peter Beattie, had won and maintained office on a platform of 'law and order'.

Only one month after Hurley's trial, the President of the Queensland Police Union of Employees and several other senior union officials were investigated by the CMC regarding fraudulent valuations of vehicles owned by the QPUE. These had been sold at substantially discounted rates to family members. The investigation did not clear Wilkinson or his union, but referred the matter to the DPP. Leanne Clare, who had refused to charge Hurley, also refused to prosecute Wilkinson. Wilkinson retired from the service soon after, citing back problems, and departed on a full police pension.[16] Leanne Clare has since been promoted to District Court Judge. Both Hurley and his friend and investigating officer, Detective Senior Sergeant Kitching, have been promoted to Inspectors.

Chris Hurley had the presence of mind, only weeks after the death, to lodge an extensive claim for compensation of his personal possessions, lost in the fires on Palm — a list totalling $100,000, and including items right down to his biro and his coffee cup. The Police Commissioner failed to follow standard procedures in lodging the paperwork, ensuring that Hurley received his payout despite the normal process of referring claims to the officers' insurance company. It has since come to light that Hurley lodged claims with both parties — the second for an amount of $34,000.[17]

Lawyer Terry O'Gorman noted that Tracey Twaddle had received no compensation for the loss of her life partner. Palm Island Mayor Alf Lacey asked, 'Is there going to be any compensation for the residents of Palm Island for their doors being knocked down and for their furniture being trashed by the SWAT team that came to Palm Island?'[18] The question remains unanswered. The doors remain kicked down.

In October 2008, Lex Wotton fronted the Brisbane Magistrate's Court facing a possible life sentence for rioting. On 23 October he collapsed outside of court while awaiting the jury verdict. Four days later the state government announced that police 'caught up in the riot' would receive awards of 'bravery' and 'valour'. The largest awards ceremony in Queensland police history took place in Townsville on 3 November.

The awards were greeted with disbelief on Palm, Denise Geia noting that some police were discovered hidden in the bushes during the disturbance, a fact she noted when she drove to the lookout in search of them. Senior Sergeant Dini, an Indigenous liaison officer who was amongst the group that asked for Geia's 'protection', would later argue that the actions of police on the day had been 'heroic'.[19]

On 7 November, 40-year-old plumber and father of four, Lex Wotton, was sentenced to seven years' jail with eligibility for parole from July 2010. Then on 18 December, in a final blow to the Palm community, Judge Robert Pack found in favour of an appeal by Hurley in the Townsville District Court. He recommended that the Coroner's Court decisions regarding the death in custody be set aside and that the inquest into Mulrunji's death be re-opened. Calls for a royal commission, from the community, petitioners and the Queensland parliamentary speaker, Mike Reynolds, met with a refusal from Premier Anna Bligh.

On 20 November 2009, as directions hearings for the inquest began in Townsville, the CMC report into widespread allegations of police brutality was tabled in State Parliament. Five years after the death in custody of Mulrinji, the report accused police of 'protecting their own'. While the report is yet to be finalised, it has condemned police handling of the initial investigation into the death and rejected the findings of the police review of that investigation. A further internal review, dealing with Hurley's claims for compensation, is ongoing.

Conclusion:
Calling Palm Island Home

...exile is a country of shifting borders, hard to quit yet hard to endure, no matter your wide shoulders, no matter your toughened heart.

Leif Enger, *Peace Like a River*[1]

You can forgive, but you can never forget.

Ivy Sam[2]

If Palm Island had begun as the backbone of the Carpet Snake — a sacred land with a Dreaming story involving Land Law, the authority of its custodians, trespass, forgiveness and of doing no harm, it is a terrible irony that it became the backbone of government policies of imprisonment, containment, punishment and control — the ultimate punitive destination in a state-wide system of post-frontier repression. From the time of 'Mad Dog Curry', through to the period controlled by Bartlam and his 'heart of stone', right into the era of power wielded by Senior Sergeant Hurley and his colleagues, Palm Islanders have been subjected to the whims of 'benevolent dictators', whose existences have each been centrally supported by the Queensland police.

It is a model built on the foundations of colonisation, moving from projections of Aboriginal people as 'pests' or 'vermin' in the way of progress, to their construction as children, in need of help and guidance. Even Sergeant Hurley is said to have seen himself as 'the daddy', with a paternalist's affection for individuals 'on a case-by-case' basis, who needed 'looking after'.[3] The belief that 'They are, and always will remain, children' echoed down through generations of practices on the part of the island's overseers.

Palm Island penitentiary was developed, in its early days, with the deliberate and articulated desire to allow conflict to foment between the various groups forced into exile there — 'if there is to be any letting off of steam, they would go for each other.' 'Horizontal violence', exacerbated so much by the introduction of alcohol, was widely tolerated until recent times.

Moreover, at each critical point of Palm Island's history, when the violence threatens to become 'vertical' and is directed at the oppressor, the mask of benevolence falls. The 'kindly uncle boss' is consumed by his fear of 'the black man', and reacts with loathing. Dissenters are flogged by Curry and confined to prison, adults and children alike. Some are dumped on nearby deserted islands, left to starve to death. Bartlam sends them to prison in their scores. Strikers are exiled to mainland reserves in leg irons, machine guns pointed at their heads. The outspoken Henry Pitt dies a suspicious death on a cell floor.

Those re-enacting the strike in the 1970s are whisked away to the mainland. Others who speak with trade unionists disappear without trace. People defending the island against unbridled tourist development are dismissed from their elected positions. In the 1980s, activists receive death threats and are followed around at night. And in 2004, almost half a century after the strike, the Palm Island people are subjected to pre-dawn raids by an anti-terrorist squad, clad in balaclavas and riot gear, in a scenario described by one observer as looking 'like Falujah'.[4] Little wonder then that Erykah Kyle should comment in this context, 'Sometimes we feel like the old Superintendent is still here.'[5]

While many of the struggles waged by the Bwgcolman have achieved gains, at times with impacts state-wide, conditions on Palm Island today remain appalling. In response to the state government's decree of tougher alcohol sanctions in May 2006, Palm Island Aboriginal Council wrote, 'We need real help for our people who are sick or who have suffered and now need support; a high school for our youth to get an education to year twelve; support for local business development; and urgent support to address overcrowding and homelessness on Palm Island. We do not need, or want, the state government imposing these laws upon us without agreement or proper consultation.'[6]

Palm Islanders have stated that they want the right to manage the store, currently owned by the government, which charges inflated prices to create profits that are then used to subsidise the transport of goods to other Aboriginal communities. Funding is needed for development and to provide jobs. Generosity, compassion and assistance are required. Palm Island was once our Alcatraz; today it is a litmus test of our 'progress' — a barometer of our capacity to respond to human crisis.

So too, reciprocity is needed. In 1995, 23.3 hectares of land at Aitkenvale, officially gazetted in 1949 as Aboriginal land, was transferred from the Queensland government to the Bwgcolman Land Trust under the Aboriginal Land Act. Approximately three hectares was excised by Queensland Health in the 1980s in order to build a hospital. The hospital was never built and proceeds from the sale of the land have never been returned.[7] Unaddressed historical issues such as this, simply add fuel to the anger felt by many Bwgcolman about conditions on the island today.

Research evidence indicates that it is not simply poverty, but the extent of inequality in societies, that determines the prevalence of ill-health and addiction. More precisely, while 'in a caring society being poor is not good for health...it is not so bad as being poor in an uncaring society.'[8] Evidence also suggests that Aboriginal youth are increasingly aware of the difference between their own socioeconomic circumstances, compared with those of non-Aboriginals around them.[9] And while current Prime Minister, Kevin Rudd, has committed to 'closing the gap' in life expectancies by 2030, recent research has indicated a widening of the gap over recent years, as non-Indigenous health improves at a far more marked pace than does that of Indigenous peoples.[10]

The Rudd government has also recently pledged its support for the United Nations Declaration on the Rights of Indigenous people. This document includes Article 23 requiring governments to actively involve Indigenous people in developing their own health, housing and social programs. Yet the Race Discrimination Act remains suspended in the Northern Territory, where more than 15,000 Indigenous people are having half of their welfare payments arbitrarily quarantined – a move affecting functional families, pensioners, people who do not drink alcohol or take drugs and families where school attendance is high. The continuation of the benevolent dictator model of intervention ensures that we keep our reputation, amongst many Indigenous Australians, as bossy hypocrites with a 'white man's law' designed to keep black people 'in their place.'

Issues of law, truth and justice linger over the death in custody of Mulrunji and all of the events connected to it. The actions of Palm Islanders in demanding answers led to the most extensive inquiry into police operations since the Fitzgerald Inquiry. The CMC inquiry into the police investigation into the death and the inquiry into the behaviour of the SERT, were followed by the state-wide CMC Inquiry into Policing in Indigenous Communities. Beginning in February 2007, the last of these entailed extensive public forums and submissions. The delivery of findings six months' later disappointed many, with the declaration that no case of substantiated abuse had been established.

Fitzgerald's investigations had exposed the 'police code' of standing by fellow officers at all costs, and of actively obstructing legal challenges to their rule. Yet perhaps there is a lesson, too, in the unfolding of events on Palm Island and the subsequent string of official failure, fiasco and insult to this most vulnerable community, that connects to wider social issues affecting all of us and to the changing nature of the dominant culture over recent decades. Anne Mann defines 'the age' as characterised by 'the new narcissism' and writes:

> With narcissism the problem is not inhibition but *disinhibition;* not too much self control, but too little. Our indulgent love affair with rage, desire, addiction, sex and ambition means there is too little restraint. We lack the kind of tough minded sobriety that comes with the awareness of our capacity to injure others.[11]

In April 2008, a Palm Island police officer fell from the balcony of the police barracks on Palm, after circumventing alcohol restrictions by partying on nearby Orpheus Island[12] — a five star glamour resort offering seven course meals, positioned across the channel from this 'Third World' community like a parallel universe. The wasteful consumption of medical and emergency services that this incident caused seems to have brought no condemnation.

Less than a month later, the Police Department's Ethical Standards Command delivered its findings in a case lodged by Palm Islander, Charlie Gibson. Gibson complained that he had been strip searched by Palm Island police who were looking for alcohol or drugs. The 26-year-old was made to disrobe and expose his genitals, in public and in front of nearby women friends and children. No intoxicants were found. Gibson's complaint was dismissed as 'unsubstantiated'.[13] Just business as usual, on this 'certain paradise for certain people'.

Palm Island
Despite the cascading sadness and despair
People live, love, work, play, pray
And continue to build hope for a future
These people call Palm Island
Home.

Written by Rachael Cummins at the handing down of the court decision: Hurley not guilty.

Notes

Chapter 1
1. Ian Gerard and Tony Koch quote Rosina Norman, 'Hell on the way to island paradise', *Weekend Australian*, 13–14 November 2004, p.6.
2. Michael Madigan and Michael McKenna, 'Paradise Lost', *Courier Mail*, 4 December 2004, p.29.
3. 'Inquest into the Death of Mulrunji, Findings of Christine Clements, Acting State Coroner, Findings of Inquest', Office of the State Coroner, Townsville, 27 September 2006, pp.2–3, http://netk.net.au/Aboriginal/Aboriginal12.asp, accessed 26 May 2007; Andrew Boe, letter to the Honourable PD Beattie, 17 February, 2005, www.boelawyers.com.au, accessed 16 June 2005.
4. 'Inquest' p.2.
5. Chloe Hooper, *The Tall Man: Death and Life on Palm Island*, Penguin, Camberwell, 2008, p. 19.
6. Jeff Waters, *Gone for a song: A death in custody on Palm Island* ABC Books, Sydney 2008, p.19.
7. Leanne Edistone, 'Officer thought dead man was foxing', *Courier Mail*, 5 August 2005, p.1.
8. Jeff Waters, 'Secrecy over Palm Island security video tape', AM, ABC Online, 1 February 2005, http://www.abc.net.au/am/content/2005/s1293303.htm, accessed 2 February 2005.
9. A Boe and P Morreau, Final submission on behalf of the Palm Island Aboriginal Council, Inquest into the Death of Mulrunji on Palm Island on 19 November 2004, Coroner's Court of Queensland at Townsville, 4 July 2006, p.40, www.boelawyers.com.au/documents/Palm/20Island/Coronial/20inquest PIAC, accessed 3 December 2005; Andrew Boe, letter to the Honourable PD Beattie, 17 February 2005; Leanne Edmonstone, 'Court shown video of inmates' final moments', *Courier Mail*, 4 August 2005.
10. Interviews, Palm Island, 23 November 2007.
11. 'Inquest', pp.9–11; Chris Graham, 'Palm Island Riot a sensible, necessary response', *National Indigenous Times*, 19 April 2007, pp.22–24.
12. 'Inquest', p.10; Michael McKenna, 'Police delay Palm death inquiry', *Australian*, 2 November 2007, p.1.

13. Tony Koch, 'Island of Distress', *Australian*, 29 March 2005, p.9; Chloe Hooper, *The Tall Man — Death and Life on Palm Island* (Penguin, Camberwell, 2008, p.46.
14. Interview with Johnnie Cummins, Brisbane, 1 June 2008.
15. Malcolm Weatherup, 'Officers feared for lives as mob rioted', *Townsville Bulletin*, 13 April 2005, p.1; Malcolm Weatherup, 'Police "told of riot but did nothing"', *Townsville Bulletin*, p.1; Interview with Johnnie Cummins, Brisbane, 1 June 2008.
16. Deborah Bird-Rose, *Reports from the Wild Country* UNSW Press, Sydney, 2004, p.22.
17. Malcolm Weatherup, 'Officers feared for their lives as mob rioted'.
18. Interviews with community members, Palm Island, 24–25 November 2007.
19. Malcolm Weatherup, 'Rioter in danger of bullet', *Townsville Bulletin*, 20 April 2005, p.1.
20. Vikki Champion, 'Tasers open to abuse: Amnesty', *Townsville Bulletin*, 21 February 2008, http://townsvillebulletin.news.com.au/html, accessed 24 February 2007.
21. Mike Head, 'Aboriginal death in custody triggers Palm Island riot', *European Network for Indigenous Australian Rights News*, http://www.enair.org/news/palmisland4.html, accessed 14 September 2005.
22. Tony Koch, 'Police accused over terror tactics', *Australian*, 29 November 2004, p.5.
23. Darrell Giles, 'Hunt for weapons as Beattie urges calm', *Sunday Mail*, 28 November 2004, pp.4–5.
24. Michael Madigan and Rae Vallaris, 'Riot island police refuse to go back', *Courier Mail*, 29 November 2004, p.1.
25. Chris Graham, 'Palm Island riot a sensible, necessary response', *National Indigenous Times*, 19 April 2007, pp.22, 24.
26. Andrew Boe and Paula Morreau, Final Submission on behalf of the Palm Island Aboriginal Council, pp.15–18; 'Inquest', pp.23–24.
27. Ian Townsend, 'Palm Island arrests questioned in court', *The World Today*, 26 July 2005, http://www.abc.net.au/worldtoday/content/2005/s1422875.htm, accessed 13 May 2008.
28. ABC Radio News Broadcast, Saturday, 27 November 2004, 7.46am.
29. Palm Island Aboriginal Council, Open Letter to the Premier, the Honourable Peter Beattie, 28 November 2004.
30. 'Indigenous insurrection in Australia over death in custody', *Friends of Grassy Narrows Newsletter*, 26 November 2004; Michael Madigan and Tanya Moore, 'Islanders flee riot', *Courier Mail*, 27 November, p.1.
31. Tony Koch and Greg Roberts, 'Injuries left Palm body "unrecognisable", activist says', *Australian*, 13 December 2004, p.1.
32. Andrew Boe, 'Something is very wrong', ANU Public Lecture Series 2005, National Centre for Indigenous Studies and Centre of International and Public Law, ANU, Canberra 25 September 2005, p.4
33. Interviews with Aboriginal residents of Townsville, 1 June 2008.
34. Hedley Thomas, 'Beattie battles bribe claim', *Courier Mail*, 24 February 2005, http://www.news.com.au, accessed 24 February 2005.

Chapter 2
1. A Queensland term for Aboriginal people.
2. Judy Watson, 'The Hope of Boggo Road', *Sunday Mail Magazine*, 7 May 1989, p.4.
3. 'Palm Island Select Committee Report', Queensland Legislative Assembly, Parliamentary service, Brisbane, Queensland, 2005, pp.16–17 & 53–54; Australian Bureau of Statistics, media release, 26 March 2008, http://www.abs.gov.au/AUSSTATS/abs@nsf/Latestproducts/2033.0.55.001Media, accessed 3 April, 2008.
4. The Honourable Desley Boyle, Ministerial Media Statement, 12 August 2009, http://statements.cabinet.qld.gov.au/MMS/StatementDisplaySingle.aspx?id=65720, accessed 6 October 2009; 'Palm Island Select Committee Report', p.14; Evan Schwarten, 'Bligh govt gears up to negotiate 40-year land leases throughout the state', *National Indigenous Times*, 7 August 2009, p.1.
5. Australian Bureau of Statistics, '2006 Census QuickStats: Palm Island (S) (Indigenous Location). 25 October 2007', http://www.censusdata.abs.gov.au/ABSNavigation/prenav/ProductSelect.html, accessed 2 April 2008.
6. Michael Madigan and Tanya Moore, 'Islanders Flee Riot', *Courier Mail*, 27 November 2004.
7. Dorothy Jones, *Cardwell Shire Story*, Jacaranda, Brisbane, 1961, p.279.
8. Les Malezer, 'Palm Island Award Wages Win Speech', 5 April 1997, www.faira.org.au.
9. *Hansard*, 24 February 2005, p.232, http://www.parliament.qld.gov.au/hansard, accessed 10 November 2009.
10. Jamie Walker, 'Wasted Lives Devoid of Hope', *Courier Mail*, 27 November 2004, p.20; Nick Squires, 'Tourism plan for Queensland Hell Hole', *New Zealand Herald*, 9 April, 2007; Jamie Walker 'Skin Deep', *Courier Mail Good Weekend*, p.18; Mark Todd, 'Tropic of Despair', *Sydney Morning Herald*, 4 December 2004.

Chapter 3
1. Nancy Williams, 'Report on Aboriginal History and Affiliation to Magnetic Island with particular reference to Nelly Bay', Report to Linkon Projects, Surfers Paradise, 1989, pp.29–31.
2. Reg Palm Island, interview with Helen Brayshaw, 1975, James Cook University, Black Oral History Project, tape no. 21A.
3. P Sutton, Preliminary Report, 1970, Official Visits, File GF/26, Townsville, Department of Aboriginal and Island Affairs records, Aitkenvale Hostel; Reg Palm Island, interview with Noel Loos, 1972, James Cook University Black Oral History Project Tape No. 16.
4. Capt WJL Wharton (ed.), *Captain Cook's Journal*, Elliott, London, 1893, p.271.
5. JC Beaglehole (ed.), *The Endeavour Journal of Joseph Banks 1768–1771*, Angus & Robertson, Sydney, 1962, p.76.
6. PP King, *Surveys of Australia 1818–1822*, Vol. 1, John Murray, London, 1969, p.196–97.

7. J Lort Stokes, *Discoveries in Australia*, T and W Boone, London, 1846, p. 338.
8. John MacGillivray, *Narrative of the Voyage of the HMS Rattlesnake Commanded by the Late Captain Owen Stanley RN, FRS, During the Years 1846–1850*, Vol. 1, T and W Boone, London, 1852, p.98.
9. Archibald Meston, *Geographic History of Queensland*, Edmund Gregory, Brisbane, 1985, p.130
10. Edmund Gregory (ed.), *Narrative of James Murrell's Seventeen Years Exile Among the Wild Blacks of North Queensland*, Edmund Gregory, Brisbane, 1896, p.22.
11. Cited in Janice Reid and Peggy Trompf (eds), *The Health of Aboriginal Australia*, Harcourt Brace Jovanovich, Sydney, 1991, p.10.
12. *Courier*, 18 March 1864; 8 December 1864.
13. Police Magistrate Cardwell to Colonial Secretary, 3 October 1864, QSA, COL/A60, No. 2828; and Henry Reynolds, 'The Unrecorded Battlefields of Queensland' in Henry Reynolds (ed.), *Race Relations in North Queensland*, James Cook University, Townsville, 1978, p.31.
14. Police Magistrate Cardwell to Colonial Secretary, 19 January 1865, QSA, COL/A63, No. 159.
15. Sir RW Cilento, *Triumph in the Tropics*, Smith and Paterson, Brisbane, 1959, p.185.
16. WRO Hill, *Forty-Five Years Experience in Northern Queensland*, Pole, Brisbane, 1907, p.31.
17. George Carrington, *Colonial Adventures and Experiences by a University Man*, Bell and Daldy, London, 1871, p.153.
18. Raymond Evans, 'Across the Queensland Frontier' in Bain Attwood and SG Foster (eds), *Frontier Conflict: The Australian Experience*, National Museum of Australia, Canberra, 2003, p.71; P Sellheim, Cooktown, to Colonial Secretary, 17 March 1875, QSA, COL/A215, No. 3239; JCH Gill, *The Missing Coast*, Queensland Museum Cultural Centre, Brisbane, 1988, pp.167, 194, 196).
19. Elizabeth Ann Kumm, Jumbun Lifestyles, Townsville, James Cook University, Grad.Dip.Material Culture, 1980, p.3; Police Magistrate Cardwell to Colonial Secretary, 26 December 1864 and 19 January 1865, QSA, COL/A63, Nos 159 and 157.
20. Cited in Williams, 'Report on Nelly Bay', pp.17–18.
21. George Carrington, *Colonial Adventures*, pp.170–171, 145–146.
22. *Queensland Votes and Proceedings [QVP]*, Vol. XIV, (1872), pp. 323–324.
23. See Roslyn Poignant, *Professional Savages: Captive Lives and Western Spectacle*, UNSW Press, Sydney, 2004.
24. J Bennett to Under-Secretary, 4 July 1914; H Butler and Thos L Francis, letter to Deputy Chief Protector, 3 September 1912; and Maps 1 June 1916 and 6 July 1914, QSA, J/200, Special Bundle on Aborigines marked 'Gall Collection'.
25. Reg Palm Island, interview with Noel Loos; Inspector Sweetman to Chief Protector, 14 June 1913 and see H Butler and Thos L Francis letter to Deputy Chief Protector, 3 September 1912, QSA, J/234, Gall Collection

26. *QPP,* Vol. III (1908), p.925.
27. Isaac Henry to Colonial Secretary, 9 September 1885, COL/A437, No. 6952, QSA.
28. Archibald Meston, 'Report on the Aboriginals of Queensland' in *QVP,* Vol. 4, (1896), pp.727 & 730.
29. Annual Report of the Northern Protector of Aboriginals for 1904, *QPP,* Vol. 1, (1905), p.767.
30. Chief Protector of Aborigines to Under-Secretary, Home Office, 8 November 1916, HOM/J214, Nos 9958–10398, QSA. Superintendents of reserves were responsible to the Chief Protector who was in turn responsible to the Home Secretary's Office. For details of the legislation and subsequent charges see Rosalind Kidd, *The Way We Civilise,* University of Queensland Press, 1997.
31. Dorothy Jones, *The Cardwell Shire Story,* Jacaranda, Brisbane,1961, p.305.
32. Peter Prior, 'Early History of Palm Island' in Aboriginal and Islander Catholic Council: *Let's Rewrite Our History,* 9th Annual Conference, Brisbane, 4–7 January 1982, p.40.
33. 'Annual Report of the Chief Protector of Aboriginals for the Year ended 1914', *QPP,* Vol. III (1915–16), pp.1680 & 1734; 'for the Year 1917', *QPP,* Vol. I (1918), p.1679.
34. Raymond Evans, 'The Duty We Owe', in DJ Murphy et al. (eds), *Labor in Power,* UQP, St Lucia,1980, p. 344; HS Martin, Constable, Cairns to Commissioner of Police, 28 August 1917, A/44743, 61M, No. 27652, QSA.
35. Raymond Evans and Jan Walker, ' "These Strangers, Where Are They Going" – Aboriginal–European Relations in the Fraser Island and Wide Bay Region 1770–1905' in *Occasional papers in Anthropology,* No. 8, March 1977, p.67.
36. 'Report of the Commissioners: Aborigines of Queensland', *Queensland Votes and Proceedings,* Vol. 1 (1874), p.442.
37. Archibald Meston, *Geographic History of Queensland,* Edmund Gregory, Brisbane,1895, p.130.
38. Chief Protector of Aboriginals to Under-Secretary, 6 May 1917 and 28 May 1917, Gall Collection, HOM J200–234, 1915–17, QSA.
39. Woodja (Annie Tallis), interview with author, Palm Island, 28 April 1990, and *Townsville Daily Bulletin,* 12 February 1986, p.13.
40. *North Queensland Register,* 18 March 1918, p.20.
41. Edward Leavy to Chief Protector, 4 April 1918, Gall Collection, A/8724, QSA.
42. *North Queensland Register,* 13 May 1918, p.1 and 8 April 1918, p.34.

Chapter 4

1. In Carol Russell (ed.), *People in Our Community,* James Cook University Union, Townsville, not dated, p.12.
2. Interviewed by Dawn May, 'The Role of the State in Fabricating a Black Working Class in the North Queensland Cattle Industry',

Deborah Wade-Marshall and Peter Loveday (eds), *Employment and Unemployment*, Australian National University, Darwin, 1985, p.210.
3. Bill Rosser, *Dreamtime Nightmares*, AIAS, Canberra, 1985, p.104 & 24; Joe McGinness, *Son of Alyandabu — My Fight for Aboriginal Land Rights*, University of Queensland Press, St Lucia, 1991, p.12.
4. WJ Gall, Under-Secretary to D Riordan, MLA Brisbane, 7 March 1923, and Petition to Riordan, 23 January 1923, HOM/J453, No. 23.593 and 23.640, QSA; Bain Attwood and Andrew Markus, *The Struggle for Aboriginal Rights – A Documentary History*, Allen & Unwin, Crows Nest,1999, p.98.
5. Home Secretary's Register of Letters 1924, HOM/B64, 'Removals', QSA.
6. *Truth*, 24 August 1930, p.13.
7. *The Age*, 31 May 1980, p.3.
8. Mark Copland, Calculating Lives: the numbers and narratives of forced removals in Queensland, 1859-1972, PhD Thesis, Griffith University, School of Arts, Media and Culture, 2005, pp.41–43
9. *North Queensland Register*, 30 June 1924, p.45.
10. *North Queensland Register*, 15 February 1930, p.12.
11. Bain Attwood and Andrew Markus, *The Struggle for Aboriginal Rights*, Allen and Unwin, Crows Nest, 1999, pp.18, 60.
12. CD Rowley, *Outcasts in White Australia*, Penguin, Ringwood, 1970, p.111.
13. 'Report on the Operations of Certain Sub-Departments for 1925', *QPP*, Vol. 1 (1926), p.1021; 'The Palm Islands Settlement and St Anne's Catholic Mission', James Cook University, Townsville, North Queensland Vertical File No. 13, p.6.
14. Bessie Lymburner, interview with author, Townsville, 17 December 1990.
15. 'Report on the Operations of the Sub-Department of Aboriginals for the Year 1919', *QPP*, Vol. II (1920), p.232.
16. *North Queensland Register*, 3 December 1923, p.31.
17. Interview with Joe Garbutt, Tape No. 1A, James Cook University (JCU) Black Oral History.
18. Henry Wilson, interview with author, Palm Island, 10 July 1989; 'The Palm Islands Settlement and St Anne's Catholic Mission', p.5; *Sydney Morning Herald*, 29 June 1929, p.11.
19. Marnie Kennedy, 'The Human Cost', *Asian Bureau Australian Newsletter*, No. 74, May 1984, p.5.
20. 'Report on the Operations of Certain Sub-Departments' for the Years 1922, 1923 and 1929, *QPP*, Vol. 1 (1923), p.1068 & 1071; Vol. 1 (1924), p.978, Vol. 1 (1929), p.953.
21. 'Billions in Stolen Wages', *Townsville Daily Bulletin*, 6 September 2007; Becky Branford, 'Aborigines fight for their money back', BBC News Online, 7 April 2004, http://newswww.bbc.net.uk.
22. Police Report, GA Cameron Inquiry into Palm Island, HOM/J712, 12 March 1929, QSA.
23. Marnie Kennedy, *Born a Half-Caste*, AIAS, Canberra, 1985, pp.8–9.

24. 'Report on the Operations of Certain Sub-Departments for the Year 1923', p.978. Police Magistrate's Report to the Secretary, QSA; Jack Sibley, interview with author, Palm Island, 30 April 1990.
25. 'Report on the Operations of the Sub-Departments', QPP, Vol. 1 (1936), p.1204.
26. Bill Congoo, interview with author, Palm Island, 13 January 1991.
27. *North Queensland Register,* 15 February 1930, p.21.
28. Marnie Kennedy, *Born a Half-Caste*, AIAS, Canberra, 1985, pp.8–9.
29. *Cummins and Campbell's Monthly Magazine*, Vol. IV, No. 21, January 1929, p.31, and Rossiter, Palm Island State School History, p.8.
30. Interview with Joe Garbutt, JCU Black Oral History.
31. Monty and Dot Prior, interview with author, Townsville, 10 January 1990.
32. Elizabeth Burr, *Things As They Were*, Aborigines Inland Mission, Burwood, 1989, p.20.
33. 'Alf Palmer Memories' in *Palm Islander*, Vol. 2, No. 4, 27 January 1978.
34. Rev. D McNab to Colonial Secretary, 9 May 1876, in *Queensland Votes and Proceedings [QVP]*, Vol. 3, (1876), p.161.
35. Richard B Howard, 'Annual Report of the Chief Protector on Aboriginals for the Year 1910', QPP, Vol. III, (1911–12), p.1305.
36. Alexander Crosby Brown, *Horizon's Rim* (Dodd, Meade, 1935), pp.52–53.
37. Cameron Inquiry, QSA.
38. WJ Gall, 'General' Report, Gall Collection, A/8724, QSA.
39. *Truth*, 16 February 1930, p.15.
40. *North Queensland Register*, 22 February 1930, p.44.
41. Statement by WJ Gall, undated, Gall Collection, A/8724, QSA.
42. Interview with Joe Garbutt, JCU Black Oral History.
43. *Truth*, 16 February 1930, p.15.
44. *North Queensland Register,* 8 February 1930, p.6.

Chapter 5
1. Townsville Supreme Court Criminal Files, Rex v. Peter Prior, QSA, A/18421, 1930, 65 A, B, C.
2. Inquest into the deaths of Robert Henry Curry, Robert Curry and Edna Curry, in ASA, JUS/N 260, 1930, 413.M; *Truth*, 17 August 1930, p.15.
3. *Daily Mirror*, 19 June 1966, Townsville, James Cook University, North Queensland, Vertical File Palm Island No. 4; Police Department Commissioner's Office, Miscellaneous Correspondence and Reports, QSA, POL/J21, 413.M; *Sydney Morning Herald*, 5 February 1930, p.15.
4. Machelle Flowers, An Oral History of the Dormitory System, Palm Island State School Library, 1988.
5. Marnie Kennedy, *Born a Half-Caste*, AIAS, Canberra, 1985, pp.12–13.
6. *Truth*, 9 March 1930; Police Department Commissioner's Office, QSA.
7. *Townsville Evening Star,* 6 February 1930; Police Department Commissioner's Office, QSA.
8. *Sydney Morning Herald*, 5 February 1930, p.15; *Townsville Daily Bulletin*, 5 February 1930; *Daily Mail*, 5 February 1930, p.7.

Notes

9. *North Queensland Register*, 10 May 1930, p.23; *Sydney Morning Herald*, 3 May 1930, p.15.
10. Sir R Cilento, letter to Mrs P Cilento, 30 September 1931, Townsville, in Sir R Cilento Collection, Ms 44/16-25b, Box 11, Fryer Library, Brisbane, Unpublished Manuscripts.
11. *North Queensland Register*, 3 May 1930, p.11 and 10 May 1930, p.23.
12. Cilento Collection, Fryer Library.
13. *Daily Standard*, 4 March 1930, Police Department Commissioner's Office, QSA.
14. *North Queensland Register*, 3 May 1930, p.11; *Truth*, 2 March 1930, p.12.
15. *Brisbane Courier*, 5 February 1930, p.15; *Townsville Daily Bulletin*, 5 February 1930.
16. *Daily Standard*, 5 February 1930, p.5; North Queensland Oral History Collection, Tape No. 52, interview by Caroline Edmondson; Alf Palmer in *Palm Islander*, Vol. 2, No. 5, 10 February 1978.
17. *Brisbane Courier*, 4 February 1993, p.13; *Daily Mirror*, 5 February 1930, p.7.
18. *Townsville Evening Star*, 6 February 1930 and *Telegraph*, 11 February 1930; Police Department Commissioner's Office, QSA.
19. *Daily Standard*, 13 February 1930, p.1.
20. *Truth*, 16 February 1930, p.15; *Daily Standard*, 7 February 1930, p.1.
21. *Truth*, 9 February 1930, p.15; Marnie Kennedy, *Born a Half-Caste*, p.12; Interview with Bessie Limburner, 17 December 1990, Townsville.
22. North Queensland Oral History Collection.
23. Sir R Cilento Collection, MS 44/16-25b, Box 11; *Smith's Weekly*, 27 April 1929, p.3.
24. GA Cameron Inquiry into Palm Island, QSA, HOM/J712, 1929.
25. *Daily Standard*, 23 March 1930, p.7.
26. *Daily Mail*, 13 February 1930, p.7.
27. *Daily Mirror*, 19 June 1966.
28. *Smith's Weekly*, 27 April 1929, p.3.
29. *Truth*, 9 March 1930, p.15.
30. *Daily Standard*, 15 April 1930, p.1; Inspector Battersley, Police Commissioner's office, letter to Inspector Loch, Townsville, 10 April 1930, Police Department Commissioner's Office, QSA.
31. *Truth*, 4 May 1930, p.10.
32. *Brisbane Courier*, 7 May 1930, p.20.
33. *Sydney Morning Herald*, 3 May 1930, p.15.
34. *North Queensland Register*, 10 May 1930, p.24.
35. *Daily Standard*, 28 March 1930, p.7; *Brisbane Courier*, 3 May 1930, p.17. *North Queensland Register*, 10 May 1930, p. 23. *Daily Standard*, 10 May 1930, p.23; *Daily Standard*, 1 May 1930, p.7.
36. *Brisbane Courier*, 15 August 1930, p.17; *North Queensland Register*, 16 August 1930, p.94.
37. *Townsville Evening Star*, 14 August 1930, Home Secretary's Department General correspondence, QSA, HOM/J791, No. 7498; *Daily Mail*, 15 August 1930, p.9; *Brisbane Courier*, 15 August 1930, p.17; *North Queensland Register*, 16 August 1930, p.94.

38. Home Secretary's Department General Correspondence, QSA; *Truth*, 16 February 1930, pp.15 and 17 August 1930, p.15.
39. *Daily Mail*, 5 February 1930, p. 7; Interview with Silas Prior, Palm Island, 13 July 1989; Australian War Memorial, Nominal Roll, Australian Imperial Force 1914–18, AWM 133; Correspondence from Central Army Records, Victoria, 8 May 1990.
40. David Kent, 'The Australian Remounts Unit in Egypt 1915–1919: A Footnote to History' in *Journal of the Australian War Memorial*, No. 1, October 1982, pp. 9–12; Correspondence from Central Army Records.
41. HS Rodie, Letter to AD Mackay, Manager for Smith's Newspapers, 17 May 1930, in Gall Collection, QSA, A/8724.
42. North Queensland Oral History Collection.
43. *Daily Standard*, 28 March 1930, p. 7.
44. Alexander Crosby Brown, *Horizon's Rim*, Dodd, Mead, 1935, p.59.
45. *Daily Standard*, 7 February 1930, p.1.
46. *Weekend Australian*, 19–20 October 1991, p.1.; *Guinness Book of Records* 1999 edition cited in Tony Koch and Brenda Malley, 'Palm Island rejects tag as "most violent place on earth" ', *Courier Mail*, 13 November 1998, p.5.

Chapter 6
1. ABC Radio Tapes, *Palm Island*, Part 1, ABC Social History Unit, 1989.
2. J Murphy and F Moynihan (eds), 'The National Eucharist Congress, Melbourne, December 2–9, 1934', *Advocate*, Melbourne 1936, p.199.
3. *Sydney Morning Herald*, 1 August 1932, p.15; Ros Kidd, cited in Palm Island – some fragments of history, The Bartlett Diaries, http://www.andrewbartlett.com, 16 January 2007.
4. Correspondence re Reservation of Palm Island for Aboriginal Purposes, Department of Health and Home Affairs, General Correspondence, QSA, A/27541, 1905–1941.
5. Dr Thos L Bancroft, *Reminiscences of Palm Island*, Brooks, Brisbane, 1933.
6. Dawn May, 'A Punishment Place', in Bill Gammage and Peter Spearritt (eds), *Australians 1938* (Broadway, Fairfax et al., 1987) p.100.
7. Jan Roberts, *Massacres To Mining*, Dove, Blackburn, 1981, p.36; 'Reports upon the Operations of Certain Sub-Departments...for the Year 1935', *QPP*, Vol. 1 (1936) p.1027.
8. Interview by Caroline Edmondson, Tape No. 52, North Queensland Oral History Collection, James Cook University.
9. Bill Rosser, *Dreamtime Nightmares*, AIAS, Canberra, 1985, pp.158–59.
10. ABC Radio Tapes, *Palm Island*, Part 2.
11. *Western Mail*, 20 May 1933.
12. Dora Birtles, *North West by North*, Jonathan Cape, London, 1935, pp.6 and 11.
13. WJ Gall, letter to Chief Protector, 7 September 1933, Department of Health and Home Affairs, General Correspondence, QSA, A/31710, 1930-50, 30; ABC, Aboriginal Reserves, No. 3243/33; 'Reports upon the Operations of Certain Sub-Departments...for the Year 1933', *QPP*, Vol. 1 (1934), p.890.

14. EM Hanlon in *QPD*, Vol. CLXVI, (1934), p.1687.
15. Willie Thaiday, *Under the Act*, Black Publishing, Townsville, North Queensland, 1981, p.27.
16. Letter from ER Gribble to Mr Morley, 2 December 1932, Gribble Papers, AIAS, MS 1515, Box 10.
17. WJ Gall, Memorandum, Impressions of Palm Island, June 1931, Gall Collection, Fryer Library, MSS 43/D/256.
18. Letter from Bishop Feetham, 15 July 1931, Gribble Papers, AIAS.
19. Letters from ER Gribble to Bishop Feetham 17 July 1933 and 21 November 1933, Gribble Papers, AIAS; ER Gribble, 'Events from Thursday September 21st 1933 to October 3rd', Gribble Papers Related to Palm Island, Mitchell Library.
20. Public Service Commissioner's Department Report to Home Secretary, 9 August 1932; 'Report upon the Operations of Certain Sub-Departments... for the Year 1932', p.896; '... for the Year 1935', p.1029; Letters from ER Gribble to Bishop Feetham, Gribble Papers, Mitchell Library.
21. Interview by Caroline Edmondson, Tape No. 52, Oral History, James Cook University, North Queensland.
22. Christine Halse, *A Terribly Wild Man*, Allen and Unwin, Crows Nest 2002, p.180.
23. Bill Congoo, interview with author, 13 January 1991.
24. *Western Mail*, 20 May 1933, John Oxley Library, S.W. Jacks, Cutting Book No. 10, p.12.
25. Elliott Murray, 'Palm Island Memories', p.15; CD Rowley, *The Remote Aborigines*, Social Science Research Council of Australia, Canberra, 1971, p.92.
26. Department of Health, Central Office Correspondence, Multi-Numbered System (First series), 1925–1949, 'Aboriginals – survey of 1932', Australian Archives CRS A1926, Item 4/5, Section 1.
27. WJ Gall, Memorandum re Protection Acts, 1934, 7 August 1934, Gall Collection, A/8724, QSA.
28. 'Reports upon the Operations of Certain Sub-Departments...for the Year 1946', p.1040.
29. Monty and Dot Prior, interview with author, Townsville, 10 January 1991.
30. ABC Radio Tapes, *Palm Island*, Part 2.
31. GD Bradbury, 'Report on the Aboriginal Settlements', p.38.
32. ER Gribble, 'Criticisms and Suggestions', Gribble Papers.
33. Tom Morgan Snr, interview with author, Palm Island, 11 January 1991; John Delaney, letter to ER Gribble, 19 July 1935, Gribble Papers Related to Palm Island, Mitchell Library.
34. Unauthored, 'Palm Island Mission' in *The Annals of the Propagation of the Faith*, 2 October 1933, p.7.
35. Bill Seaton, interview with author, Townsville, 2 July 1991.
36. Bill Rosser, *Dreamtime Nightmares*, p.132.
37. 'Reports upon the Operations of Certain Sub-Departments...for the Year 1932', p.890.
38. GD Bradbury, 'Report on the settlements', p.112.

39. Nancy M Williams, Report on Aboriginal History and Affiliation to Magnetic Island with Particular Reference to Nelly Bay, Report to Linkon Projects, Surfers Paradise, 1989, p.43.
40. *Sydney Morning Herald*, 5 March 1932, p.14.
41. 'Hooligan', *North Queensland Register*, 20 July 1935; 'Hooligan recaptured', *Cairns Post*, 4 December 1935; 'Aborigines Capture', *North Queensland Register*, 7 December 1935.
42. 'Report on the Operations of Certain Sub-Departments...for the Year 1937', *QPP*, Vol. 2 (1938), p.1112; Bain Attwood and Andrew Markus, *The Struggle for Aboriginal Rights*, Allen and Unwin, Crows Nest, 1999, p.102. *Australian Abo Call* was a monthly journal published by the Aborigines Progressive Association.
43. *Courier Mail*, 20 February 1940 p.4; 'The Palm Islands...Missions', p.7; ER Gribble to Canon Garland, 20 January 1937, *Gribble Papers* AIAS, Box 11 Item 63; Willie Thaiday, *Under the Act*, pp.21–22.
44. Bain Attwood and Andrew Markus, *The Struggle for Aboriginal Rights*, pp.60, 101–02; *North Queensland Guardian*, 11 September 1937, p.4; 6 November 1937, p.3 and 20 January 1938, p.2 and 12 February 1938, p.2.
45. Rosalind Kidd, *The Way We Civilise*, University of Queensland Press, St Lucia, 1997, p.171
46. RH Hall, *The Black Diggers*, Allen and Unwin, Crows Nest, 1989, p.116.
47. FA Krause. *The Illustrated Story of a Beautiful Pacific Isle*, Willmetts Print, Townsville, 1946, no page numbers.
48. 'Reports Upon the Operations of Certain Sub-Departments' for the Years 1949, *QPP*, Vol. 3, (1950) p.869, 1950, *QPP*, (1950–51) p.1053.

Chapter 7

1. Cited in DJ McClay, Surviving the Whiteman's World: Adult Education in Aboriginal Society, PhD thesis, University of Queensland, 1988.
2. John Maguire, 'The Fantome Island Leprosarium', Roy MacLeod and Donald Denoon (eds), *Health and Healing in Tropical Australia and Papua New Guinea*, James Cook University, Townsville, 1991, p.148.
3. Queensland Department of Health and Home Affairs, *What is Their Destiny?* Brisbane, s.n., 1933.
4. Dr Elliott Murray, 'Palm Island Memories', *Sydney University Medical Journal*, Vol. 29, August 1935, p.16.
5. 'Report upon the Operations of Certain Sub-Departments' for the Years 1932, *QPP*, Vol. 1, (1933), p.888; 1933, p.884.
6. RW Cilento, letter to Mrs P Cilento, 28 October 1933, Cilento Collection, Fryer Library, MS 44, Box 3, Item 10, New Guinea Letter Book; Bessie Lymburner, interview with author, Townsville, 17 December 1990.
7. RW Cilento, letter to Mrs P Cilento, 25 September 1931, Cilento Collection.
8. Interview by Carol Edmondson, Tape No. 52, North Queensland Oral History Collection, James Cook University; Notes and Diary Entries, Fantome Island Sisters, Townsville, James Cook University, North Queensland Vertical File, Palm Island No. 3.

9. Allan Brandt, 'Aids in Historical Perspective: Four Lessons from the History of Sexually Transmitted Diseases', *American Journal of Public Health*, Vol. 78, No. 4, April 1988, pp.369–370; 'Annual Report of the Director-General of Health and Medical Services, 1934/35', p.8; 'Report upon the Operations of Certain Sub-Departments for the Year 1933', p.883; Saunders and Taylor, 'To Combat the Plague', *Hecate*, No. 1, 1988, p.25.
10. Report Nos 1 & 3 re Palm and Fantome Islands, Department of Health and Home Affairs General Correspondence, QSA, A/4232, 27 December 1940 & No. 8300 of 1941, QSA.
11. JW Bleakley, *The Aborigines of Australia*, Jacaranda, Brisbane, 1961, p.146.
12. 'Report upon the Operations of Certain Sub-Departments' for the Years 1936, pp.1195, 1197 & 1937, p.1102.
13. *Northern Churchman*, No. 542, 1 September 1936, p.6.
14. Annual Report of the Director-General of Health and Medical Services, 1937/38, p.12.
15. Matron A O'Brien to EM Hanlon, 12 March 1940, Department of Health and Home Affairs General Correspondence, A/31756, 1927–1940, No. 2472, QSA; Ludlow, *Peel Island*, p.39.
16. Notes and Diary Entries, Fantome Island Sisters.
17. Cliff Wyles, interview with author, Townsville, 15 July 1990.
18. RW Cilento, Director-General to Under-Secretary, Department of Health and Home Affairs, 9 August 1940, A/31756, QSA; DW Johnson to Deputy Director, Health and Medical Services, 4 April 1940, Home Secretary's Office General Correspondence, 1927–1940, A/31756, 30 a b c, QSA.
19. John Maguire, 'The Fantome Island Leprosarium', p.147.
20. Peter Ludlow, *Peel Island*, Peter Ludlow, Brisbane, 1989, p.104; 'Annual Report of the Director-General of Health and Medical Services, 1949/50', p.19; Sister Paul, interview with author, Palm Island, 14 July 1989.
21. 'Annual Report on the Health and Medical Services of the State of Queensland, 1951/52', p.18; 1952/53, p.20; Paddy Tanner, interview with author, Palm Island, 7 July 1990.
22. Report upon the Operations of Certain Sub-Departments...for the Year 1950, *QPP*, Vol. 2 (1950–51), p.1054.
23. Stephen Hagan, 'A testimony of injustice', On Line opinion, http://www.onlineopinion.com.au/print.asp?article=5425, accessed 11 February 2009.

Chapter 8
1. Willie Thaiday, *Under the Act* (Townsville, North Queensland Black Publishing, 1981); ABC Radio Tapes, *Palm Island — A Punishment Place*, Part II, (ABC Social History Unit, 1989); Alessandro Cavadini and Carolyn Strachan, *Protected*, Australian Film Institute, Melbourne, 1976.
2. See Joanne Watson, 'We couldn't tolerate any more: the Palm Island Strike of 1957', in Ann McGrath & Kay Saunders with Jackie Huggins (eds), *Aboriginal Workers, Special Issue Labour History 69*, November 1995.
3. *Telegraph*, 12 June 1957, p.26.
4. *Telegraph*, 13 June 1957, p.3.

5. List of Deportees, Date Departed Palm and Destination, 1956–59, Palm Island General Correspondence, 1956–59, Townsville, Department of Native Affairs, GF/140, Aitkenvale Hostel.
6. Townsville Daily Bulletin, 19 June 1957, p.2.
7. Telegraph, 13 June 1957, p.3.
8. Tribune, 24 July 1957, p.3.
9. Director of Native Affairs to Superintendents, Woorabinda and Cherbourg, 14 June 1957, 3A/239, Palm Island General Correspondence, 1956–59, GF/140.
10. C O'Leary, Director of Native Affairs to Superintendent, Palm Island, Confirmation of Advice Given to Aboriginals Assembled on Parade, 8am, 3 July 1957, Palm Island, 5 July 1957, Palm Island General Correspondence, 1956–59, GF/140.
11. Angela Burger, *Neville Bonner — a biography*, Macmillan, Melbourne, 1979, p.33.
12. Director of Native Affairs to Palm Island Superintendent, 16 July 1957, Palm Island General Correspondence, 1956–59, GF/140.
13. *Queensland Parliamentary Debates*, Vol. 219, (1957–58), pp.882–883.
14. C O'Leary, Director of Native Affairs to Superintendent, Palm Island Confirmation...5 July 1957, GF/140.
15. *Courier Mail*, 18 January 1958, p.3.
16. 'Select Committee on Voting Rights of Aborigines', Minutes of Evidence, *Commonwealth Parliament*, 1961, Part II, p.85.
17. TDB, 19 January 1974, p.3.
18. Bobbi Sykes, *Love Poems and Other Revolutionary Actions*, University of Queensland Press, St Lucia, 1988, pp.23–24.

Chapter 9
1. 'Director Meets the Press', *Aboriginal Quarterly*, July–September 1968, p.8.
2. 'We say Palm Island is a penal settlement', *Smoke Signals*, Vol. 8, No. 4, June 1970, p.21.
3. 'Select Committee on Voting Rights of Aborigines', *Commonwealth Parliament* [CP], Minutes of Evidence, 1961, Part II, p.92.
4. *Courier Mail*, 21 June 1961, p.9.
5. Inquest into the Death of Henry Pitt, Depositions and Findings in Coroner's Inquests, 1961, 313, JUS/N 1394, QSA; Leonie Daisy, interview with author, Palm Island, 16 January 1991; Jack Sibley, interview with author, Palm Island, 30 April 1990.
6. Ivy Sam, interview with author, Palm Island, 15 January 1991.
7. Leonie Daisy, interview with author, Palm Island, 29 June 1991.
8. *Queensland Parliamentary Debates*, Vol. 230 (1961–62), p.702.
9. Dr Allen Saltau, interview with author, Brisbane, 6 September 1992.
10. Jan Mills, interview with author, Brisbane, 6 November 1991.
11. 'Palm Island Report', *Trend*, February 1970, p.27; Jim Keeffe, 'Island Without Hope', *Aboriginal Quarterly*, June 1969, p.6.

12. Bain Attwood and Andrew Markus, *The 1967 referendum: Race, power and the Australian Constitution*, Aboriginal Studies Press, Canberra, 2007.
13. John Chesterman and Brian Galligan, *Citizens without rights: Aborigines and Aboriginal Citizenship*, Cambridge University Press, Melbourne, 1997, pp.61 & 3.
14. Faith Bandler, *Turning the Tide*, Aboriginal Studies Press, Canberra, 1989, p.33.
15. Bill Rosser, *Dreamtime Nightmares*, AIAS, Canberra,1985, p.140.
16. 'Island looking for its sun', *ATSIC News,* September 2000, http://www.atsic.gov.au/News Room/; Rosalind Kidd, *The Way We Civilise*, University of Queensland Press, St Lucia,1997, p.279.
17. *Australian*, 2 June 1971, p.5; Gordon Bryant, 'Palm Island seen by Labor MPs', *Smoke Signals,* Vol. 9, No. 4, June–August 1971, p.21; Erykah Kyle, 'Breaking the Cycle: A community Initiative', paper presented at the Best Practice Interventions in Corrections for Indigenous Peoples Conference, Australian Institute of Criminology, Sydney, 8–9 October 2001, p.2.
18. HC Coombs, Chairman, Council for Aboriginal Affairs, Premier's Department to Chairman, Aboriginal Council Palm Island, 30 October 1968, Townsville, Department of Aboriginal and Island Affairs Records, Aitkenvale Hostel; Garth Nettheim, 'A Matter of Management?', *University of New South Wales Law Journal*, Vol. 2, 1978, p. 321; D Walker et al., *Conspiracy By The State*, Ad Hoc committee for Defence, Brisbane,1975, pp.14–15 & 22.
19. *Courier Mail,* 4 July 1974, p.1.
20. *QPD*, Vol. 265 (1974), p.719.
21. *Courier Mail,* 11 September 1974, p 1; *Tribune,* 10 September 1974, p.7.
22. *Courier Mail,* 17 September 1974, p.7; Garth Nettheim, 'A Matter of Management?', p.321.
23. *QPD*, Vol. 265 (1974), p. 547; Rosser, *Dreamtime Nightmares*, pp.170–75; Aba Johnson and Leonie Daisy, interview with author, Palm Island, 28 April 1990; *Sunday Mail*, 15 December 1974, p.10; *Australian,* 11 December 1974, p.4.
24. James G Barber et al., 'Alcohol and Power on Palm Island', *Australian Journal of Social Issues,* Vol. 23, No. 2, May 1988, p.92.
25. *Courier Mail,* 22 May 1973, p. 16; Barber et al., 'Alcohol and Power on Palm Island', p.93.
26. *Alcohol Problems of Aboriginals, Final Report, House of Representatives Standing Committee on Aboriginal Affairs*, AGP, Canberra, 1977, p.12.
27. Anastasia M. Shkilnyk, *A Poison Stronger Than Love: The Destruction of the Ojibwa Community*, Yale University, New Haven,1985, p.152.
28. Garth Nettheim, 'A Matter of Management?', p.330.
29. *Sydney Morning Herald,* 1 November 1985, p.1.
30. Erykah Kyle, 'Self Management...A Palm Island Perspective'.
31. Paul Wilson, *Black Death White Hands*, Allen and Unwin, Sydney 1981, p.123.

32. David S Trigger et al., 'Mortality Rates in 14 Aboriginal reserve communities', *Medical Journal of Australia*, Vol. 1, No. 8, April 1983, p.363.
33. John Cavanagh et al., *The World Alcohol Industry*, Transnational Corporations Research, Sydney,1985, p.184.
34. David McKnight, *From Hunting to Drinking: The Devastating Effects of Alcohol on an Australian Aboriginal Community*, Routledge, London, 2002; Richard Trudgeon, *Why Warriors Lie Down and Die*, Aboriginal Resource and Development Services, Darwin, 2000.
35. Barber et al., 'Alcohol and Power on Palm Island', pp. 95–97.
36. S Pitois et al., 'Problems Associated with the presence of cyanobacteria in recreational and drinking waters' in *International Journal of Environmental Health Research*, Vol. 10, No. 3, September 2000, pp. 203–218; Susan Byth, 'Palm Island Mystery Disease', *Medical Journal of Australia*, Vol. 2, 1980.
37. Judith Atkinson, *Trauma Trails — recreating songlines: the transgenerational effects of trauma in Indigenous Australia*, Spinifex Press, North Melbourne, 2003.
38. Judith Hermann, *Trauma and Recovery*, Basic Books, New York, 1997, p. 2, 9, 44–45, 87, 101.

Chapter 10
1. Joanne Watson, 'Always will be: Musgrave Park', in Raymond Evans and Carole Ferrier (eds), *Radical Brisbane, An Unruly History*, Vulgar Press, Carlton North 2004; Queensland's Darkest Days, *The Guardian*, 8 June 2005.
2. Frank Brennan, Forty Years On — The Spirit of the 1967 Referendum after the Hurley Trial and the Howard intervention on Northern Territory Child Abuse, Townsville Catholic Council, Inaugural NAIDOC dinner, Jupiter's Casino, Townsville, 6 July 2007.
3. Rosalind Kidd, *The Way We Civilise*, University of Queensland Press, St Lucia, 1997, p.330.
4. 'Island looking for its sun', *ATSIC News,* September 2000, http://www.atsic.gov.au/News Room/.
5. *Townsville Bulletin*, 27 March 1992, p.3. *Weekend Australian*, 7–8 November 1992, p.60.
6. Frank Brennan, *Land Rights Queensland Style: The Struggle for Aboriginal Self Management*, University of Queensland Press, St Lucia, 1992, pp.33–34, 68.
7. 'Stolen wages, missing Trust funds – the fight for justice in Queensland,' European Network for Indigenous Australian Rights, http://www.enair.Org/action/stolen.html;
8. Chris Graham, 'War waged on black workers', 21 July 2004, http://www.enair.Org/action/stolen.html; Dr Rosalind Kidd, 'Queensland Stolen Wages Fact Sheet, May 2002, http://www.enair.Org/action/stolen.html; Scott Mc Dougall, ' "A Certain Commonality": Discriminating Against

the Discriminated in the Compensation of Queensland's Underpaid Workers', *Indigenous Law Bulletin*, Vol. 5, No. 14, 2002.
9. Submission to the Senate Legal and Constitutional References Committee Inquiry into Stolen Wages, Human Rights and Equal Opportunity Commission, http://www.hreoc.gov.au/legal/submissions/2006/stolen_wages_2006.html, accessed 16 April 2008, accessed 16 April 2008.
10. Lisa Scott, 'Tragedy Island', *Weekend Australian Magazine*, 27–28 July, 1996, p.13.
11. Noel Pearson, Cape York Peninsula Substance Abuse Strategy, September 2002, www.capeyorkpartnerships.com, accessed 11 October 2005.
12. LF Wyvill, *Report of the Inquiry into the Death of Vincent Roy Ryan*, AGPS, Canberra, 1991, p.68.
13. Profiles: Indigenous Deaths in Custody, ATSIC Issues, http://www.atsic.gov.au/issues/law_and_justice/rciadic/indigenous_deaths_custody/ci, accessed 25 August 2005.
14. Race Discrimination Commissioner, *National Inquiry Into Racist Violence, Summary*, Human Rights and Equal Opportunity Commission, Sydney, 1991, pp.2, 4.
15. Henry Reynolds, *Why Weren't We Told?* Viking, Ringwood, 1999, pp.256–57; Interview with Aboriginal community member of Townsville, 25 June 2008
16. Peter Lindsay, Forum concerning Palm Island, http://www.able2know.com/forums/about38727-0.html, accessed 2 February 2005.
17. Roslyn Poignant, *Professional Savages: Captive Lives and Western Spectacle*, UNSW Press, Sydney, 2004; see also, Walter Palm Island, Tambo, in Fforde, Cressida (ed.), *The Dead and Their Possessions*, Routledge, London, 2002.
18. Mark Ludlow, 'Herron Denies Stolen Generation', Courier Mail, 1 April, 2000, p.1; 'Besieged Hayden hits "sorry" campaign', *Courier Mail*, 13 October 2000, p.6.
19. *The 7.30 Report*, Australian Broadcasting Corporation, 16 April 2001, http://www.abc.net.au/7.30/content/2001/s277922.htm, accessed 17 April 2008.
20. Malcolm Brown, 'Life and death on island of despair', *Sydney Morning Herald*, 20 January 2007, p1; Email correspondence, Rachael Cummins, Townsville, 25 June 2008.
21. *Meeting Challenges, Making Choices* Evaluation Report No. 2, September 2005, The State of Queensland, Department of Premier and Cabinet Brisbane, 2005, p.63 and executive summary.
22. *Townsville Bulletin*, 21 January, 2005; Margaret Wenham, 'Aboriginal alcohol fines top $250,000', *Courier Mail*, 22 December 2004; Michael McKenna, 'Leaders warn of grog ban backlash', *Courier Mail*, 26 November 2004, p.5.

23. Carla Schlesinger et al., 'The development and validation of the Indigenous Risk Impact Screen (IRIS)', *Drug and Alcohol Review*, Vol. 26, Issue 2, March 2007, pp.109–117.

Chapter 11
1. Chloe Hooper, *The Tall Man — death and life on Palm Island*. (Camberwell, Penguin, 2008), pp.126, 5–7
2. 'Inquest into the Death of Mulrunji, Findings of Christine Clements, Acting State Coroner, Findings of Inquest', Office of the State Coroner, Townsville, 27 September 2006, pp.2–3, netk.net.au/Aboriginal/Aboriginal12.asp, accessed 26 May 2007, pp.23–24; Malcolm Weatherup, 'That's rubbish', Townsville Bulletin, 3 March 2006, http://www.townsvillebulletin.news.com.au/05942,18333328.00html, accessed 3 March 2006.
3. 'Inquest', p24; Chloe Hooper, The Tall Man: Death and Life on Palm Island, (Camberwell, Penguin 2008), pp126, 125–127; Paul Benedeck, 'Police admit lying during Palm Island trial', Green Left Weekly, 17 October 2008, http://www.greenleft.org/2008/771/39754, accessed 21 October 2008.
4. Michael Madigan, 'Inquest hears abuse claim', *Courier Mail*, 1 March 2006, p.10.
5. Neil Hickey and Amanda Watt, 'Island Outrage', *Courier Mail*, 29 September 2006, p.1.
6. 'A Line in the Sand', *Message Stick*, ABC Television, 6pm, 17 November 2006.
7. Interviews with Aboriginal residents of Townsville, 1 June, 2008.
8. Catherine Donnelly and Stewart Levitt, Media Alert, 'Calls for a fair trial', Thursday 13 July 2006.
9. Chloe Hooper, *The Tall Man*, pp.248–49.
10. 'Opposition calls for Palm Island police commendations', ABC News, 4 June 2008, http://www.abc.net.au/news/stories/2008/06/04/2265439.htm
11. 'Inquest', p.6.
12. Chloe Hooper, *The Tall Man*, pp.2 & 217; *Sunday Arts*, Interview with Chloe Hooper, 9 November 2008, ABC television.
13. Linda Christmas, 'The Tall Man: Death and Life on Palm Island by Chloe Hooper', *Telegraph*, 5 February 2009, http://www.telegraph.co.uk/culture/books/bookreviews/4527913/TheTall Man. accessed 9 February, 2009; Jane Jakeman, 'The Tall Man: Death and Life on Palm Island by Chloe Hooper', *Independent*, 4 February 2009, http://www.independent.co.uk/arts-entertainment/books/reviews/the tall man, accessed 4 February 2009.
14. Chloe Hooper, 'Under the Rainshadow', *The Monthly*, September 2008.
15. 'Inquest', pp.2, 9–10.
16. Chris Graham, 'The Big Read: the thin blue lines', National Indigenous Times, 17 April 2008, http://www.nit.com.au/News/story.aspx?id=14706, accessed 9 November 2009; Michael McKenna, 'Police union chief investigated over auto deal', Australian, 20 October 2007,

www.theaustralian.news.com.au/.../0,25197,22610741-2702,00.
html, accessed 9 November 2009; Ruby Ironside, 'Police union car deals revealed', Courier Mail, 1 February 2008, www.news.com.au/couriermail/...0,23146136-3102.00htm, accessed 9 November 2009
17. Sean Parnell, 'Palm death cop chris Hurley got $100,000 payout', Australian, 28 May 2008, http://www.theAustralian.news.com.au/story/0,25197,2377064-601,00.html, accessed 28 May 2008.
18. Sean Parnell, 'Palm officer paid triple items' value', Australian, 29 May 2008. http://www.theaustralian.news.com.au/story/0,25197, 23775557-5013945,00.html, accessed 2 June 2008.
19 'Palm Island Mayor orders bravery medal cop out of community', National Indigenous Times, 13 November 2008, p.1.

Conclusion
1. Leif Enger, *Peace Like a River* (London, Black Swan, 2002), p.64.
2. Ivy Sam, interview with author, Palm Island, 15 January 1991.
3. Chloe Hooper, *The Tall Man — Death and Life on Palm Island* (Camberwell, Penguin, 2008), p.118.
4. Vince Mundraby, Palm Island resident, *Courier Mail*, 29 November 2004, p.1; Murrandoo Yanner, 'Palm Island family urged to take action', *The West*, 21 June 2007, http://www.thewest.com.au, accessed 21 June 2007.
5. Mark Todd, 'Decades of despair', *Sydney Morning Herald*, 4 December 2004, http://www.smh.com.news/National/Tropic-of-despair/2004/12/03/1101923341699, accessed 2 March, 2006.
6. Palm Island Alcohol Management Plan (AMP) – an issues paper prepared by the Palm Island Aboriginal Shire Council, http://www.kalkadoon.org/index.php/2006/07/02/palm-island-management-plan.html,_accessed 20 November 2006.
7. Palm Island Select Committee Report, Queensland Legislative assembly, Parliamentary service, Brisbane, Queensland, 2005, pp.16–17 & 53–54.
8. Gavin H Mooney, 'Addictions and social compassion', *Drug and Alcohol Review*, March 2005, 24, p.137.
9. Terri Elliott-Farrelly, 'Australian Aboriginal suicide: The need for an Aboriginal suicidology?' *Australian e-Journal for the Advancement of Mental Health*, Vol. 3, Issue 3, 2004, p.5.
10. Joel Gibson, 'Black-white life gap gets wider', *Sydney Morning Herald*, 25 June 2008, http://www.smh.com.au/news/national/black-white-life-gap-gets-wider/2008/06/02/4124073247003.html, accessed 28 June 2008.
11. Anne Manne, 'What about me? The new narcissism', *Monthly*, June 2006, p.39.
12. 'Palm Island police officer falls off balcony', *ABC News*, 24 April 2008, http://www.abc.net.au/news/stories/2008/04/24/2226929.htm, accessed 17 June 2008.
13. Peter Michael, 'Tension rises on Palm Island', *Courier Mail*, 6 June 2008, p.2.

Bibliography

Official sources, unpublished

Department Of Family Services And Aboriginal And Islander Affairs, Brisbane.
Uncatalogued Bundles, Correspondence and Reports re Palm Island, 1950–1965.

Department Of Family Services And Aboriginal And Islander Affairs, Townsville, Aitkenvale Hostel
Department of Native Affairs:
. Fantome Island General, 1968–1973, GF/1.
. Staff General, Palm Island, 1957–August 1966, GF/20.
. Official Visits, Palm Island, April 1967–November 1970, F/26.
. Requisitions for Supplies, Palm Island, GF/60.
. Palm Island, General Correspondence, 1956–1959, GF/140.

Queensland State Archives
Clerk of Petty Sessions, Cardwell Letterbook, CPS 12J/W9.
Colonial Secretary's Office:
    General Correspondence: 1861 to 1894.
    In-Letters: 'Escorts — Prisoners, Aboriginals and Lunatics', 61, 1906–1951.
Department of Health and Home Affairs:
    General Correspondence: 1925 to 1942.
    Correspondence re Aboriginal Reserves: A/27541, re Reservation of Palm Island (1905–41); A/31710, 30 ABC (1930–50); A/3811, 14001–14200 (1935); A/4291, 5201–5400 (1942).
    Correspondence re Lazarets: COL/323 (1904–40); COL/325 (1905–40); A/31756, 30 ABC (1927–40); A/31757 (1941–44).
    Institutional Registers: A/4751 (1926); A/4065 (1939); B/573 (1941).
Department of Public Instruction:
    EDU/Z, Palm Island School Files (1925–36).
Gall Collection, Home Office:
    HOM/J234, 4774-5375 (1912–17); A/8724, Memorandum re Protection Acts (1934).
Home Office:
    Registers of General Correspondence: HOM/B1–B77 (1896–1930).
Home Secretary's Department:
    Correspondence re Barambah: A/31708, 30 ABC (1909–25).
    General Correspondence: 1911 to 1930.

In-Letters: HOM/A23, 4589-8961 (1899); HOM/J56, 55-1777 (1910); HOM/J60, 4305-4759 (1910).
Re Staff: COL/150, 30 ABC (1927-58); HOM/J66, 2799 (1930).
Register of Letters, B64, Removals (1924).
Justice Department:
Depositions and Findings in Coroners' Inquests: JUS/N37, 101-200 (1873); JUS/N712, 558 (1920); JUS/N907, 260, 413.M (1930); JUS/N1394, 313 (1961).
Lands Office:
General Correspondence: A/27541, Palm Island Papers, (1937).
Police Department:
Police Files: POL/J21, M413, Aboriginal Reserves (1903-48); POL/J21, M417, Burial of Aboriginals (1903-46); POL/J30, M510, 516/30, Aboriginal Deserters from Settlements (1930).
Premier's Department:
In-Letters: PRE/A436, 7003-7464 (1913); PRE/A969, 4402-4672 (1929).
Protector of Aborigines, Letterbook, A/20595 (1916-30).
Survey Office:
Survey Files: A/27541 (1905-41); A/27767 (1940-46).
Townsville Supreme Court:
Criminal Files: A/18421, 57-99, (1930).
Treasury Department:
Reports: TRE/A18, 1130-2774 (1877).
Works Department:
WOR/B61, 26/16682 (1892-1928).

Official sources, published

Alcohol in Australia: A Summary of Related Statistics, Commonwealth Department of Health Central Statistics Unit, Canberra, 1979.

Alcohol Problems of Aboriginals, Final Report, House of Representatives Standing Committee on Aboriginal Affairs, AGPS, Canberra, 1977.

Annual Reports, Departments Pertaining to Aboriginal Affairs, 1899-1979, *Queensland Parliamentary Papers*.

Annual Reports, Director-General of Health and Medical Services, 1934/35-1937/38.

Annual Reports, Health and Medical Services, State of Queensland, 1945-1975.

Racist Violence, Report of National Inquiry into Racist Violence in Australia, AGPS, Canberra, 1991.

Report on Aboriginal and Torres Strait Islanders on Queensland Reserves, Senate Standing Committee on Constitutional and Legal Affairs, Australian Senate, Canberra, 1978.

Royal Commission into Aboriginal Deaths in Custody
Johnston, Commissioner Elliott, National Report — Overview and Recommendations, AGPS, Canberra, 1991.
Muirhead, Commissioner JH, Interim Report, AGPS, Canberra, 1988.

Wyvill, Commissioner LF, *Regional Report of the Inquiry in Queensland*, AGPS, Canberra, 1991.
Wyvill, Commissioner LF, *Report of the Inquiry into the Death of Vincent Roy Ryan*, AGPS, Canberra, 1991.
Select Committee on the Voting Rights of Aborigines, Vol. 2, 1961, Australian House of Representatives Report.
The Epidemiology of Leprosy in Australia, Cecil Cook. Report of Investigation in Australia during the Years 1923–1925, Commonwealth of Australia, Department of Health, Service Publication No. 38, 1927.
Queensland Parliamentary Debates, 1912–1974.
Queensland Votes and Proceedings, 1897–1901.

Unpublished manuscripts

Australian Institute of Aboriginal and Torres Strait Islander Studies, Canberra
    Gribble Papers, MS 1515.
    Laycock, Donald, Port Stewart Languages, 1964, MS 270.
    Tsundda, Tasuku, Report on Fieldwork, 1974, MS 709.
Fryer Library, Brisbane
    Cilento Collection, MSS 44/16–266, Box 20; MSS 44/144, 143–156, Box 21; MSS 44/150.
    Gall Collection, MSS 43/D245; MSS 43/D256; MSS 43/D260.
    Gribble, John B, Papers, MSS 2/130.
    Hayes Scrapbooks, Boxes 22, 23.
Mitchell Library, Sydney
    Gribble Papers, ML MSS 4503.

Primary books

Bancroft, Thos L, *Reminiscences of Palm Island*, Brooks, Brisbane, 1933.
Beaglehole, JC (ed.), *The Endeavour Journal of Joseph Banks 1768–1771*, Angus and Robertson, Sydney, 1962.
Birtles, Dora, *North West by North – a Journal of a Voyage*, Jonathan Cape, London, 1935.
Bleakley, JW, *The Aborigines of Australia*, Jacaranda, Brisbane, 1961.
Brassie, T Alnutt, *Sixteen Months' Travel 1886–87*, Spottiswood and Co., London, 1988.
Brown, Alexander Crosby, *Horizon's Rim*, Mead, Dodd, 1935.
Carrington, George (ed.), *Colonial Adventures and Experiences by a University Man*, Bell and Daldy, London, 1871.
Carron, WM, *Narrative of the Expedition Undertaken Under the Direction of the late Mr Assistant Surveyor EB Kennedy*, Kemp and Fairfax, Sydney, 1849.
Cilento, Sir RW, *Triumph in the Tropics*, Smith and Paterson, Brisbane, 1959.
Congoo, Bill, *Stories from Palm Island*, Townsville Cultural Association et al., Townsville, 1981.

Gribble, ER, *The Problem of the Australian Aboriginal*, Angus and Robertson, Sydney, 1932.
Hill, WRO, *Forty-Five Years Experience in Northern Queensland*, Pole, Brisbane, 1907.
Hooker, Sir Joseph D (ed.), *Journal of the Right Hon. Sir Joseph Banks*, Macmillan, London, 1989.
Huxley, TH (ed.), *Diary of the Voyage of the HMS Rattlesnake*, Chatto and Windus, London, 1935.
Jack, Logan R, *North Most Australia* Vols 1 and 2, George Robertson, Melbourne, 1922.
Johnstone, Richard Arthur, *Spinifex and Wattle — Reminiscences of Pioneering in North Queensland*, Bolton, Cairns, not dated.
Jukes, J Beete (ed.), *Narrative of the Surveying Voyage of HMS Fly* Vol. I, T&W Boone, London, 1847.
King, PP, *Survey of Australia 1818–1822* Vol. I, John Murray, London, 1969.
Krause, FA, *The Illustrated Story of a Beautiful Pacific Isle*, Willmetts Print, Townsville, 1946.
Lang, Gideon, *The Aborigines of Australia*, Wilson and Mackinnon, Melbourne 1865.
MacGillivray, John, *Narrative of the Voyage of the HMS Rattlesnake Commanded by the Late Captain Owen Stanley RN, FRS During the Years 1846–1850*, Vols I and II, T&W Boone, London, 1852.
Moresby, Capt John, *Discoveries and Surveys in New Guinea and D'entrecasteaux Islands*, John Murray, London, 1876.
Moresby, John, *Two Admirals*, John Murray, London, 1909.
Perry, Harry C, *A Son of Australia — Memories of WE Parry-Okeden 1840–1926*, Watson and Ferguson, Brisbane, 1928.
Roth, Walter E, *Ethnological Studies Among the North West — Central Queensland Aborigines*, Edmund Gregory, Brisbane, 1897.
Spry, WJJ, *The Cruise of the HMS Challenger*, Sampson, Low et al., London, 1880.
Stokes, J Lort, *Discoveries in Australia*, Vols 1 and 2, T. & W. Boone, London, 1846.
Wallis, Arthur E, *The Cruise of the Ellengowan*, New Century Press, Sydney, 1924.
Wharton, Capt WJL (ed.), *Captain Cook's Journals*, Eliot, London, 1893.

Primary serials and articles

AIA News, Queensland, 1979–84.
Australian Board of Missions Review, 1930–34.
Cummins and Campbell's Monthly Magazine, 1927–48.
Houzé, E and Jacques, V, 'Les Australiens du Musee du Nord', *Bulletin of Social Anthropology de Bruxelles*, Vol. 3, 1884.
Murray, R Elliott, 'Palm Island Memories', *Sydney University Medical Journal*, Vol. 29, August 1935.
Northern Churchman, 1936–51.

North Queensland Ethnography Bulletin, No. 5, 1903.
North Queensland Naturalist, 1945.
Parsons, EW, 'Palm Islands, Townsville', *Bank Notes*, November 1931.
Queensland Geographic Journal, 1907–09.
Queensland Naturalist, 1929–30, 1974.

Primary newspapers

Age, 1980.
Argus, 1933, 1950.
Australian, 1970–74, 2004–2008.
Brisbane Courier, 1930.
Bulletin, 1929–30.
Cooktown Courier, 1874–78.
Courier, 1864.
Courier Mail, 1930–58, 1973–74, 1988–93, 2004–2009.
Daily Mail, 1930.
Daily Standard, 1929, 1930.
Land Rights News, 1988.
Leader, 1918–19.
National Indigenous Times, 2005–2009.
North Queensland Guardian, 1937–38.
North Queensland Register, 1918, 1923, 1930, 1937.
Palm Islander, 1977–78.
Queenslander, 1885, 1889, 1918.
Smith's Weekly, 1929.
Smoke Signals, 1962, 1970–74.
Sydney Morning Herald, 1926–37, 1957, 1985.
Telegraph, 1957, 1973–74.
Townsville Bulletin, 1986–92; 2004–2008.
Townsville Daily Bulletin, 1885, 1887–88, 1919–20, 1928, 1930, 1957.
Townsville Evening Star, 1930.
Townsville Herald, 1918.
Tribune, 1957, 1961.
Truth, 1930, 1955.
Warwick Daily News, 1973.

Newspaper cutting books

John Oxley Memorial Library, Brisbane
   Aboriginal Cutting Book
   Collinson, J, Cutting Book.
   Hurd, RS, *Cutting Book No. 2*.
   Illidge, *Cutting Book*.
   Jacks, SW, *Cutting Book*.
Oral history collections and interviews

ABC Social History Unit, *Palm Island, A Punishment Place*, Parts 1 and 2 (1989).
James Cook University of North Queensland
. James Cook University Black Oral History Project
. North Queensland Oral History Project Tapes 1, 2 and 52.

Private Collection

Interview with Reg Dodd, by Therese Forde (1990).
Interviews with George Sturges, Sister Paul and Mrs Krause by Chris Halse (1985).
Interviews by author (1989–2008)
    Burns, Arthur and Ryan, Betty
    Congoo, Bill
    Cummins, Johnnie and Rachael
    Daisy, Leonie and Johnson, Aba
    Lymburner, Bessie
    McAvoy, Thelma
    Miller, Sissy
    Mills, Jan
    Morgan, Tom
    Paul, Sister
    Prior, Monty and Dot
    Prior, Silas and Kippy
    Ryan, George
    Saltau, Allen
    Sam, Ivy
    Seaton, Bill
    Sibley, Jack and Jean
    Tallis, Annie
    Wilson, Henry
    Wyles, Cliff

Secondary books

Altman, John and Hinkson, Melinda, *Coercive Reconciliation*, Arena, North Carlton, 2007.
Atkinson, Judy, *Trauma Trails: Recreating Song Lines. The Transgenerational Effects of Trauma in Indigenous Australia*, Spinifex Press, Melbourne, 2003.
Attwood, Bain, *The Making of the Aborigines*, Allen and Unwin, Sydney 1989.
—— *Rights for Aborigines*, Allen and Unwin, Crows Nest, 2003.
Attwood, Bain and Markus, Andrew, *The Struggle for Aboriginal Rights – A Documentary History*, Allen and Unwin, Crows Nest, 1999.
—— *The 1967 referendum: Race, power and the Australian Constitution*, Aboriginal Studies Press, Canberra, 2007.

Attwood, Bain and Foster, SG (eds), *Frontier Conflict: The Australian experience*, National Museum of Australia, Canberra, 2003.
Bandler, Faith, *Turning the Tide*, Aboriginal Studies, Canberra, 1989.
Bird-Rose, Deborah, *Reports from a Wild Country*, UNSW, Sydney, 2004.
Bolton, GC, *A Thousand Miles Away*, Jacaranda, Brisbane, 1963.
Brady, Maggie. *Indigenous Australia and Alcohol Policy*, University of New South Wales Press, Sydney, 2004.
—— (ed.) *Giving away the Grog: Aboriginal accounts of drinking and not drinking*, Drug Offensive, Commonwealth Department of Human Services and Health, Canberra, 1995.
Brayshaw, Helen, *Well Beaten Paths*, James Cook University Department of History, Townsville, 1990.
Brennan, Frank, *Land Rights Queensland Style, The Struggle for Aboriginal Self-Management*, UQP, St Lucia, 1992.
Brennan, Frank and Egan, John, *Finding Common Ground, An Assessment of the Bases of Aboriginal Land Rights*, Dove, Blackburn 1985.
Brugger, Suzanne, *Australians and Egypt, 1914–1919*, MUP, Melbourne, 1980.
Burger, Angela, *Neville Bonner, A Biography*, Macmillan, Melbourne, 1979.
Burr, Elizabeth, *Things As They Were*, Aboriginal Inland Mission, Burwood, 1989.
Chesterman, John, *Civil Rights: How Indigenous Australians Won Formal Equality*, University of Queensland Press, St Lucia, 2005.
Chesterman, John and Galligan, Brian, *Citizens without rights: Aborigines and Aboriginal citizenship*, Cambridge University Press, Melbourne, 1997.
Connors, Libby, Finch, Lynette, Saunders, Kay and Taylor, Helen, *Australia's Frontline, Remembering the 1939–45 War*, UQP, St Lucia, 1992.
Cunneen, Chris, *Conflict, Politics and Crime – Aboriginal Communities and the Police*, Allen and Unwin, Crows Nest, 2001.
Doyal, Lesley with Penell, Imogen, *The Political Economy of Health*, Pluto Press, London, 1983.
Dudgeon, Pat with Garvey, Darren and Pickett, Harry, *Working with Indigenous Australians: A Handbook for Psychologists*, Gunada Press, Curtin University Research Centre, Perth, 2000.
Enger, Leif, *Peace Like a River*, Black Swan, London, 2004.
Evans, Raymond, *Loyalty and Disloyalty. Social Conflict on the Queensland Homefront, 1914–18*, Allen and Unwin, Sydney, 1987.
—— *The Red Flag Riots, A Study of Intolerance*, UQP, St Lucia, 1988.
—— *A History of Queensland*, Cambridge University Press, Melbourne, 2007.
Evans, Raymond et al., *Exclusion, Exploitation and Extermination. Race Relations in Colonial Queensland*, ANZ, Brookvale, 1975.
Evans, Raymond and Ferrier, Carole (eds), *Radical Brisbane – an unruly history*, Vulgar Press, Carlton North, 2004.
Finnane, Mark (ed.), *Policing in Australia – Historical Perspectives*, New South Wales University Press, Kensington, 1987.
Forde, Cressida (ed.), *The Dead and Their Possessions*, Routledge, London, 2002.
Foucault, Michel, *Discipline and Punish*, Penguin, Harmondsworth, 1977.

Gibson-Wilde, Dorothy, *Gateway to a Golden Land — Townsville to 1884*, James Cook University Studies in North Queensland History Unit No. 7, Townsville, 1984.
Gill, JCH, *The Missing Coast*, Queensland Museum Cultural Centre, Brisbane, 1988.
Graham, Duncan, *Dying Inside*, Allen and Unwin, Crows Nest, 1989.
Guthrie, Gerard, *Cherbourg, A Queensland Aboriginal Reserve*, University of New England Department of Geography, Armidale, 1976.
Haebich, Anna, *Broken Circles*, Fremantle Arts Press, Fremantle, 2002.
Hall, Robert A, *The Black Diggers*, Allen and Unwin, Crows Nest, 1989.
Hazlehurst, Kayleen M (ed.), *Ivory Scales — Black Australia and the Law*, NSW University Press, Sydney, 1987
Hercus, Louise and Sutton, Peter (eds), *This is What Happened*, AIAS, Canberra, 1986.
Hermann, Judith, *Trauma and Recovery*, Basic Books, New York, 1997.
Hooper, Chloe, *The Tall Man — death and life on Palm Island*, Penguin, Camberwell, 2008.
Human Rights and Equal Opportunity Commission, *The Provision of Health and Medical Services to the Aboriginal Communities of Cooktown, Hopevale and Wujal Wujal*, Human Rights and Equal Opportunity Commission, Canberra, 1991.
Hunter, Ernest, *Aboriginal Health and History: Power and prejudice in remote Australia*, Cambridge University Press, Cambridge, 1993.
Hunter, E, Brady, M and Hall, W, *National Recommendations for the Clinical Management of Alcohol-Related Problems in Indigenous Primary Care Settings*, Common Department of Health and Aged Care, Canberra, 1999.
Hunter, Ernest, Reser, Joseph, Baird, Mercy and Reser, Paul, *An Analysis of Suicide in Indigenous Communities of North Queensland: The Historical, Cultural and Symbolic Landscape*, Commonwealth Department of Health and Aged Care, Commonwealth of Australia, Canberra, 2001.
Jones, Dorothy, *The Cardwell Shire Story*, Jacaranda, Brisbane, 1961.
—— *Hurricane Lamps and Blue Umbrellas*, Bolton, Cairns, 1973.
—— *Trinity Phoenix, A History of Cairns*, Cairns and District Centenary Committee, Cairns, 1976.
Keen, Ian (ed.), *Being Black – Aboriginal Cultures in 'Settled' Australia*, Aboriginal Studies Press, Canberra, 1988.
Kennedy, Marnie, *Born a Half-Caste*, AIAS, Canberra, 1985.
Kerr, James Semple, *Out of Sight – Out of Mind: Australia's Places of Confinement 1788–1988*, Australian Bicentennial Authority, Sydney, 1988.
Kidd, Rosalind, *The Way We Civilise*, UQP, St Lucia, 1997.
—— *Black Lives, Government Lies*, University of New South Wales Press, Sydney, 2000.
—— *Lectures on North Queensland History*, James Cook University Department of History, Townsville, 1974.
—— *Lectures on North Queensland History*, Second Series, James Cook University, Townsville, 1975.
Lippmann, Lorna, *Generations of Resistance, The Aboriginal Struggle for Justice*, Longman Cheshire, Melbourne, 1981.

Lishman, WA, *Organic Psychiatry, the Psychological Consequences of Cerebral Disorder*, Blackwell Scientific, Oxford, 1978.

Long, JPM, *Aboriginal Settlements — A Survey of Institutional Communities in Eastern Australia*, ANU, Canberra, 1970.

Ludlow, Peter, *Peel Island, Paradise or Prison?*, Peter Ludlow, Brisbane, 1989.

McGrath, Ann and Saunders, Kay, with Jackie Huggins, *Aboriginal Workers*, Special Issue, *Labour History* 69, November 1995, University of New South Wales, Sydney.

McGinness, Joe, *Son of Alyandabu, My Fight For Aboriginal Land Rights*, UQP, St Lucia, 1991.

McKernan, Michael, *The Australian People, The Great War*, Nelson, Melbourne, 1980.

McKnight, David, *From Hunting to Drinking: The Devastating Effects of Alcohol on an Australian Aboriginal Community*, Routledge, London, 2002.

MacLeod, Roy and Denoon, Donald (eds), *Health and Healing in Tropical Australia and Papua New Guinea*, James Cook University, Townsville, 1991.

Malezer, Les et al., *Beyond the Act*, FAIRA, Brisbane, 1979.

May, Dawn, *From Bush to Station – Studies in North Queensland History* No. 5, James Cook University, Townsville, 1983.

Nairn, Bede and Serle, Geoffrey (eds), *Australian Dictionary of Biography*, Vol. 7, 1891–1931, MUP, Carlton, 1979.

Nettheim, Garth, *Outlawed*, ANZ, Sydney, 1973.

—— *Victims of the Law*, Allen and Unwin, Sydney, 1981.

Patience, Allan (ed.), *The Bjelke-Petersen Premiership 1968–1983, Issues in Public Policy*, Longman Cheshire, Melbourne, 1985.

Patrick, Ross, *A History of Health and Medicine in Queensland 1824–1960* (St Lucia, UQP, 1987).

Peterson, Nicholas (ed.), *Tribes and Boundaries in Australia*, AIAS, Canberra, 1976.

—— *Aboriginal Land Rights, A Handbook*, AIAS, Canberra, 1981.

Phillips, Gregory, *Addictions and Healing in Aboriginal Culture*, Aboriginal Studies Press, Canberra, 2003.

Phillips, Sandra, Phillips, Jean, Whatman, Sue and McLaughlin, Juliana (eds), *(Re) Contesting Indigenous Knowledges and Studies*, The Australian Journal of Education Supplement, Vol. 36, 2007.

Pike, Douglas (ed.), *Australian Dictionary of Biography* Vol. 2, 1788–1850, MUP, Melbourne, 1967.

—— *Australian Dictionary of Biography* Vol. 4, 1851–1890, Melbourne University Press, Melbourne, 1972.

Plomley, NJB (ed.), *Weep in Silence*, Blubber Head, Hobart, 1987.

Poignant, Roslyn, *Professional Savages: Captive Lives and Western Spectacle*, UNSW Press, Sydney, 2004

Pryor, Boori (Monty) with Meme McDonald, *Maybe Tomorrow*, Penguin, Ringwood, 1998.

Read, Peter, *A Hundred Years War*, Pergamon, Rushcutters Bay, 1988.

Reid, Janice (ed.), *Body Land and Spirit, Health and Healing in Aboriginal Society*, UQP, St Lucia, 1982.

Reynolds, Henry, *Aborigines and Settlers*, Cassell, Melbourne, 1972.

—— *The Other Side of the Frontier*, Penguin, Ringwood, 1982.
—— *Dispossession*, Allen and Unwin, Sydney, 1989.
—— *Why weren't we told?*, Penguin, Ringwood, 1999.
—— *An Indelible Stain? The question of genocide in Australia's History*, Viking, Ringwood, 2001.
—— *North of Capricorn. The Untold Story of Australia's North*, Allen and Unwin, Crows Nest, 2003.
Reynolds, Henry (ed.), *Race Relations in North Queensland*, James Cook University, Townsville, 1978.
Rosser, Bill, *This is Palm Island*, AIAS, Canberra, 1978.
—— *Dreamtime Nightmares*, AIAS, Canberra, 1985.
Rowley, CD, *Outcasts in White Australia*, Penguin, Ringwood, 1970.
—— *The Remote Aborigines*, Social Science Research Council of Australia, Canberra, 1971.
Russell, Carol, *People in Our Community*, James Cook University Union, Townsville, not dated.
Saggers, Sherry and Gray, Dennis, *Dealing with Alcohol: Indigenous Usage in Australia, New Zealand and Canada*, Cambridge University Press, Cambridge, 1998.
Sargent, Margaret, *Australian Studies, Drinking and Alcoholism in Australia, A Power Relations Theory*, Longman Cheshire, Melbourne, 1979.
Shkilanyk, Anastasia H, *A Poison Stronger Than Love, The Destruction of an Ojibwa Community*, Yale University Press, New Haven, 1985.
Stevens, FS (ed.), *Racism — The Australian Experience* Vols 1 and 2, ANZ, Sydney, 1972.
Swain, Tony and Bird-Rose, Deborah (eds), *Aboriginal Australians and Christian Missions*, Australian Association for the Study of Religions, Bedford Park 1988.
Sykes, Bobbi, *Love Poems and Other Revolutionary Actions*, UQP, St Lucia, 1988.
Taffe, Susan, *Black and white together: FCAATSI: the Federal Council for the Advancement of Aborigines and Torres Strait Islanders 1958–1973*, University of Queensland Press, St Lucia, 2005
Tatz, Colin, *Race Politics in Australia* University of New England Press, Armidale, 1979.
Thaiday, Willie, *Under the Act*, North Queensland Black Publishing, Townsville, 1981.
Tindale, Norman B, *Aboriginal Tribes of Australia*, University of California, Berkeley, 1974.
Trigger, David S, *Whitefella Comin', Aboriginal Responses to Colonialism in Northern Australia*, Cambridge University Press, Cambridge 1992.
Trudgeon, Richard, *Why Warriors Lie Down and Die*, Aboriginal Resource and Development Services, Darwin, 2000.
Walker, D, Garcia, J and Lacey, L, *Conspiracy by the State*, Ad Hoc Committee for Defence, Brisbane, 1975.
Waters, Jeff, *Gone for a song — a death in custody on Palm Island*, ABC Books, Sydney, 2001.

Watson, Lilla J, *Minority Groups in America, Their Struggle and Ours*, Race Relations Committee, Surry Hills, 1975.
Williams, Nancy M, *Two Laws, Managing Disputes in a Contemporary Aboriginal Community*, AIAS, Canberra, 1987.
Wilson, Paul, *Black Death, White Hands*, Allen and Unwin, Sydney, 1981.

Secondary serials and articles

Aboriginal Law Bulletin, 1981–87.
Aboriginal Quarterly, 1968–69.
Advocate, 1936.
Anderson, Christopher, 'Queensland Aboriginal Peoples Today' in Holmes, JH (ed.), *Queensland, A Geographical Interpretation, Queensland Geographical Journal*, 4th Series, Vol. 1, 1986.
Attwood, Bain. 'Understandings of the Aboriginal Past, History or Myth', *Australian Journal of Politics and History*, Vol. 34 and Supp. No. 2, 1988.
—— 'Aborigines and Academic Historians, Some Recent Encounters', *Australian Historical Studies*, No. 94, April 1990.
Australia Productivity Commission. Overcoming Disadvantage: Key Indicators 2007: Indigenous Report, Australian Government Printer, Canberra, 2007.
Barber, James G. et al., 'Alcohol and Power on Palm Island', *Australian Journal of Social Issues*, Vol. 23, No. 2, May 1988.
Behrendt, Larissa and Watson, Nicole. 'Good intentions are not good enough', *The Australian Literary Review*, 2 May 2007.
Bourke, ATC et al., 'An Outbreak of Hepato-Enteritis (The Palm Island Mystery Disease) Possibly Caused by Algal Intoxication', *Toxicon*, Suppl. 3, 1983.
Brady, Maggie, 'Broadening the Base of Interventions for Aboriginal People with Alcohol Problems', National Drug & Alcohol Research Centre, Technical Report 29, UNSW, 1966.
Brady, M, Dawe, S and Richmond, R, 'Expanding Knowledge among Aboriginal service providers on treatment options for excessive alcohol use', *Drug and Alcohol Review*, Vol. 17, No. 1, 1998.
Brandt, Allan M, 'AIDS in Historical Perspective, Four Lessons from the History of Sexually Transmitted Diseases', *American Journal of Public Health*, Vol. 78, No. 4, April 1988.
Brown, Ron, 'Australian Indigenous Mental Health', *Australian and New Zealand Journal of Mental Health Nursing*, Vol. 10, No. 1, 2001.
Byth, Susan, 'Palm Island Mystery Disease', *The Medical Journal of Australia*, Vol. 2, 1980.
Collinson, JW, 'Cardwell, A Gateway to the West', *Historical Society of Queensland Journal*, Vol. IV, No. 2, December 1949.
Colliver, FS, 'The Endeavour and Aboriginal Australian Contacts', *Queensland Naturalist*, Vol. 20, 1–3, 1971.
de Maria, William, '"White Welfare, Black Entitlement", The Social Security Access Controversy, 1939–59.' *Aboriginal History*, Vol. 10, Part 1, 1986.

Eckermann, AK, 'Half-Caste ... Out-Caste.' *Occasional Papers in Anthropology*, No. 6, July 1976.
Evans, Raymond, 'Queensland's First Aboriginal Reserve', *Queensland Heritage*, Vol. 2, No. 4, 1971.
—— 'The Hidden Colonists' in Roe, Jill (ed.), *Social Policy in Australia – Some Perspectives*, Cassell, Stanmore, 1976.
—— 'Aborigines – The Duty We Owe' in Murphy, DJ et al. (eds), *Labor in Power*, UQP, St Lucia, 1980.
—— 'A Permanent Precedent, Dispossession, Social Control and the Fraser Island Reserve and Mission, 1897–1904', *Ngulaid*, No. 5, 1991.
Evans, Raymond and Walker, Jan, '"These Strangers, Where Are They Going?" Aboriginal-European Relations in the Fraser Island and Wide Bay Region 1770–1905.' *Occasional Papers in Anthropology*, No. 8, March 1977.
Frawley, K, 'European Exploration and Early Images of Northeast Queensland 1770–1880', *Journal of Australian Studies*, No. 10, June 1982.
Graham, Mary, 'The Philosophical Underpinnings of Aboriginal World Views', *Insight*, February 2004.
Guthrie, Gerard, 'Authority at Cherbourg', *Occasional Papers in Anthropology*, No. 6, July 1976.
Healy, Bill et al., 'Aboriginal Drinking, A Case Study in Inequality and Disadvantage', *Australian Journal of Social Issues*, Vol. 20, No. 3, 1985.
Horner, Jack, 'Blacks and Whites Together, Memories of Anti-Racist Campaigning 1956–1973', *Politics*, xi, No. 1, 1976.
Hooper, Chloe, 'The Tall Man', *The Monthly*, March 2006.
—— 'Under the Rainshadow', *The Monthly*, September 2008.
Human Rights Commission, 'Aboriginal Reserve By-Laws and Human Rights', *Occasional Papers*, No. 5, AGPS, Canberra, 1983.
Hunter, Catherine, 'Palm Island – the truth behind the media portrayal. An Interview with Erykah Kyle', *Indigenous Law Bulletin*, Vol. 6, No. 12, July 2005.
Hunter, Ernest, 'Aboriginal Mental health awareness: an overview', *Aboriginal and Torres Strait Islander Health Worker Journal*, Vol. 17, No. 1, January/February 1993.
—— 'What are the prospects of harm reduction approaches in aboriginal Australia?', *Drug and Alcohol Review*, Vol. 15, No. 4, 1996.
—— 'Staying tuned to developments in Indigenous health: reflections on a decade of change', *Australasian Psychiatry*, Vol. 11, No. 4, 2003.
Jebb, Mary Ann, 'The Lock Hospitals Experiment: Europeans, Aborigines and Venereal Disease' in Reece, Bob and Stannage, Tom (eds), *European-Aboriginal Relations in Western Australian History*, Vol. VIII, December 1984.
Jones, Dorothy, 'The Centenary of Cardwell, The Story of a Frontier Outpost', *Royal Historical Society of Queensland*, Vol. VII, No. 2, 1963–64.
Jose, DG et al., 'A Survey of Children and Adolescents on Queensland Aboriginal Settlements 1967', *Australian Paediatric Journal*, No. 5, 1969.
Laurie, Arthur, 'The Black War in Queensland', *Royal Historical Society of Queensland Centenary Journal*, Vol. VI, No. 1, September 1959.

Lincoln, Robyn A et al., 'Mortality Rates in 14 Queensland Aboriginal Reserve Communities', *The Medical Journal of Australia*, Vol. 1, No. 8, 16 April 1983.

Loos, NA, 'Aboriginal Resistance on the Mining, Rainforest and Fishing Frontiers', *Lectures on North Queensland History*, Vol. 1, 1974.

—— 'Aboriginal Resistance in North Queensland', *Lectures on North Queensland History*, 3rd Series, James Cook University Department of History, Townsville, 1979.

—— 'Queensland's Kidnapping Act, The Native Labourers' Protection Act of 1884', *Aboriginal History*, Vol. 4, No. 2, December 1980.

Manne, Anne, 'What about me? The New Narcissism', *The Monthly*, June 2006.

Marchisotti, Daisy, 'History of the Land Rights Struggle in Queensland', *Australian Left Review*, No. 64, 1978.

May, Dawn, 'The Articulation of the Aboriginal and Capitalist Modes on the North Queensland Pastoral Frontier', *Journal of Australian History*, No. 12, 1983.

—— 'The Role of the State in Fabricating a Black Working-Class in the North Queensland Cattle Industry' in Wade-Marshall, Deborah and Loveday, Peter (eds), *Employment and Unemployment, A Collection of Papers*, ANU North Australian Research Unit, Darwin, 1985.

McCausland, Ruth, 'Shared Responsibility Agreements: Practical reconciliation or paternalist rhetoric?', *Indigenous Law Bulletin*, Vol. 6, No. 12, July 2005.

McDougall, Scott, '"A Certain Commonality": Discriminating Against the Discriminated in the Compensation of Queensland's Underpaid Workers', *Indigenous Law Bulletin*, Vol. 5, No. 14, 2002.

Mitchell, Kathleen, 'Reflections on Palm Island', *Nelen Yubu*, No. 15, March 1983.

Mooney, Gavin H, 'Addictions and social compassion', *Drug and Alcohol Review*, 24, March 2007.

Moran, M, 'Housing and Health in Indigenous Communities in the USA, Canada and Australia: the significance of economic empowerment', *Aboriginal and Torres Strait Islander Health Bulletin*, No. 7, 2003.

O'Neil, Shorty, 'Green Mangoes?', *Care Newsletter*, No. 18, 1980.

O'Shane, Pat, 'The psychological impact of white settlement on Aboriginal people', *Aboriginal and Islander Health Worker Journal*, Vol. 19, No. 3, 1995.

Palm Island Aboriginal and Islander Council, 'Palm Island Report', *Trend*, February 1970.

Pearson, Noel, 'The Deed of Grant in Trust', *Aboriginal Law Bulletin*, Vol. 2, No. 38, June 1989.

Reynolds, Henry, 'The Other Side of the Frontier', *Historical Studies*, Vol. 17, No. 66, 1966.

—— 'Violence, The Aboriginals and the Australian Historian', *Meanjin Quarterly*, Vol. 31, 1972.

—— 'Aboriginal Resistance in Queensland', *Australian Journal of Politics and History*, Vol. XXII, 1976.

—— 'The Land, the Explorers and the Aborigines', *Historical Studies*, Vol. 19, No. 75, October 1980.

Rigby, Bruce, 'Land Rights in Queensland', *Social Alternatives*, Vol. 2, No. 2, 1981.

Rowland, MJ, 'The Distribution of Aboriginal Watercraft on the East Coast of Queensland', *Australian Aboriginal Studies*, No. 2, 1987.

Sanders, DF, 'Parasitology, Palm Island Aboriginal Settlement', *Institute of Medical Research Nineteenth Annual Report*, 1964 and 1965.

Saunders, Kay and Taylor, Helen, '"To Combat the Plague", The Construction of Moral Alarm and State Intervention in Queensland During World War II', *Hecate*, Vol. 14, No. 1, 1988.

Schlesinger, Carla et al., 'The development and validation of the Indigenous Risk Impact Screen (IRIS): a 13 item screening instrument for alcohol and drug and mental health risk', *Drug and Alcohol Review*, Vol. 26, Issue 2, March 2007.

Stevens, Frank, 'Protection or Persecution Board, Aboriginal Policy in North Australia', *Dissent*, No. 24, 1969.

Sutton, Peter, 'The politics of suffering: Indigenous Policy in Australia since the Seventies', *Anthropological Forum*, Vol. 11, No. 2, 2001.

Tatz, CM, 'Queensland's Aborigines: Natural Justice and the Rule of Law', *The Australian Quarterly*, Vol. XXXV, No. 3, September 1963.

—— 'The Politics of Aboriginal Health', Supplement to *Politics*, Vol. VIII, No. 2, November 1972.

Thorpe, William, 'Archibald Meston and Aboriginal Legislation in Colonial Queensland', *Historical Studies*, Vol. 21, No. 82, April 1984.

Trigger, David, 'Blackfellas and Whitefellas, The Concept of Domain and Social Closure in the Analysis of Race Relations', *Mankind*, Vol. 16, No. 2, August 1986.

Trigger, David S et al., 'Mortality Rates in 14 Queensland Aboriginal Reserve Communities', *The Medical Journal of Australia*, Vol. 1, No. 9, April 1983.

Unauthored, 'Palm Island Mission', *The Annals of the Propagation of the Faith*, October 1933.

Welbourne, Suzanne, 'Politicians and Aborigines in Queensland and Western Australia', *Studies in Western Australian History*, No. 11, March 1978.

Wilson, MJ, 'Northern Territory Diocese and Missions', *Nelen Yubu*, No. 12, June 1982.

Wilson, Paul, 'Black Death, White Hands Revisited – The Case of Palm Island', *Australian and New Zealand Journal of Criminology*, No. 18, March 1985.

Unpublished secondary theses

Anderson, Christopher, The Political and Economic Basis of Kuku-Yalanji Social History (PhD Thesis, University of Queensland, 1984).

Blake, Thomas, A Dumping Ground, Barambah Aboriginal Settlement 1900–45 (PhD Thesis, University of Queensland, 1991).

Brayshaw, Helen, Aboriginal Material Culture in the Herbert/ Burdekin District, North Queensland (PhD Thesis, James Cook University, 1977).

Copland, Mark, Calculating Lives: the numbers and narratives of forced removals in Queensland 1859–1972. (PhD Thesis, Griffith University, 2005).
Evans, KE, Missionary Effort Towards the Cape York Aborigines 1880–1910, A Study of Culture Contact (BA Hons Thesis, University of Queensland, 1969).
Evans, Raymond L, Charitable Institutions of the Queensland Government to 1919 (Masters Thesis, University of Queensland, 1969).
Ford, Therese, Confinement and Control, A History of Woorabinda Aboriginal Community 1927–1990 (BA Hons Thesis, University of Queensland, 1990).
Griffin, HM, Frontier Town, The Early History of Townsville and Its Hinterland, 1864–1884 (BA Hons Thesis, James Cook University, 1983).
Kumm, Elizabeth, Jumbun Lifestyle (Graduate Diploma in Material Culture, James Cook University, 1980).
McClay, DJ, Surviving the Whiteman's World: Adult Education in Aboriginal Society, (PhD Thesis University of Queensland, 1988).
Trigger, David Samuel, Doomadgee – A Study of Power Relations and Social Action in a North Australian Aboriginal Settlement (Honours Thesis, University of Queensland, 1985).

Other sources, published

Aboriginal and Islander Catholic Council, *Let's Rewrite Our History* (9th Annual Conference, Brisbane, 4–7 January 1982).
Abschol, *Apartheid in Queensland, Abschol Seminar 1968* (Brisbane, Abschol, 1968).
Alcohol and Drugs Working Group, Apunipima Cape York Health Council and Cape York Partnerships under direction of Noel Pearson, Cape York Peninsula Substance Abuse Strategy, September 2002. www.capeyorkpartnerships.com.
Australian Bureau of Statistics, 2006 Census QuickStats: Palm Island (S) (Indigenous Location).25 October 2007. http://www.censusdata.abs.gov.au/ABSNavigation/prenav/ProductSelect.html Accessed 2 April 2008.
Boe, Andrew, Final submissions on behalf of Palm Island Aboriginal Council, attachment B — Summary of relevant prior complaint evidence, Inquest into the death of Mulrunji on Palm Island on 19 November 2004, www.boelawyers.com.au/documents/Palm/20Island/Coronial/20inquest   PIAC. Accessed 3 December 2005.
Indigenous Male Health Report, Canberra, Office of Aboriginal and Torres Strait Islander Health, Commonwealth Dept Health & Ageing, 2002.
Inquest into the Death of Mulrunji, Findings of Christine Clements, Acting State Coroner, Findings of Inquest, Office of the State Coroner, Townsville, 27 September 2006, pp.2–3, netk.net.au/Aboriginal/Aboriginal12.asp Accessed 26 May 2007.
Legislative Assembly of Queensland, Palm Island Select Committee Report, August 2005. (Brisbane, The State of Queensland).
North Queensland Vertical File, Miscellaneous Published Items re Palm Islands, Townsville, James Cook University Library.

Palm Island Alcohol Management Plan (A.M.P.) – an issues paper prepared by the Palm Island Aboriginal Shire Council, http://www.kalkadoon.org/index.php/2006/07/02/palm-island-management-plan.html. Accessed 20 November 2006.

Pearson, Noel, Outline of a Grog and Drugs (and therefore Violence) Strategy, July 2001. www.capeyorkpartnerships.com.

Protected, Australian Film Institute, Melbourne, 1976.

Queensland Government, *Commission of Inquiry into Abuse of Children in Queensland institutions*, Queensland Government, Department of Families, Youth and Community care, Brisbane, 1999.

—— *Meeting Challenges, Making Choices: Evaluation Report*, The State of Queensland, Department of Premier and Cabinet, Queensland Government, Brisbane, 2005.

—— *The Aboriginal and Torres Strait Islander Women's Task Force on Violence Report*, The State of Queensland, Department of Aboriginal and Torres Strait Islander Policy and Development, Brisbane, 1999.

Remote Aboriginal and Torres Strait Islander Community Futures, ATSIS, Canberra, 1990.

Submission to the Senate Legal and Constitutional References Committee Inquiry into Stolen Wages, Human Rights and Equal opportunity commission, http://www.hreoc.gov.au/legal/submissions/2006/stolen_wages_2006.html. Accessed 16 April 2008.

Uncivilized, Expeditionary Films, 1933.

Other sources, unpublished

Blakely, Robert, Palm Island Visions: A Local Government Perspective. The Brisbane Institute seminar, 6 March 2001.

Boe, Andrew, Something is very wrong, ANU Public Lecture Series 2005, National Centre for Indigenous Studies and Centre of International and Public Law, ANU, Canberra, 25 September 2005.

Brady, Maggie, Brief Interventions with Indigenous People. APSAD Alcohol and Drug Conference, Brisbane 16–19 November 2003.

Frank Brennan, Forty Years On — The Spirit of the 1967 Referendum after the Hurley Trial and the Howard intervention on Northern Territory Child Abuse, Townsville Catholic Council, Inaugural NAIDOC dinner, Jupiter's Casino, Townsville, 6 July 2007.

FAIRA, Aborigines, Archaeologists and the Rights of the Dead. World Archaeological Congress Inter-Congress on Archaeological Ethics and the Treatment of the Dead, University of South Dakota, 7–10 August 1989.

Gibons, Merv., Anthropology and Tradition, A Contemporary Aboriginal Viewpoint. ANZAAS Congress, Townsville, James Cook University, 1987.

Kidd, Michael, Aboriginal Mental Health and Economic Rationalism. Social Justice, Social Judgment Conference, University of Western Sydney, April 1998.

Kyle, Eryka, Self-management ... A Palm Island Perspective. Remote Aboriginal and Torres Strait Islander Communities Futures Conference, James Cook University, Townsville, 1990.

Langton, Marcia, A New Deal? Indigenous development and the Politics of Recovery. Charles Perkins Memorial Lecture, Canberra, 2002.
Maguire, Dr J, The Fantome Island Leprosarium, Health and Health Issues in Tropical Australia. ANZAAS Congress, James Cook University, Townsville, 1987.
Needham, John, Report on the Aborigines of Australia for Australian Board of Missions, April 1925. Australian Institute of Aboriginal Studies, Miscellaneous Items.
North Queensland Vertical File, Miscellaneous Unpublished Items re Palm Island, James Cook University Library, Townsville.
Pearson, G, 'Man Cannot Live by Service Delivery Alone', Opportunity and Prosperity Conference, Melbourne, 13 November 2003.
Powder, P and Law, E 1991, 'The Powder-Law Report on the Incidence of Rising Suicides by Aborigines on Queensland Communities Whilst in Custody', Report to RC Katter, Northern Development and Community Services.
Reser, P et al., Alcohol Consumption Patterns and Consequences in North Queensland, A Report of Preliminary Findings Concerning the Association Between Alcohol Use and Attempted Suicide in Aboriginal Communities in North Queensland. Remote Aboriginal and Torres Strait Islander Community Futures Conference, James Cook University, Townsville, 1990.
Spruyt, Danielle, Who's Dysfunctional? The Drawing Board: An Australian Review of Public Affairs. Symposium: Indigenous Futures, University of Sydney, Sydney, 7 June 2004.

Palm Island State School Library
Flowers, Machelle, An Oral History of the Dormitory System (1988).
List of Removals to Palm Island, 1921 (Townsville, Roman Catholic Archives).
Maguire, John, Catholic Missions to the Aborigines in North Queensland (1984).
Nutley, David, Palm Island, Five Oral Histories.
Rossiter, Alan, Palm Island State School History, 1918–1988.
Willis, Patricia, Palm Island History.

St Michael's Catholic Primary School, Palm Island
Catholic Church Register of Births, Deaths and Marriages, 1930.
Catholic Church Register of Baptisms, 1932–42.

Index

ABC, 11, 102, 149
Aboriginal and Torres Strait Islanders' (Queensland Discriminatory Laws) Act, 127
Aboriginal Coordinating Council, 129, 139
Aboriginal councils, 18, 128, 139
 alcohol, 131–133
 Deeds of Grant in Trust (DOGITS), 136
 dismissals, 130
 Mapoon, 78
 see also Palm Island Aboriginal Council
Aboriginal Land Act 1991, 137, 159
Aboriginal Legal Service, 15
Aboriginal Legal Services, 139
Aboriginal Protection Acts (Queensland Acts), 31, 39, 42–43
 1930s changes, 80, 93–94
 1965 changes, 125
 1970s, 127, 128; alcohol provisions, 131–132
 1970s protests against, 128–130
 employment under, *see* employment
 exemption under, 43, 101, 116
 removal under, *see* removals
 State Children's Act 1911, 78–79
Aboriginal Protection Property Account, 44
 see also Trust Fund
Aboriginal Quarterly, 125, 127
Aborigines and Torres Strait Islander (Land Holding) Act, 136
Aboud, J, 123
abscondings, *see* escapes
Act Confrontation Committee, 128, 129

activism, 39, 88–89, 102–103, 125–131, 135–136
 wages campaign, 126, 127, 128, 137, 138–139
 see also protests; strikes
African-Americans, 89–91, 125
agriculture, 29, 33, 42–43, 79, 115
 child labour, 85
 pig farms, 30
 removal of infrastructure, 136
 Second World War, 89
 stockmen, 37, 43, 126
 Superintendents' expertise, 81
Aikens, Tom, 116
Aitkenvale, 21, 118, 139, 159
alcohol, 131–134, 139, 154, 158
 deaths in custody related to, 140–141
 Mulrunji's consumption, on day of arrest, 2, 13
alcohol canteen, 18, 131–132
alcohol consumption by whites, 50, 53, 75, 82, 112
 Curry, Robert, 51–52, 65, 68, 74, 75
 Pattison, Dr Charles, 46, 52
alcohol restrictions, 144–145, 158, 160
 after Mulrunji's death, 6, 12
 punishment for drinking in 1960s, 121
 supply to Murri residents in Curry's time, 52, 66
Alley, Charles, 55, 66
America, 29, 142
Americans, 89–91
Amnesty International, 128
Anglican Church, 49, 119
 Fantome Island, 97, 99
 Gribble, Reverend Ernest, 80–83, 84, 85–86, 88, 91

197

Index

Anning, Caesar, 60, 69, 70, 71
Arnhem Land, 133
arrests, 105, 129, 136, 144–145
   Cannon, Noel, 148
   escapees, 88
   Mulrunji, 2–3, 146
   after Mulrunji's death, 9–14, 149–150, 152
   after Nevitt Inquiry, 66
   Pitt, Henry, 122
   Prior, Peter, 69
   strikers, 110, 112–113, 118
   see also deaths in custody
assault charges and allegations, 81, 82
   Curry, Robert, 44–46, 50, 51, 52, 54–75
   Pattison, Dr Charles, 46, 52
   see also deaths in custody
assimilation, 43, 49, 83, 105–106
Atkinson, Judy, 134
Aurukun, 118, 130–131, 144
Aurukun Associates Agreement Act 1975, 130
Australian (newspaper), 10, 128
Australian Abo Call, 88
Australian Broadcasting Corporation (ABC), 11, 102, 149
Australian Council of Trade Unions, 126
Australian Labor Party, 128, 129
   Bligh government, 18, 156
   Gair government, 115
   Goss government, 137
   Keating government, 142, 143
   Tucker, Percy, 124, 127
   Whitlam government, 127, 130
   see also Beattie, Peter
Australian Sisters of Our Lady of Help, 94, 99
autopsies and autopsy reports, Mulrunji's death, 5, 6–7, 13, 15, 146, 149

Baira, Jacob, 133
Baira, Jacob Jnr, 6
Ballard, Elizabeth, 52, 58, 60, 63, 67, 70–71
Ballard, Leonard, 56, 57, 60, 63, 75
   assaults by Curry, 50, 51
   Curry's letter to *Truth*, 67, 68
   Curry's words to, before death, 62
   home, 41
   relationship with Pattison, 46, 52, 65

   testimony at Curry deaths inquest, 67, 73
Bamaga, 115, 118
Bancroft, Dr Thomas L, 77, 79, 81, 84, 86
Bandler, Faith, 126
bandroom, 60–61
bands, 49, 83, *between pp. 110–111*
banking, *see* Trust Fund
Banks, Joseph, 25, 26
Barambah, *see* Cherbourg
Barambah, Willie, 60
Barnes, Michael, 15, 16
Barnum, Bailey and Hutchinson's 'Greatest Show on Earth', 29, 142
Barrett, Coroner BD, 140
Barry, Police Sergeant Greg [Jack], 113
Barry, Police Sergeant Jack, 111
Bartlam, Roy Henry, x, 91, 103–125, 155
bauxite mining, 118, 130
Beagle, 26
Beattie, Peter, and Beattie government, 10, 11, 13, 137, 153, 155
   Cape York Justice Study, 144
   description of Palm Islanders, 19
   Queensland Public Prosecutor's Volkers decision, 150
   reparation for underpaid and stolen wages, 43, 138–139
   state of emergency after Mulrunji's death in custody, 7–13, 153
   visits to Palm Island, 12–13, 15–16, *between pp. 110–111*, 150
bêche-de-mer fishing, 29, 30, 85, *between pp. 110–111*
Beckett, Clive, 59, 60, 61, 70, 71
Beckett, Les, 153
beer, *see* alcohol
Bell, Diamond, 124
bells, 41, 85, 104, 111, 120
Bengaroo, Police Liaison Officer Lloyd, 2, 3, 5, 6, 146, 152
Bessie Point, 119
Big Snake, *see* Carpet Snake
'Binagury', 82
Birri Gubba, 40
Bismark, Robert 'Bobby', 100–101
Bjelke-Petersen, Johannes, and Bjelke-Petersen government, 125, 127–131, 135–137
Black Cat squadron, 89–91

Blackman, William, 10, 152
Blanket, Dwayne, 152
Bleakley, Chief Protector JW, 32, 73, 78, 80, 84
  applications for exemptions, 43
  Curry's correspondence with, 46, 67, 68–69
  dormitory system, 38
  education, views on, 49, 87
  escapes, reports on, 47, 88
  Fantome Island reports, 93, 95–96
  gazettal of Palm Island group, 77
  Hull River, 33
  Palm Island visits, 34, 35, 51
  recommendations to establish Palm Island reserve, 33–34
  sexual relations policy, 48
Bligh, Anna, and Bligh government, 18, 156
Bligh, Keith, 123
Bligh, Kitchener, 137
Blue, Archie, 46
Bly, Nellie, 61
boatshed, 57, 60, 61
Boe, Andrew, 4, 14, 15, 16, 151, 153
Bonner, Alfred, 3
Bonner, Neville, 107, 116–117, 129
Bonner, Patrick, 130
Borbidge government, 137–138
'bottom end', 22
Bowen, 27
boys' dormitories, *see* dormitories
Brackenbridge, Fred, 88
Bradbury, GD, 85
Brady, Pastor Don (Qwanji), 104, 109, 127, 128
Bramble Reef, 29
Bramwell, Patrick, 2, 3, 4, 14–15, 147
  death, 150–151
  rumours about release from police cells, 5
Bramwell, Roy, 2, 3–4, 5, 150, 152
  at inquests, 15, 147
brass bands, 49, 83, *between pp. 110–111*
Brennan, Frank, 135–136
Bringing Them Home Report, 143
Brisbane, 14, 20–21
  Commonwealth Games, 135–136
Brisbane Exhibition Grounds, 44
Brisbane Legal Services, 128
Brisk Island, 77, 88

Britton, Detective Sergeant, 12
Brown, Alexander Crosby, 74
Buchanan, Jimmy, 122
Bulsey, David, 13–14
Buluguyban, 25, 30–31, 40
Burketown, 3, 37, 147
Butler, Harry, 29–30
Butler Bay, 6, 10, 29–30
Butler's Guest House, 29–30, 50, *between pp. 110–111*
Butlervale, 83
Bwgcolman, 19–23, 143
Bwgcolman Land Trust, 159

Cairns, 13, 37, 38, 129
  police, 9, 33
Cairns Trades and Labour Council, 117
Cameron, GA, 52
  Curry deaths inquest, 62–63, 64–71
  inquiry into alleged flogging by Curry, March 1929, 45–46, 65
Campbell, Jack, 57–58, 59, 60
Canada, 133–134
Cannon, Noel, 147, 148
Cannon Bay, 91
canteen, 18, 131–132
Cape Cleveland, 27
Cape Pallarenda, 25
Cape York Justice Study, 144
Cardwell and Cardwell region, 18, 27–29, 34, 106
  Hooligan's escape to, 87–88
  Hull River, 32–33, 34–35
Carpet Snake, 19, 24–25, *between pp. 110–111*
Carpet Snake Creek, 24
Carrington, George, 28
Carter, Commissioner William, 138
Casement Bay, 21
cash economy, 126
Castors, Beryl, 127
Catholic Church, xi, 21, 48–49
  church seating, 83
  Fantome Island, 83, 94, 97, 99–100
Cavadini, Alessandro, 102, 120
Cavanagh, James, 129
Cavendish Road High School, 20
census, 126
Central Australasian, 28–29
Cerico, Sid, 88
Challenger Bay, 40, 60, *between pp. 110–111*

Chances, 50, 74
Cherbourg (Barambah), 34, 41, 75, 89
  removals from Palm Island, 46, 115, 117
  removals to Palm Island, 17
child endowment, 139
child labour, 78–79, 85
children, 9–11, 13–14
  deaths, 29, 89, 91, 124, 134
  evacuation during Second World War, 90
  Fantome Island admittances, 95–96
  punishment, 44, 47, 48, 49, 86, 128
  see also dormitories; schooling
children, removal of, 33, 38, 78–79, 142
  after Mulrunji's death in custody, 6, 150
  Bringing Them Home Report, 143
  Gribble's views, 83
  RCIADIC findings, 139, 140
Chillagoe, 25
Christianity, *see* church and religion
Christmas Day, x
  1929, 52, 65, 73
church and religion, 48–49, 86, 110, 122, 127
  Presbyterian Church, 118, 130
  see also Anglican Church; Catholic Church
Chuter, CE, 73
Cilento, Dr Raphael, 84, 94–95, 98
citizenship, 126
Clare, Leanne, 150, 151, 155
Clay, Assan, 10
Clay, Douglas, 147, 148–149
Clay, Fred, 109, 127, 130
  Council Chair, 128–129, 131
  escape to mainland, 88
  recollections of dormitory life, 86
Clay, Iris, 22, 125, 127, 130
  recollections of queuing for rations, 39
  recollections of removal to Palm, 78
Clay, Noby, 2
Clay, Ricky, 130
Clements, Deputy Coroner Christine, 16, 146–147, 149, 152
  comments on police investigation, 5, 12
Cleveland Bay, 27
Cleveland Bay Express, 28
Cloncurry, 78
clothing, 39, 89, 90, 107–108
Clumpoint, John, 152

colonisation, *see* invasion and frontier conflict
Comalco, 118
Committee to Defence Black Rights, 139
Commonwealth Constitution, 126
Commonwealth Electoral Act 1962, 125–126
Commonwealth Games, 135–136
Commonwealth Select Committee on Voting Rights of Aborigines, 119, 121
Community Justice Groups, 142
Community Services (Aborigines) Act 1984, 136
'Concerned Palm Islanders' group, 127, 137
Congoo, Bill, 103, 104, 105
  Councillor, 128, 129
  escape attempts, 47, 108
  recollections of work, 85, 106
  strike, 109, 110, 111, 112, 113, 114, 115
Constitution, 126
Conway, Harold, 69, 71
Cook, Captain James, 25–26
Cooke, Sub-Inspector, 111, 113
Cooktown, 30
Coolburra, Edna, 2
Coolgaree Bay, 19, 30
Coolgaree Bay Hotel, 139
Copland, Mark, 38
Cordelia Rock, 24
Cornell, Edward Arnold, 81
coronial inquiries, *see* inquests
corporal punishment, *see* floggings
corroborees, 49, 83, *between pp. 110–111*
Council for Aboriginal Reconciliation, 142
councils, *see* Aboriginal councils
Courier, 27
Courier Mail, 11, 84, 119, 129, 148
court trials and actions, 138, 142, 150
  after Curry's rampage, 71–72
  after Mulrunji's death in custody, 147, 149–150, 152, 155, 156; Hurley's, 151, 152–153, 156
  see also inquests
Courtney, Dr CA, 82, 97–99
Coutts, Buller, 137
Cowderry, Nicholas, 150
Crime and Misconduct Commission (CMC), 4, 6, 16, 146, 149, 153

findings on Queensland Public Prosecutor's Volkers decision, 150
fraudulent valuations of QPUE vehicles investigation, 155
Inquiry into Policing in Indigenous Communities, 159–160
replacement of initial investigating team, 11–12
report into policy brutality allegations, 156
Croker (overseer), 109
cultural traditions, 19, 21–25, 48
  medicine practices, 94
Cummins, Rachael, 127, 132, 135, 137, 161
  author's friendship with, 20–21
Cunnamulla, 100–101
Cunningham, RA, 142
Curacoa Island, 44, 59, 60, 71, 73, 77
curfews, 13, 29, 41, 104
  avoiding detection when walking out after, 87
Currie, Donnie, 22
Curry, Agnes, 41, 49, 64–65, 67, 74
Curry, Edna, 65, 67
  death, 56, 59, 62, 74
Curry, George, 63–64
Curry, Robbie, 65, 67
  death, 56, 59, 62, 74
Curry, Robert Henry, 35, 40–75, 81, *between pp. 110–111*
  Hooper's parallels with Hurley, 154–155
  residence site, 22, *between pp. 110–111*
cyclone salvage, 40
cyclones, 34–35, 51, 93

Daily Standard, 64, 74–75
Daisy, Jimmy, 22, 122, 124
Daisy, Leonie, 21, 22–23, 124
Daley, Constable, 63, 73
Daly, T, 69
Davis, Peter, 152
Davison, Eric, 57, 60, 63
  gathering outside residence, 58, 70
de Jersey, Chief Justice Paul, 150
De Satge, Ruby, 36
deaths and death rates, 39, 47–48, 76, 89, 91
  alcohol-related, 131, 132, 133
  children and infants, 89, 91, 124
  Curry's rampage, 55–75

Fantome Island, 92, 93, 97, 98, 100
frontier massacres, 18, 27–29, 81
Hull River, 33, 34
Kukamunburra, 142–143
life expectancy, 18, 159
from police brutality, 104
during and after removal, 77, 78, 98
see also suicide
deaths in custody, 139–141, 143
  Mulrunji, 1–16, 19, 146–156; *see also* Hurley, Senior Sergeant Chris
  Pitt, Henry, 122–124
Dee Street, 4, 151
Deeds of Grant in Trust, 136
Delaney, J E, 81–82
Department of Aboriginal and Island Affairs, 101, 120, 125, 128, 132
Department of Health, 84
Department of Health and Home Affairs, 96, 98–99
Department of Labour and National Service, 119
Department of Native Affairs, 99, 103, 117, 118, 123
  consequences of writing to, 108
  name change in 1958, 120
  reports on finance, 106
  Sonny Sibley's removal to Woorabinda, 116
Department of Public Instruction, 49
Department of Public Prosecutions (DPP), 149, 150, 151, 155
Dijiri, 29
Dillon, John, 129
Dimbulah, 25
Dinduck, Rosie, 67
Dini, Senior Sergeant, 156
diseases, *see* health and living conditions
dispossession, 93, 118
  see also removals
doctors, *see* medical officers
Dodd, Beatrice, 123
DOGITS, 136
Donaldson, Billy, 60, 71
Donnelly, Mark, 6, 8
Doolan, Fred, 109, 111, 116
Doomadgee, 147, 154
Doomadgee, Cameron (Mulrunji), 1–16, 19, 146–156
Doomadgee, Carol, 5
Doomadgee, Elizabeth, 14, 22
Doomadgee, Eric, 1, 149
Doomadgee, Jane, 5

dormitories and dormitory system, x–xi, 38, 43, 48, 96
  during Curry's rampage, 56–57, 69
  food supplies, 47, 79, 86
  'industrial schools', 49, 78–79
  punishment regimes, 44, 45–46, 47, 49, 86, 107–108, 128
  World War II, 90–91
  see also girls' dormitories
Dormitory Women's Reunion, 76
Douglas, Justice RJ, 71
Dreamtime Snake, *see* Carpet Snake
Drew, Dr J Grahame, 82, 86
Drones, xi

Eclipse Island, 22, 39, 44, 86
  escapes from, 47, 88
  gazettal as reserve lands, 77
education, *see* schooling
employment and forced labour, 1, 18, 30
  1920s, 39, 42–43, 47
  1930s, 78–79, 82, 84–85; Fantome Island, 95
  Second World War, 89
  1950s, 105–106, 107, 108, 115, 117
  1960s, 127
  late 1970s, 131, 132, 133
  1980s, 131, 136
  after arrival from Hull River, 40
  at Hull River, 33
  reasons for removal to Palm, 37
  see also strikes; wages and earnings
Endeavour, 25–26
entertainment, *see* recreation and entertainment
escapes, 38–39, 47, 55, 87–88, 108
  from Hull River, 33
  Hull River as punishment reserve after, 32
Esme, 57–58, 72
Ethical Standards Command, 6, 160
Etteridge, David, 150
eugenic theories, 31, 32, 48, 84
Evans, Coroner DG, 140–141
evening curfews, *see* curfews
exemptions under Act, 43, 101, 116

FAIRA, 20, 127, 137
Fantome Island, 42, 83, 92–101, between pp. 110–111
  Curry's trip to during rampage, 58–59, 63
  gazettal as reserve land, 77

Farrell, Inspector James, 51
Faulkner, Bishop, 101
Federal Council for Aboriginal Advancement, 125
Federal Council of Aborigines and Torres Strait Islanders (FCAATSI), 120, 127, 128
Feetham, Bishop John, 81
finance, 17–18, 106, 127
  Aitkenvale, 139, 159
  alcohol canteen sales, 18, 31–132
  Beattie's threats and offers following Mulrunji's death, 12, 13, 15–16
  brass band funding, 49
  Curry's allegations about accounts, 50, 52, 67–68
  during depression, 79, 81–82; income derived from trochus shell trade, 85
  Fantome Island, 94, 95, 96, 99
  secondary education, 83
  see also wages and earnings
Fingleton, Di, 150
First World War, Curry's military service during, 72
fishing, 1–2, 23, 30, 31, 40
  ban at Yarrabah, 119
  Bartlam's expeditions, 108
  to supplement rations and food supplies, 44, 47, 80
fishing industry, employment in, 29, 30, 43, 79
  abscondings, 47
  income generated, 85
  wages, 42, 85
Fitzgerald, Tony, 144
Fitzgerald Inquiry, 137, 160
Fitzpatrick, Denis, 11
floggings, 36
  on Palm Island, 44–46, 54, 66–67, 68
Florence, Lisa, 12
Flynn, Dr, 122–123
food supplies, 29, 30, 40, 53
  1930s, 47, 79–80, 81, 84, 86, 96
  1940s, 89, 90, 98–99
  1950s, 106–107, 110, 112
  1960s, 124–125
  Fantome Island, 96, 98–99
  prisoners exiled to other islands, 22, 44, 86
  during state of emergency following Mulrunji's death, 12
  see also rations
football, 91, 154

football team, 44, 49–50, *between pp. 110–111*
  stolen funds allegation, 52, 67–68
Foote, Cecil, 82
Forrest River, 80, 81
Foster, Father, 83, 99
Foster, Delena, 144
Foster, Leslie, 121
Foster, Mavis, 137
Foundation for Aboriginal and Islander Research and Action (FAIRA), 20, 127, 137
Francis, Thos, 30
Fraser Island, 33, 34, 95
Friday, George Snr, 136
frontier, *see* invasion and frontier conflict
Fulford, Fred, 38, 123–124
Fuller, Constable, 148
funding, *see* finance
funeral, Mulrunji, 13, 14

Gabriel, Dr Morgan, 100
Gair government, 115
Gall Under-Secretary WJ, 49, 80, 81, 84
  relations with Curry, 45, 46, 51–52, 68, 73
gambling, 44, 51, 88, 105, 110, 127
Garbutt, Joe, 42, 49, 50, 53, 121
Garcia, John, 129
Gayndah, 81
Geia, Albie, 109–110, 111, 112, 115
  family, 114
Geia, Denise, 156
Geia, Joe, 102
Geia, Tom, 110, 127, 135, 137
Gibson, Charlie, 160
Gibson, Merv, 144
girls' dormitories, 41, 48, 78–79, *between pp. 110–111*
  during Curry's rampage, 56–57
  Dormitory Women's Reunion, 76
  male visitors, 86, 87, 90–91, 107
  punishment regimes, 44, 45–46, 47, 86, 107–108
Glasgow, Chief Magistrate David, 13
Gold Coast, 14, 149, 151, 153
gonorrhoea, 94, 97
Goss government, 137
Graham, Chris, 11
Gribble, Reverend Ernest, 80–83, 84, 85–86, 88, 91
Gubbbal, *see* Carpet Snake
Gundy, David, 127

Gunnawarra, Constable Jack, 122, 123
Gurundji, 126, 130

Haebich, Bob, 137
Hagan, Stephen, 100–101
Halberstater, Leslie, 122
'half-castes', 31, 32, 48, 84
Halifax, 25, 27, 30, 52
Halifax Bay, 1, 25, 28
Hall, Robert A, 90
Hamilton, Jan, 20
Hamilton, Joseph, 41, 51, 56, 60, 63, 72
Hanlon, EM, 80, 89, 93, 98
Hanson, Pauline, 150
Harvey, Jimmy, 59, 60, 69, 70, 71
Harvey, Kirsten, 10
Harvey, Rene, 45–46, 66–67, 68
Hawkins Point, 29
Hazeldine, Ellen, 41, 52
Health Act 1937, 98
health and living conditions, 29, 92–93, 159
  1920s, 39, 47–48
  1930s, 82, 83–84, 93
  1940s, 89, 91
  1960s, 124–125
  1970s, 127, 132, 134
  1980s, 136
  Hull River, 33
  see also deaths; hospitals; housing
Henry, Isaac, 31
Herbert River, 24, 87–88
Herman, Judith, 134
Heron, John, 143
Hewitt, Neville, 129
Hickey, Inspector, 148
high school education, 20, 83, 158
Hill, WRO, 27–28
Hinchinbrook Island, 28, 29, 142
Hinze, Russ, 131
Hippi, Albert, 37
Hoffman, Thomas, 42, 55–63, 66–73, 75
  charges laid against, 69–71
  home, 41, 56
  Murri patrol stationed by, 58, 60, 69–70
  relationship with Curry, 51, 61; stolen funds allegation, 52, 67–68
  statement at inquiry into Pattison–Ballard feud, 52
  statements at inquest by, 62–63, 66, 67, 69–70; about Pattison, 65, 66
  strap made by, 45

Hoffman, Mrs Thomas, 56
Home Office/Department, 54, 64, 68, 73, 74–75
  depression economic policies, 81
  Fantome Island reports, 96–98, 99
  see also Bleakley, Chief Protector JW; Gall Under-Secretary WJ
Hooligan, 87–88
Hooper, Chloe, 154–155
Hopevale, 118
Horseshoe Reef, 27
hospitals, 40, 84, 136
  Aitkenvale, 159
  Curry's death, 62
  Curry's threat to burn, 57, 62
  Pitt in, 122–123
  during state of emergency following Mulrunji's death, 8, 9, 12
  Townsville, 14–15, 64, 148, 153
  see also Fantome Island; medical officers
hotels, 132, 139
  Lowth's, 51–52
housing, 17, 18, 21
  1940s, 89, 91, 97
  1950s, 105–106, 107, 108–109, 110, 118; police raids, 112–113, 114
  1957 strikers deported to other reserves, 115
  1960s, 124
  1980s, 131, 136
  after arrival from Hull River, 40
  at Hull River, 33
  King's 1819 observations, 26
  police raids following Mulrunji's death, 9–11, 14
housing for white staff, 40–41
  Bartlam residence, 103–104
  Curry residence, 40, 41, 56; site, 22, between pp. 110–111
  Kenny residence, 35
Houston, John, 129
Howard, John, and Howard government, 143, 155
Howard, Richard B, 30
Hull River, 32–33, 34–35
human rights, 88–89, 119–121, 125–131, 135–145
  Catholic Church advocacy, 83
  Gribble's advocacy, 80, 82–83
  see also land rights
Human Rights and Equal Opportunity Commission (HREOC), 141, 143

Human Rights Commission inquiry into wage discrimination, 137, 138
Hunter, Ernest, 143
Hurley, Senior Sergeant Chris, 2–6, 11, 146–156, 157
  appeal, 156
  compensation claims for loss of personal possessions, 155, 156
  DPP Clare's decision, 150
  Hooper's research, 154–155
  inquests, 16, 146–149; Patrick Bramwell's testimony, 14–15, 151
  trial, 151, 152–153, 161

'industrial schools', 49, 78–79, 87
infectious diseases, see health and living conditions
Ingham, 25, 50, 87, 88
inquests, 140–141
  Curry deaths, 62–63, 64–71
  Pitt, Henry, 122–124
inquests into Mulrunji's death, 2, 15, 16, 146–149, 150, 156
  autopsies and autopsy reports, 5, 6–7, 13, 15, 146, 149
  Clements' comments on police investigation, 5, 12
invasion and frontier conflict, 20, 25–35, 92–93
  massacres, 18, 27–29, 81
Ipswich, 32

Jackson, Clem, 62
jails, see prisons
James, Peggy, 36
James Noble Fund, 83
Johnni, Delsey, 149
Johnson, Abe, 22–23, 130
Johnson, DW, 96–98
Johnson, George, 122, 123
Johnson, RL, 128
Johnstone, Sub-Inspector, 28–29
Jones, Robert, 122
Julian, FH, 82, 88, 94, 96, 98
Jumbo, Johnny, 21, 123
Juno Bay, 96

Kalkadoon Wars, 18
Kandju, 40
Keating government, 142, 143
Keefe, Senator Jim, 129, 131
Kennedy, Marnie, 42–43, 44, 47, 48, 56–57

Index

Kenny, JM, 32–33, 34, 35
Kidd, Roslyn, 43, 137
kidnappings, *see* removals
Kidner, Terence, 152
Killoran, Pat, 101
King, Phillip Parker, 26
Kirrima station, 88
Kissing Point, 87
Kitching, Detective Senior Sergeant Raymond, 5, 155
Knight, David, 133
Kokoimudji, 40
Kongkanji, 40
Kornmann (carpenter), 52
Krause, FA, 91
Kukamunburra, 142–143
Kuku Yalanji, 40
Kurandah, 35
Kyle, Alby, 58, 88
Kyle, Dan, 55, 66
Kyle, Erykah, 127, 137
  comments on beer canteen, 132
Kyle, Erykah, and Mulrunji's death, 1, 10, 13, 158
  description of Mulrunji, 2
  in Hooper's account, 154
  inquest submission, 16

'laboratory model' of public health programs, 95–101
labour, *see* employment; trade union movement
Lacey, Alf, 18, 139, 155
Lacey, Lionel, 129
Lampe, Dr Guy, 6, 146
Land Act (Aboriginal and Islander Land Grants) Amendment Act, 136
land rights, 128, 130–131, 135, 137
  native title, 142, 143
land tenure, 31, 159
  Bligh government proposals, 18
  Deeds of Grants in Trust (DOGITS), 136
  Dick Palm Island's letter to Chief Protector, 30
Land Use Agreement, 19
languages and language groups, 24, 25, 40, 143
  English, 82
  punishments for speaking, 44, 49
Largactil, 122
Lass O'Gowrie, 35
Laura, 78

Lavarack barrack, 141
lazaret, *see* Fantome Island
Leafe, Sergeant, 3, 4, 6, 146
Leahy, Dr Clinton, 148
legislation, 130, 136, 137, 159
  leprosy (1892), 95
  state of emergency declared under, 7–13, 153
  voting rights, 125–126
  see also Aboriginal Protection Acts
legislation, federal, 98, 125–126, 137, 138
  land rights, 135
  native title, 142, 143
  to redress Queensland discriminatory legislation, 127, 130
Lenoy, Edith, 128, 129
Lenoy, Fred, 137
Lenoy, Yvette, 14
leprosy, 82, 83, 94, 95, 98–100
Levitt, Stuart, 149, 152
life expectancy, 18, 159
Lightning, Paddy, 130
Lindsay, Peter, 141
Lingiari, Vincent, 130
Loch, Inspector, 81
lock hospital, *see* Fantome Island
Lowth's Hotel, 51–52
Lymburner, Bessie, 40, 113, 114, 115
Lymburner, Eric, 109, 112, 113, 115

McAvoy, Thelma, 43, 107
McBride, Renee, 21
MacGillivray, John, 26
McGinness, Joe, 37, 39
McNab, Duncan, 50
'Mad Dog', 35
Magnetic Island, 24–25, 29, 87
Main Street, 56, 57
Malanda, 41
malaria, 33, 66
Malcolm, Bob, 46
Malezer, Les, 19
Maloney, Detective, 59, 63, 69–70, 73
Maloney, Father, 83
Mam, Pam, 127
Mam, Steve, 127
Manbarra, 19, 24–25, 29–31, 40
Mango Avenue, 8, 40–41, 44, 57, 58, 128
  Curry residence site, *between pp. 110–111*
  protest march during strike, 110–111

Index

Mann, Anne, 160
Mapoon, 40, 50, 78, 118
Mareeba, 25
Maria, 29
Martin, Constable, 33
matrons, 41, 44, 86, 91
   O'Brian, Avonia, 98–99
   see also Pattison, Matron Ethel
Matthews, Ralph, 59–60, 66, 67, 69
Maxwell, Col, 116
media reports, 75, 89, 128, 129, 134, 135–136, 145
   Bancroft's statements in 1930s, 79, 84
   Bartlam's administration, 104, 109, 111, 112, 114–115, 116; film about strike, 120
   colonial, 27, 28–29
   Curry's administration, 41, 44–45, 53, 66–68
   Curry's rampage, 63–64, 67–68, 69, 70, 74–75; trials, 71–72
   escapes and attempted escapes, 38–39, 87–88
   Hull River, 34–35
   removals, 38–39; police bribery allegations, 37
   Yarrabah strike, 119
media reports on Mulrunji's death and aftermath, 1, 7, 8, 11, 14, 19
   inquest, 147–148
   Message Stock, 149
   SERT raid on Wotton's home, 9–10
medical inspections, 48
   Fantome Island clearances, 93–94, 97–99, 101
medical officers and staff, 82
   Bancroft, Thomas L, 77, 79, 81, 84, 86
   Fantome Island, 83, 93, 95–98, 100; Morecombe, Albert, 58–59, 62, 63, 75
   Murray, Dr Elliot, 84
   Pitt's death in custody, 122–123
   Saltau, Dr Allen, 124–125
   Smith, Dr Hilyard, 91
   see also Pattison, Dr Charles Maitland
medicine practices, 94, 95–101, 122–123
Meeting Challenges, Making Choices policy, 144
Melbidir, 35
men's group, 13, 143
Mermaid, 26
Message Stick, 149

Meston, Archibald, 26, 31, 34
Miller, Dougie, 10
Mills, Jan, 125
mining, 118, 130
missionaries, *see* church and religion
Missionaries of Mary, 83
Mitchell, Bruce, 59
Moloney, Father Patrick, 48
Mona Mona, 50, 118
Moore government, 64, 69, 74
Morecombe, Albert, 58–59, 62, 63, 75
Morgan, Tom Snr, 86, *between pp. 110–111*
morning roll call and parade, 42, 80, 85, 104, 116, 117
Mornington Island, 130–131, 133
Morrill, James, 27
Morton, Chevez, 10
Mt Garnet station, 87
Mulholland, Robert, 153
Mullan, J, 37
Mulrunji, 1–16, 19, 146–156
Mumford, Bruce, 152
Murdock, Arthur, 58
Murphy, Sergeant Darren, 8
Murray, Arthur, 148
Murray, Dr Elliott, 84
Murray River, 28, 106
music, 49, 83, *between pp. 110–111*

National Health and Medical Research Council, 98
National Tribal Council, 125
native council, 88
Native Police, 27–29, 31, 32
Native Police on Palm Island, 41, 42, 45, 46, 48
   1930s, 80, 82, 85–86
   1950s, 104–105, 107, 109; during strike, 110
native title, 142, 143
Neill, Hope, 17
Nevitt Inquiry, 52, 53–54, 64, 65–66, 68
New South Wales, 77, 88
Nobby Point, 29
Noble, Henry, 116–117
Noble, James, 83
Norman, Alissa, 149–150
Norman, Rosina, 1
Normanton, 38–39, 77, 78
North East Bay, 23
North Queensland Guardian, 89

Index

North Queensland Register, 34–35, 38–39, 41
Northern Territory, 126, 130, 135, 159
novocaine, 65, 73
Nugent, Gladys, 2
nurses, 8, 14, 40, 91
   Fantome Island, 95, 96
   Hazeldine, Ellen, 41, 52
   see also matrons

Obah, Andrew, 105
Obah, Ellison, 59, 60, 61, 69, 70, 71
   brass band, 49
O'Brian, Matron Avonia, 98–99
O'Brien, CD, 96–98
O'Gorman, Terry, 150, 155
Ojibwa community, 133–134
O'Leary, Cornelius, 70, 75
   Deputy Chief Protector, 81, 88
   Director of Native Affairs, 109, 110, 112, 114, 115, 116
Orpheus Island, 130, 160
outstation movement, 130

Pack, Judge Robert, 156
Pallarenda, 25, 87
Palm Island, Dick, 25, 30, 143
Palm Island, Mary, 45
Palm Island, Mick, 25, 30
Palm Island, Reg, 24–25, 30, 40
Palm Island, Walter Jnr, 142, 143
Palm Island Aboriginal Council and Councillors, 1, 9, 127, 137
   alcohol, 131–133, 139; restrictions, 144, 158
   community administration transferred to, 136
   dismissals, 15, 128–130
   finance, 17–18, 131–132, 139; Beattie's threats and offers, 12, 13, 15–16
   Lacey, Alf, 18, 139, 155
   Mulrunji's death and aftermath, 6, 12–13, 15–16, 155
   see also Kyle, Erykah
Palm Island Brass Band, 49, *between pp. 110–111*
Palm Island football team, *see* football team
Palmer, Alf, 50
Palmer, Maurice, 137
Parker, Russel Jnr, 149, 150

Parker, Wayne Russel Snr, 149–150
parliamentary committees, 33
   Commonwealth, 119, 121
parliamentary questions, 124
parliamentary reports, 33, 156
parliamentary statements, 117
Pattison, Dr Charles Maitland, 52, 55–63, 65, 66, 68–69, 70, 75, *between pp. 110–111*
   assault of Archie Blue, 46
Pattison, Matron Ethel, 65, 70, *between pp. 110–111*
   assault by Curry, 55, 56, 57, 58, 59, 61, 63
pearl shell fishing, 29, 85
Pearson, Karl, 31
Pearson, Noel, 139, 144, 150
Pedro, Henry, 57–58, 67, 72
Peel Island, 98, 99, 100
Pencil Bay, 47, 108
penitentiary, Palm Island as, 17, 18–20, 36–50, 76–88, 157–158
   1960s, 107, 119, 121
   Bleakley's recommendations, 33–34
Peruvian, 27
Peters, Father Mick, 21
Pickles, Frank, 57
Picnic Point, 29
pigs, 30, 40
Pilot, Barbara, 147–148
Pitt, Henry, 122–124
police, 1–16, 32, 139–141, 146–156, 159–160
   Bartlam's superintendentship, 117;
   during strike, 111, 112–115, 116, 118
   Cairns, 9, 33
   colonial, 27–29
   Fraser Island, 34
   Hooligan pursuit, 87–88
   see also arrests; Native Police; removals; Townsville police
police cells, *see* deaths in custody; prisons
Police Citizens Youth Club (PCYC), 15–16
Police Commissioners, 6, 28, 155
Police Ethical Standards Command, 6, 160
police magistrates, 27, 28
   inquiries, 45–46, 50, 52, 65; Curry deaths, 62–63, 64–71
police unions, 11, 12

Index

CMC investigation into fraudulent valuations of vehicles, 155
inquests into Mulrunji death, 16, 149
rallies in support of Hurley, 151
political activism, *see* activism
population, 17, 18
  1929, 43
  1930s and 1940s, 39, 77
  1957, 111–112
  1980s, 136
  Halifax, before and after white occupation, 27
  people removed, 38
poverty, 1, 17, 135, 159
  alcohol and, 131, 132, 133, 139, 144
  Cilento's emphasis upon 'material betterment', 84
  see also wages
Poynter, Jayson, 149–150
Poynter, Lance, 152
Poynter, Richard, 10
Pratt, Constable, 87–88
Presbyterian Church, 118, 130
press reports, *see* media reports
prisons, prisoners and confinement, 10, 80, 143
  alcohol-related, 139, 140–141, 144–145
  Bartlam's superintendentship, 103, 104, 105, 106, 108, 109; strikers, 110
  children, 44, 86
  following civil unrest after Mulrunji's death, 9–14, 149–150, 151, 152, 155, 156
  following Clay Council dismissal, 129
  Curry's superintendentship, 41, 44, 49, 55, 56, 66
  Delaney's superintendentship, 81
  Pencil Bay, 108
  for 'tribal killing', 50
  see also deaths in custody; Eclipse Island; penitentiary, Palm Island as; Townsville police watch house; Townsville Prison
Protected, 102, 120
Protection Acts, *see* Aboriginal Protection Acts
Protectors, 30, 32
  Cunnamulla, 101
  see also Bleakley, Chief Protector JW; Superintendents
protests, 89, 103, 129
  after Mulrunji's death in custody, 6–14, 15, 151; by police, *between pp. 110–111*, 151–152
  Commonwealth Games, 135–136
  see also strikes
Provident Fund, *see* Trust Fund
Prior, Kippy, 22
Prior, Monty, v, 85, 127
Prior, Peter, 32, 59–61, 64, 69–71
  grandson, 10
Prior, Renata, 10
Prior, Silas, v, 22, 110
Pryor, Tom, 82
Public Safety Preservation Act 1986, state of emergency declared under, 7–13, 153
Public Service Commissioner, 42
Punishment Island, *see* Eclipse Island
punishment regimes, 85, 86, 128
  Bartlam's superintendentship, 104–105, 106, 107–108, 109, 122–124
  Curry's superintendentship, 44–47, 48, 49, 54, 66–67, 68
  offences causing removal to Palm, 19, 37–38, 40, 106, 121
  Yarrabah, 118–119
  see also Eclipse Island; removals from Palm
Puttaburra, Jimmy, 58

Queensland Aboriginal Advisory Council, 136
Queensland Aboriginal and Islander Legal Service Secretariat, 138–139
Queensland Parliament, 117, 124, 156
Queensland Police Service, *see* police
Quinn, JP, 70
Quinn, Mary, 62
Qwanji (Brady, Pastor Don), 104, 109, 127, 128

Racial Discrimination Act 1975, 137, 138, 159
racial segregation, *see* segregation
rations, 39, 42, 105
  Christmas dinner provided by Bartlam, x
  during Depression, 76, 79, 86
  exiles on Curacoa and Eclipse Islands, 44, 86
  findings of 1930 inquiry, 47

strike in 1957, 110, 112; as reason for, 106–107, 108; result, 118
wages secured for those receiving only, 88
Rattlesnake, 26
Rattlesnake Island, 34
recreation and entertainment, 49–50, 83, 107, 108, *between pp. 110–111*
  Christmas – New Year, x, 14, 49, 52
  see also football; tourism
referendum in 1967, 126
religion, *see* church and religion
removals, 29, 31–34, 89, *between pp. 110–111*
  deportations from reserves, 118–119, 131
  to Fantome, 93–95, 96, 97–98, 100–101
  overseas, 29, 142–143
  to Palm, 36–39, 77–79, 107, 119, 140;
  reasons for, 18–19, 37–38, 40, 106, 121
  see also children, removal of; penitentiary, Palm Island as
removals from Palm, 46, 126–127, 130
  Manbarra and Buluguyban, 31, 34
  removals from Palm during Bartlam's superintendentship, 108, 109, 111, 117–118
  after Pitt's death, 124
  strikers and their families, 113–116
Reser, Dr Josef, 140, 143
reserve regulations, breaches of, 41, 87, 90–91
  corporal punishment provisions, 45–46, 107–108
resistance, 19, 20
  against invasion, 26–29, 31, 32
  see also protests
Returned Soldiers' League, 64
Reynolds, Henry, 27, 141
Reynolds, Mike, 156
Richardson, Senior Constable Kathleen, 8
rights, *see* human rights; land rights
Rita, 58–59, 60, 73
Roberts, GR, 82, 86
Robinson, Detective Sergeant Darren, 5, 6, 7, 8, 14, 148
Rockhampton, 34, 115, 116
Rodie, HS, 73

roll call and parade, 42, 80, 85, 104, 116, 117
Rollingstone, 58, 63
Roman Catholic Church, *see* Catholic Church
Ross, BA, 71
Ross River, 25
Rosser, Bill, 36, 128
Roth, Northern Protector, 32
Royal Commission into Aboriginal Deaths in Custody (RCIADIC), 139–140, 142, 143, 144, 145, 152
Rudd, Kevin, and Rudd government, 159
Ryan, George, 88
Ryan, Vincent Roy, 140

St George's Church, 83
Saltau, Dr Alan, 124–125
Salvarsan, 96
Sam, Ivy, 22, 78–79, 86, 106–107, 108, 123
Sam, Zacky, 130
sanitation, 84, 124, 136
Santayana, George, 145
Sarabo, Paddy, 123
Saxby Downs Station, 37
schooling, 49, 78–79, 87
  secondary education, 20, 83, 158
schools, 41, 56, 107
  after Mulrunji's death, 9, 10, 12;
  Beattie's visit, 15
  Bartlam's visits, 103
  fruit supplies, 132
  models used to establish, 49
  for white children, 41, 49, 64, 107, 128
schoolteachers, 8, 83, 90, 91
  aids and attendants, 85
  see also Davison, Eric
Seaton, Bill, 86, 110
Seaton, Michael, 117
Second World War, 89–91, 100
secondary education, 20, 83, 158
segregation, 27, 31, 32, 40–41, 128
  American troops during Second World War, 90
  Bartlam's time, 103, 107, 125
  church seating, 83
  Cilento's recommendations, 84, 98
  schooling, 41, 49, 87, 107, 128
  see also dormitories and dormitory system

sewage and sanitation, 84, 124, 136
sexual relations, 48, 86, 107–108
  Curry, Robert, 54, 66, 67, 74; with Nellie Bly?, 61
  Delaney, JE, 81–82
  Mapoon, 78
  Second World War, 90–91
  venereal disease, 48, 52, 92–100, 122
Seymour, Police Commissioner, 28
Shadford, Ron, 122, 123
Shanahan, Chief Judge Pat, 150
Shepherd, David (man in 'frock'), 8, 13
Shevill, Bishop, 91, 119
Shine, Kerry, 149
shipwrecks, 27, 29
Shkilnyk, Anastasia, 133–134
shops, *see* stores
Sibley, Alice, 116
Sibley, Cecilia, 9–10
Sibley, Jack, 90, 137
Sibley, Jean, 137
  recollections of Americans, 90–91
  recollections of Bartlam's time, 103, 105; strike, 110–111, 113
Sibley, Penny, 3
Sibley, Schanara, 9–10
Sibley, Sonny, 109, 111, 112, 115, 116
  family, 114, 116
Simian, Charles, 49
Sisters of Our Lady of Help, 94, 99
Skuthorp, Bill, 108, 118
Small Carpet Snake, 24
Smallwood, Percy, 88
Smith (Pattison's medical assistant), 57
Smith, Cappy, 42
Smith, Dr Hilyard, 91
Smith's Weekly, 66–67
Solomon, Willie, 49
South Mission Beach, 33
Special Emergency Response Team (SERT), 9–10, 12, 153
Spence, Police Minister Judy, 10, 12, 13, 151, 152, 153
sport, 49–50, 107
  see also football
St George's Church, 83
State Children's Act 1911, 78–79
state of emergency, 7–13, 153
Steadman, Constable Kristopher, 3, 154
sterilisation, 84
Stevens, Colin, 70, 71
Stewart's Creek, 47, 70, 71

stockmen, 37, 43, 126
Stokes, J Lort, 26
Stolen Children, *see* children, removal of
Stopford (Under-Secretary's Office), 51
storekeepers, 80
  see also Ballard, Leonard
stores, 44, 79–80, 124–125, 158
  construction, 40, 42, 118
  destruction, 56, 57, 136
Strachan, Carolyn, 102, 120
Street, Chief Justice Sir Lawrence, 151
strikes, 102, 108–120, *between pp. 110–111*
  Taroom, 32
  Wave Hill, 126
  Yarrabah, 119
Stuart Prison, *see* Townsville Prison
Sturgess, George, 82
Sub-Department of Native Affairs, 99
substance abuse, 1, 139–140, 144, 145
  see also alcohol
suicide and attempted suicide, 18, 143
  in custody, 140
  Eclipse Island exiles, 22
  after Mulrunji's death and inquest, 12, 15, 149, 151
Sullivan, Tom, 39
sulphone treatment, 100
Superintendents, Assistant
Superintendents and managers, 20, 32, 80–82, 86
  Bartlam, Roy Henry, x, 91, 103–125, 155
  Courtney, Dr CA, 82, 97–99
  Dillon, John, 129
  Julian, FH, 82, 88, 94, 96, 98
  Kenny, JM, 32–33, 34, 35
  Mapoon, 78
  O'Leary, Cornelius, 70, 75, 81
  Peel Island, 100
  see also Curry, Robert Henry; Hoffman, Thomas
Swann, Mrs, 107
Sweetman, Inspector, 30
Sydney Morning Herald, 87, 135
Sykes, Bobbi, 128
syphilis, 93, 94, 96, 97

The Tall Man, 154
Tallis, Annie, 34
Tambo, 142–143
Tanner, Paddy, 100

Tapau, Gordon, 112, 115
Taroom, 32, 34, 49
Taser stun guns, 9, 10, 11
teachers, *see* schoolteachers
Tedman (clerk), 50
Telegraph, 63–64, 109, 114–115
Thaiday, Madge, 113, 115
Thaiday, Mick, 127
Thaiday, Willie, 102, 109, 110
   arrest, 113, 114, 118
   banana farm manager, 106
   native council, 88
   trochus shell diver, 85
   Woorabinda, 115
theft
   allegations against Hoffman, 52, 67–68
   Anglican Church launch, 88
Thimble, Vincent, 143
Thursday Island, 11, 32, 67, 82
timber collection, 42, 79, 85, 123–124
timber mill, 40, 136
Tippo, 87
Tippo, Polly, 45
tobacco, 30, 79, 85, 90, 115
Tom O'Shanter Point, 29
'Tomato Face', 103
'top end', 21–22
tourism, 39–40, 42, 53, 104
   Bjelke-Petersen's proposals, 128–130
   Butler's Guest House, 29–30, 50, *between pp.* 110–111
   Orpheus Island, 130, 160
Townsville, 25, 27, 29, 34, 127, 140–141
   Aitkenvale, 21, 118, 139, 159
   Curry's visit to Gall and Stopford, 51–52, 68
   Drones, xi
   food supplies from, 79–80
   after Mulrunji's death in custody, 12, 13, 14–15; survey on attitudes towards Aborigines and Palm Islanders, 152
   Second World War, 89
   shopping trips to, x, 43
Townsville Bulletin, 9–10
Townsville Dairy Bulletin, 114, 120, 145
Townsville Evening Star, 71–72
Townsville Hospital, 14–15, 64, 148, 153
Townsville police, 28, 30, 81, 130, 141
   Curry's rampage, 58, 59, 63, 69–70
   Mulrunji's death in custody, 5–6, 8, 9, 14, 151, 152
   Palm Island strike, 111, 112–115, 116
Townsville police watch house, 43, 71, 114–115, 127
   deaths in custody, 140–141
Townsville Prison (Stewart's Creek), 47, 50
   Bramwell's confinement, 150
   deaths in custody, 140
   Prior's confinement, 70, 71
Townsville Shire Council, 128–129
Townsville Trades and Labour Council (TLC), 117, 122, 124
trade union movement, 89, 116, 117, 119
   equal wages campaign, 126, 127, 128
   Pitt's death in custody, 122, 124
trauma, 134
travel to mainland, x, 43, 108
   football team, 49–50, 52
   original Islanders, 25, 31
   residences during, 43, 107, 118
   see also escapes; removals; tourism
trials, *see* court trials and actions
tribal camps, 40, 50, 106
Tribune, 104, 115, 116
trochus shell trade, 42, 43, 79, 85
Trudgeon, Richard, 133
Trust Fund (Provident Fund, banking system), 43–44, 85, 89, 105, 138–139
   deductions for hospital care, 96
   Taroom strike, 32
Truth newspaper, 37, 53, 64, 69, 72
   Curry's letter to, 67–68
tuberculosis, 98
Tucker, Percy, 124, 127
Tully, 35
Tully River, 18, 28, 29, 31
Turn Off Lagoon, 37, 78
Turtle Rock, 22–23
Twaddle, Mary, 128, 129
Twaddle, Tracey, 2, 5, 155

'Uncle Boss', 35
'Uncle Willie', 102
unemployment, 1, 37, 131, 132, 133
United Nations Declaration on the Rights of Indigenous people, 159
United States, 29, 142
   troops in Australia, 89–91, 125
Upper Murray River, 106

Index

Valley of Lagoons, 27–28
venereal disease, 48, 52, 92–100, 122
video surveillance of police cells, 140
   tapes of Mulrunji, 4, 11, 153
violence and conflict, 1, 81–82, 104–105, 157–158
   alcohol-related, 132, 133, 134, 139, 144, 145; *see also* alcohol consumption by whites
   within Curry administration, 50–75
   HREOC inquiry, 141
   inter-tribal feuds, 50
   Mulrunji's death in custody aftermath, 6, 7–13, 150–151, 153
   during strike, 112–113, 116
   see also deaths in custody; invasion and frontier conflict; punishment regimes
Volkers, Scott, 150
voting rights, 119, 125–126

wages and earnings, 39, 42, 53
   1930s, 81, 84–85, 88
   1950s, 104, 105, 106, 109, 110, 115; after strike, 118
   campaign for equal, 126, 127, 128, 137, 138–139
   see also Trust Fund
Walker, Denis, 128, 129
Walsh, Algan, 107
Walsh, Aubrey, 70
Walsh, Keith, 71
Walsh, Steve (Stumbo), 131
Warner, Charlie, 113, 116
water and waste system, 84, 89, 124, 134, 136
Waters, Jeff, 4
Waterside Workers' Union, 119
Watson, George, 109, 112, 115
   family, 114
Watson, John, 129
Watson, McGregor, 77
Wattie Creek, 126, 130
Wave Hill, 126

Weber, Inspector Warren, 3, 5, 6
Webster, Detective Ken, 12
Weipa, 50, 118
Welfare Officers, 107, 131
West Point, 24
Whitlam government, 127, 130
Wilcox, Captain J, 119
Wilkinson, Gary, 149, 155
Will O' the Wisp, 26
Williams, Inspector , 3, 6
Williams, Nancy, 87
Wilson, Robert, 123
women, 28, 29, 33
   alcohol-related violence against, 133, 139, 145
   employment and forced labour, 42–43, 105, 106
   evacuation during Second World War, 90
   Fantome patients, 94, 97
   punishment regimes, 44, 56, 66, 105, 106, 107–108; Curry's flogging of Rene Harvey, 45–46, 66–67, 68
   reasons for removal to Palm, 37, 40
   during strike, 110
   see also sexual relations
Wondai, Jack, 57
Woodward report, 130
Woorabinda, 89, 97, 101, 115–116, 117, 140
World War I, Curry's military service during, 72
World War II, 89–91, 100
Wotton, Lex, 8–10, 154, 155, 156
Wyles, Cliff, 99
Wyles, Virginia, 24

Yanner, Murrandoo, 14
Yarrabah, 32, 50, 89
   Gribble at, 80, 91
   music, 49
   Noble, James, 83
   strike, 118–119
Yidangi, 40